This bo
themes
united It
status o
Fascism.

The Fasc
propagan
source m
material.
topics su
actions c

John Po
sources, as well as a glossary and guide to further reading. He reassesses the status of the Fascist movement as a coalition rather than a monolith and details the images of energy and violence which were crucial to the success of Fascism, both within Italy and internationally.

John Pollard is Professor of Modern History at Anglia Polytechnic University.

ROUTLEDGE SOURCES IN HISTORY
Series Editor
David Welch, University of Kent

OTHER TITLES IN THE SERIES
The Suez Crisis
Anthony Gorst and Lewis Johnman

Resistance and Conformity in the Third Reich
Martyn Housden

The Russian Revolution 1917–1921
Ronald Kowalski

FORTHCOMING
The Third Republic
William Fortescue

The German Experience
Anthony McElligott

The Rise and Fall of the Soviet Union
Richard Sakwa

The Fascist Experience in Italy

John Pollard

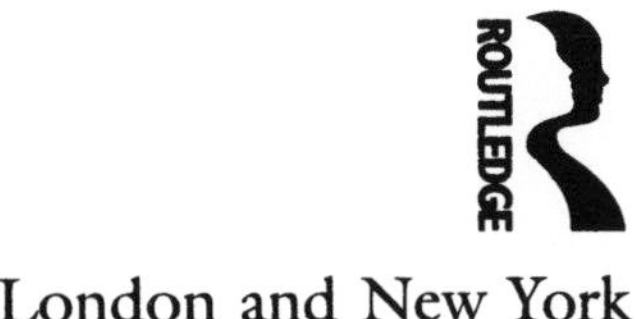

London and New York

First published in 1998
by Routledge
2 Park Square, Milton Park, Abingdon, Oxon, OX14 4RN

Transferred to Digital Printing 2005

Simultaneously published in the USA and Canada
by Routledge
270 Madison Ave, New York NY 10016

Typeset in Galliard and Gill by Keystroke, Jacaranda Lodge, Wolverhampton

British Library Cataloguing in Publication Data
A catalogue record for this book is available from the British Library

Library of Congress Cataloging in Publication Data

Pollard, John F. (John Francis). 1944–
The Fascist experience in Italy / John Pollard.
p. cm. — (Routledge sources in history)
Includes bibliographical references and index.
1. Fascism—Italy—History. 2. Italy—Politics and government—1922–1945. I. Title. II. Series.

DG571.P592 1998
945.091—dc21 97–31359
CIP

ISBN 0–415–11631–7 (hbk)
ISBN 0–415–11632–5 (pbk)

Printed and bound by Antony Rowe Ltd, Eastbourne

Contents

Series editor's preface

Sources in History is a new series responding to the continued shift of emphasis in the teaching of history in schools and universities towards the use of primary sources and the testing of historical skills. By using documentary evidence, the series is intended to reflect the skills historians have to master when challenged by problems of evidence, interpretation and presentation.

A distinctive feature of *Sources in History* will be the manner in which the content, style and significance of documents is analysed. The commentary and the sources are not discrete, but rather merge to become part of a continuous and integrated narrative. After reading each volume a student should be well versed in the historiographical problems which sources present. In short, the series aims to provide texts which will allow students to achieve facility in 'thinking historically' and place them in a stronger position to test their historical skills. Wherever possible the intention has been to retain the integrity of a document and not simply to present a 'gobbet', which can be misleading. Documentary evidence thus forces the student to confront a series of questions which professional historians also have to grapple with. Such questions can be summarised as follows:

1 What type of source is the document?
- Is it a written source or an oral or visual source?
- What, in your estimation, is its importance?
- Did it, for example, have an effect on events or the decision-making process?

2 Who wrote the document?
- A person, a group, or a government?
- If it was a person, what was their position?
- What basic attitudes might have affected the nature of the information and language used?

3 When was the document written?
- The date, and even the time, might be significant.
- You may need to understand when the document was written in order to understand its context.
- Are there any special problems in understanding the document as contemporaries would have understood it?

4 Why was the document written?
- For what purpose(s) did the document come into existence, and for whom was it intended?

- Was the document 'author-initiated' or was it commissioned for somebody? If the document was ordered by someone, the author could possibly have 'tailored' his piece.

5 What was written?

- This is the obvious question, but never be afraid to state the obvious.
- Remember, it may prove more revealing to ask the question: what was *not* written?
- That is, read between the lines. In order to do this you will need to ask what other references (to persons, events, other documents, etc.) need to be explained before the document can be fully understood.

Sources in History is intended to reflect the individual voice of the volume author(s) with the aim of bringing the central themes of specific topics into sharper focus. Each volume will consist of an authoritative introduction to the topic; chapters will discuss the historical significance of the sources, and the final chapter will provide an up-to-date synthesis of the historiographical debate. Authors will also provide an annotated bibliography and suggestions for further reading. These books will become contributions to the historical debate in their own right.

In this volume, Professor John Pollard provides students of history and languages with an accessible introduction to the study of Italian Fascism. The study includes a detailed breakdown of the origins of Fascism, its development and its characteristics. Particular emphasis is placed on Fascist economic and social policies and on Mussolini's foreign policy. By his skilful analysis of a wide range of sources the author has illustrated the key issues with extraordinary clarity and insight. The author has also translated a significant number of new sources. This work also offers important insights into the historiographical debate on the nature and shape of Italian Fascism. The author reappraises the conditions that led to the rise of Fascism in Italy, he charts its development and its manifestations in Italian society and in a provocative and challenging conclusion discusses the legacy of Fascism. John Pollard contends that the Fascist legacy still has a potentially important role to play in shaping Italy's future. This book will become an indispensable aid to all students who wish to possess a better understanding of the nature of Italian Fascism and its long-term impact on post-war politics in Italy.

David Welch

Canterbury 1997

Acknowledgements

I must first of all thank the generations of A-level and undergraduate students to whom I have taught courses in Italian history over the years and from whom I have learnt so much as a result. I am also grateful to Luisa Quartermaine for her help with the section on the Fascist Social Republic. Roger Absalom and Roger Griffin did me the enormous favour of reading the first draft at very short notice. As a result, they saved me from serious factual errors and forced me to rethink some of my interpretations of events, but I alone take responsibility for the finished product. For the third time in my life I am immensely grateful to Noel Currer Briggs for his excellent index. I must also thank Heather McCallum and David Welch for their encouragement and their superhuman patience in awaiting the manuscript. Last, but by no means least, I must thank Pompey for his moral support.

The author and publisher are grateful to the following for permission to reproduce copyright material:

> The pictures of Mussolini from U. Silva, *Ideologia e arte del fascismo*, 1973 are reproduced by permission of Edizioni Gabriele Mazzotta srl and the picture of Piazza Della Vittoria, Brescia is reproduced by permission of Publifoto, Milan. The extract from S. Woolf (ed.), *The Italian Risorgimento*, 1969, is reproduced by permission of Addison, Wesley & Longman; the extract from C. Seton-Watson, *Italy from Liberalism to Fascism*, Methuen, 1967, is reproduced with the author's permission; the extracts from P. Kennedy, *The Rise and Fall of the Great Powers*, 1988 are reproduced by permission of HarperCollins Publishers Ltd.; the extracts from A. Lyttelton (ed.), *Italian Fascism: From Pareto to Mussolini*, 1973 are reprinted by permission of Peters Fraser & Dunlop Group Ltd; the extract from J.A.S. Grenville, *The Major International Treaties, 1914–1945. A History and Guide with Texts*, Methuen & Co., 1974 is reproduced by permission of Routledge; the extract from G. Carocci, *Italian Fascism*, 1972 trans. by I. Quigley (first published as *Storia del fascismo* by Editore Aldo Garzanti, 1972, translation copyright, Pelican Books Ltd., 1974 is reprinted with their permission; the extract from P. Sparke, *Italian Design: 1870 to the Present*, 1988 is reproduced by permission of Thames & Hudson Ltd.; the extract from A. Acquarone, *L'organizzazione dello stato totalitario*, 1965, is reprinted by permission of Gulio Einaudi Editore; the extracts from, *Mediterranean Fascism, 1919–1945*, C.F. Delzell, are reprinted by permission of Walker and Company,

435 Hudson Street, New York, New York 10014, 1-800-289-2553. All Rights Reserved; the extract from J. Whittam, *Fascist Italy*, 1995 is reproduced by permission of Manchester University Press; extracts from G. Bonfanti, *Il fascismo, vol. I, la conquista del potere*, 1976, are reprinted by permission of Editore La Scuola; the extract from G. Rochat, *Militari e politici nella preparazione della campagna d'Etiopia; Studio e documenti, 1932–1936*, are reproduced by permission of Franco Angeli s.r.l.; an extract from *Ciano's Diplomatic Papers*, edited with an introduction by M. Muggeridge, 1948, pp. 142–6 is reproduced by permission of Odhams Press and the extracts from D. Hine, *Governing Italy: the Politics of Bargained Pluralism*, 1993 and from R. Griffin, *Fascism*, 1995 are reproduced by permission of Oxford University Press.

While the author and publisher have made every effort to contact all copyright holders of material used in this volume, they would be grateful to hear from any they were unable to contact.

Glossary

anarcho-syndicalism	a working-class movement combining elements of the anarchism of the Bakunin type with revolutionary syndicalism.
Anschluss	the union of Austria and Germany brought about by Hitler's invasion and occupation of Austria in March 1938.
avant-guardist	a cultural or political movement in the forefront, or vanguard, of ideas.
blitzkrieg	literally 'lightning war', as applied to Hitler's rapid airborne and armoured campaigns against Poland (1939) and Western Europe (1940) which brought him quick victory against his opponents.
bourgeoisie	the French middle class. In Marxist terminology, the class which has control of the means of production and distribution.
carabinieri	semi-military, state police force in Italy.
centrifugal forces	those forces – natural or human – which pull away from the centre.
CGL	the General Confederation of Labour, the socialist-controlled trade union organisation.
CIL	the Italian Labour Confederation, the Catholic trade union organisation.
clientelism	a form of electoral 'exchange' in which the elector gives the vote in expectation of a very precise, individual material reward.
corporate state	a state which is allegedly organised around the professions and economic interest groups, and which seeks to regulate labour relations on a statutory basis, e.g. Austria, 1934–8, Italy under Fascism and Franco's Spain.
constituent assembly	an elected assembly whose primary purpose is to draw up a constitution for a country, e.g. France in 1790 and 1946, the Weimar National Assembly in Germany in 1919 and Italy in 1946.

Deputy	a member of the lower house of the Italian parliament (the Chamber of Deputies).
franchise	the right to the vote.
gleichschaltung	the process whereby Hitler and the Nazis established their dictatorship in Germany between March 1933 and August 1934.
latifondo	a very large agricultural estate in Southern Italy and Sicily, usually owned by an aristocrat. The extensive cultivation was rather inefficient.
lebensborn	the Nazi practice of selectively breeding 'pure' Aryan Germans, often outside of marriage.
lebensraum	the 'living space' demanded by Hitler for the survival and expansion of the German race, especially in Eastern Europe.
Liberal Italy	the name we give to Italy between 1861 and 1922, which was created by the moderate liberal politicians of Northern Italy. In Anglo-Saxon political terminology, the political class and its 'liberal' ideology would more precisely be defined as liberal-conservative.
lockout	industrial action on the part of employers whereby they lock out the workers from their establishments,
Locarno	the treaties of 1925 between Britain, Italy, Belgium, France and Germany, whereby the first two powers guaranteed to defend the western frontiers of the last three, as defined by the Treaty of Versailles of 1919.
misogyny	male intolerance of, and hostility towards, women.
putsch	a violent seizure of power, or attempted seizure of power; most notably, Hitler's failed attempt in Munich in 1923.
proportional representation	an electoral system which awards seats to political parties in a parliamentary body in direct proportion to the number of votes cast in a given area. The precise workings of the system can vary enormously.
quadumvirs	literally 'one of four men'. A commander of the Fascist 'March on Rome' in October 1922.
risorgimento	the resurgence, or rebirth, of Italy.
suffrage	the right to vote: the 'suffragettes' were the women who struggled to secure female suffrage in pre-First World War Britain.

Introduction

In the last twenty to thirty years there has been an enormous increase in the output of historical studies of Italian Fascism both in Italy and elsewhere. British and American historians have made a very substantial contribution to this output, particularly in the field of Fascist foreign policy, and have produced some of the best short but comprehensive histories, most notably those by Cassels and De Grand, and more recently by Morgan and Whittam. This latest volume has a rather different purpose from the others. It does not seek to offer a radically new interpretation of Italian Fascism, though it does note the important insights of recent works. Rather, it seeks to provide sixth-form and undergraduate students of history and languages with an introduction to the study of Italian Fascism: its long-term origins in the history of Liberal Italy, its development as a political movement, its rise to power and its characteristic policies as a regime. It analyses the decline and collapse of the regime and its brief, tragic reincarnation as the 'Italian Social Republic'. After an examination of Fascist ideology, it considers the consequences of the experience of Italian Fascism for an Italy which is still living with parts of its legacy today.

It also provides students with a representative selection of source materials – including maps, statistics and photographs – to illustrate the key issues. These sources supplement written documents which include items long available in English and a significant number of newly translated ones. (Unless otherwise stated, I have translated all new documents which come from Italian sources.) These source materials are, generally speaking, intended to be integral parts of the text.

The structure of the volume is deliberately neither wholly chronological nor wholly thematic, though themes are dealt with in broadly chronological order. It is my experience that economic and foreign policy, and the ideology of Fascism, are best studied separately from the broad chronological account of the movement and the regime. Where appropriate, developments in Italy are related to their European context and an account of major historiographical developments and debates is provided. In addition, full bibliographies of published documents and secondary sources in English, with a representative sample of works in Italian for language students, and audio-visual material, are appended to assist students pursuing further, in-depth studies, as well as non-specialist teachers constructing reading lists.

1 The 'pre-history' of Italian Fascism

Introduction

Though Italian Fascism was to a great extent a child of its time, it did not suddenly appear from nowhere. It had roots in pre-First World War political and cultural movements, and also in the war itself. Moreover, its success cannot be properly understood outside the broader context of Italy's political, economic and social development following its emergence as a unified state in the middle of the nineteenth century. Denis Mack Smith, for example, sees it as the logical consequence of all the weaknesses and defects of the Liberal state created at unification, and above all the failure after unification to bridge the gap between 'legal' Italy, the rulers, and 'real' Italy, the ruled (Mack Smith, in A. W. Salamone, 1970, pp. 103–11). Fascism was not inevitable in this historical context, but it would have been impossible without it.

The Unification of Italy

The emergence of the united Italian state between 1861 and 1870 was ultimately the outcome of a complex of interrelated processes of cultural, social and political change known as the 'Risorgimento', meaning the resurgence or rebirth of Italy, stretching back into the mid-eighteenth century. Though the great prophet and leader of Italian nationalism, Giuseppe Mazzini, had urged that Italy would only win her freedom from foreign rule and achieve unification through popular revolution, Italian independence and unification were brought about by a small, dynamic elite, the moderate Liberals led by Camillo Cavour, and a pre-national state, Piedmont, using the unrevolutionary means of diplomacy and war in 1859–61 (unification of all Italy except Venetia and the area around Rome), 1866 (incorporation of Venetia) and 1870 (conquest of Rome). Despite popular participation in the manning of the barricades in the revolts of 1848, and the romantic role played by Garibaldi, his 'Thousand Redshirts' and their peasant followers in 1860, the masses were notably absent from the events which brought about independence and unification.

Liberal Italy and its Problems

The unified state – 'Liberal Italy' – which emerged from the Risorgimento was largely the creation of a tiny elite, the northern and central Italian ruling class. The failure to involve the masses in the struggles for independence and unification was primarily due to that class's fear of social revolution on the one hand, and the lack of an agrarian programme by the more radical, Mazzinian, wing of the national movement on the other. This 'failed' or 'passive revolution' was to have serious consequences, for the unified state was really two Italys rather than one – 'real' Italy and 'legal' Italy. According to Christopher Seton-Watson, '"Legal" Italy was the King and parliament, the politicians and bureaucrats concentrated in a distant capital: "real" Italy was the mass of the peasant population. Communication between the two was rare and unfriendly' (Seton-Watson 1967, p. 25). Contact between the two Italys was most rare in the Southern regions, and indeed became extremely hostile during the 'Great Brigandage', a virtual civil war that ravaged the South in the years immediately following unification. The brigands were a mixture of organised criminal bands, demobilised soldiers from the Neapolitan and Garibaldinian armies and peasants escaping both the taxes and conscription imposed by the new state and the exactions of their grasping landlords. Setting the pattern for the future treatment of lower-class discontent by the state, the new national government suppressed the brigands by brute, military force. This reinforces claims by later commentators, most notably the Southerner Gramsci, that the South was 'conquered' by the North, rather than united to it, and had thus become its 'colony' rather than an integral part of a new nation state.

The failure of successive governments to solve the appalling problems at the root of recurrent peasant discontent and violence in the South was the result of the alliance which the Northern ruling class had concluded with its Southern counterpart, an alliance which was one of the main bases of the Italian political system after unification. This ruling class was given a virtually free hand in its relations with the peasantry and its corrupt control of local government in return for supporting national government at election time. One long-term consequence was that some of the worst features of Southern society, clientelism and even collusion with organised criminality – mafia – eventually passed into the general Italian political culture and practice.

Given the leading role played by Piedmont during the struggles for independence and unity, it is hardly surprising that the political system of the new Italy should have been fashioned in her image. Thus, Italy in 1861 received not a new 'tailor-made' constitution drawn up by a widely elected constituent assembly, as Mazzini and the republicans had desired, but the *Statuto*, the existing constitution of Piedmont. Under this constitution, D'Azeglio, Cavour and their moderate liberal successors in the premiership developed a system of parliamentary government in which, in practice, the power of the monarch was limited. But the King still retained considerable powers, should he choose to use them.

Document 1.1 The Statuto Albertino: 1848

The ministers are responsible . . . The executive power belongs to the King alone. He is the supreme head of the state: he commands all the land forces and naval forces; he declares war, he makes treaties of peace, alliance, commerce, etc., informing parliament of them as soon as the interests and security of the state permit.

Source: S.J. Woolf, The Italian Risorgimento, *1969, pp. 51–3*

The document does not say to whom the ministers were responsible but it did provide a constitutional basis for the King to play a decisive role in Italian politics at times of national emergency, which is exactly what he did during the 'End of Century Crisis', in the Intervention Crisis of 1915, at the time of the March on Rome in October 1922 and at the collapse of Fascism in July 1943. Monarchs always held themselves a little aloof from the hurly-burly and 'squalor' of parliamentary politics; more closely involved, in fact, in what Martin Clark has described as 'high politics', the activities of the diplomatic and military elites (Clark, 1996, p. 44).

Though parliament was undoubtedly Italy's most truly national institution, it was also a weak, flawed one, its main weakness lying in the very narrow franchise which was restricted by age, gender, literacy, tax and property qualifications to less than 2 per cent of the population. Even after the electoral reform of 1882 a mere 8 per cent had the vote. In these circumstances, until the suffrage was extended to the bulk of the male population in 1912, Italy was ruled by a tiny, exclusive political class whose essential homogeneity of ideology and socio-economic class interests, that is, those of the urban upper bourgeoisie and the landed aristocracy, prevented the emergence of a party system. Apart from the Radicals and Republicans (and after 1892 the Socialists and 1903 a handful of Catholics), almost all Italian politicians before the First World War were merely of different shadings of a broadly liberal-conservative hue. As a result of small constituencies, electoral corruption and clientelism was commonplace, especially in the South. At a national level, political leaders, most notably Agostino Depretis, who was prime minister three times between 1876 and 1887, resorted to 'transformism', a superior form of bribing their opponents, in order to create and sustain parliamentary majorities. Francesco Crispi, a leading politician of the 'Left' between 1861 and 1896, provided a description of transformism in action in a speech to his constituents.

Document 1.2 Transformism in Operation

You should see the pandemonium at Montecitorio (the Chamber of Deputies) when the moment approaches for an important division. The agents of the government run through the rooms and corridors, to gather votes. Subsidies, decorations, canals, bridges, roads, everything is promised:

sometimes an act of justice long denied, is the price of a parliamentary vote.

Source: quoted in C. Seton-Watson,* Italy from Liberalism to Fascism, *1967, p. 92

It should be pointed out, however, that Crispi was to use exactly the same methods himself when he became prime minister. Clientelism, the winning of votes at a constituency level through the distribution of favours to 'clients' was the other side of the coin of 'transformism'. As one member of parliament wrote in 1886, 'A Deputy has to find jobs for people, secure verdicts for his supporters in criminal and civil cases alike, help others to pass their examinations or get pensions, promote or oppose public and private contracts. He has to get convicts released, civil servants punished or removed, obtain roads and bridges for his constituents' (quoted in King and Okey, 1909, p. 24). Such was the stuff of Italian politics in the Liberal era.

It also has to be said that some of Italy's most powerful leaders, most notably Cavour between 1854 and 1861, Francesco Crispi in the 1880s and 1890s and Giovanni Giolitti in the early 1900s, while paying lipservice to parliamentary institutions, often treated them with scant respect. Cavour has frequently been condemned for his 'parliamentary dictatorship', which included a habit of arbitrarily quashing his opponents' elections wholesale; Crispi both reduced the electorate and shut down parliament for long stretches when it suited him; and Giolitti achieved political stability through a parliamentary majority which, in the South at least, was largely produced by extensive bribery and corruption. As a result, parliament enjoyed little prestige, even among sections of the political class itself.

The other most characteristic feature of the new Italian state was the rigidly centralised control of local government through the Napoleonic system of prefects (provincial governors) and the police. Initially, the adoption of this system was largely a matter of administrative convenience, but it was also seen as an essential corrective to the strong, centrifugal tendencies of regionalism and localism that survived from the pre-unification period. In the 1860s at least, Italy's rulers were afraid that without it the new state which they had created would fall to pieces. Later it also served as a defence for the country's tiny ruling class against the violent protests of the discontented and disenfranchised masses, and in the late 1920s it would serve as an ideal base on which the Fascists could build their one-party police state.

The Roman Question

The isolation of the ruling class of Liberal Italy was exacerbated by the hostility of the Catholic Church, which could have been such a powerful source of moral support and legitimacy for the new state, as it was in Austria and the France of Napoleon III. The conflict between Church and state, which after 1870 was conventionally referred to as the 'Roman Question', originated in the Risorgimento.

The moderate Liberals' modernising programme led to the enactment of legislation which wrested control of marriage law and education from the Church and severely cut back its property and legal privileges. But the Church–state conflict in Italy possessed a dimension which differentiated it from similar disputes elsewhere, for the process of unifying the Italian states necessarily involved the destruction of the Pope's 'temporal power': his territorial sovereignty over the Papal States of Central Italy. Despite all the attempts of Cavour and his successors to find a compromise solution, Pope Pius IX did not accept the loss of his temporal power and refused to recognise the Kingdom of Italy. This policy was continued, on a formal basis at least, until 1929.

The Roman Question had damaging consequences for Italy, which Mussolini and the Fascists were eventually able to exploit. The conflict widened the gulf between 'real' and 'legal' Italy, because the Church's hostility reinforced the natural diffidence of many of the peasantry towards the new state. In addition, the Papal decree 'Non Expedit', which forbade Catholics from participating in the politics of the Italian state, reduced the tiny electorate still further. A Catholic movement or 'subculture', organised around the *Opera dei Congressi*, developed in intransigent opposition to the Liberal state and its political class; this confirmed the strong anti-clerical tendencies of that class. But the most damaging effect of the conflict was the way in which it bred a lack of confidence in and commitment to the parliamentary institutions of the Liberal state among the clergy and elements of the laity. Aggrieved by the treatment of the Church at the hands of the Liberal political class, which was in any case compromised in the eyes of many Catholics by its Masonic connections, these groups were eventually to turn to the Fascists to provide an authoritarian solution to the Roman Question.

Economic and Social Development in Liberal Italy

Italy was a latecomer to the economic developments of the nineteenth century. At her unification in 1861, whereas Great Britain, Belgium and Germany had already undergone major processes of industrialisation, and France was also in the throes of industrial change, Italy by comparison was economically backward and underdeveloped. Several factors hindered economic progress: poor communications, as a result of mountainous barriers, few navigable rivers or canals and no integrated or fully developed railway system; lack of raw materials and sources of energy (in particular an absence of significant coal deposits); and the appalling financial condition of the new state due to the cost of the wars of independence and unification.

One of the most characteristic features of Italian economic development since unification has been its spasmodic pattern of growth. Industry grew slowly in the first two and a half decades after unification, slowed into recession in the late 1880s and 1890s and then speeded up again in the so-called 'big spurt' between 1896 and 1910. In this period, helped by improving world conditions, remittances from millions of emigrants and the development of hydro-electric power (which enjoyed favourable conditions in Northern Italy), some of the household names of Italian manufacturing industry appeared – FIAT, Olivetti and Pirelli. But further periods of industrial expansion were required – during the First World War, during the Fascist period and in the economic 'miracle' of the late 1950s and early 1960s – before Italy began to display some of the main characteristics of a 'modern', urban industrial nation.

On the eve of the First World War, therefore, Italy, despite the undoubted economic progress which she had made, was still lagging far behind in the world industrial-manufacturing league tables. Thus, her limited and sometimes ineffective role in international diplomacy, as 'the Least of the Great Powers' (Bosworth, 1979, p. 1) was a true reflection of her economic weakness, which would hamper her efforts to wage war in both world conflicts.

Document 1.3 Statistical Indicators of Italy's Relative Economic Weakness

Table 1 Relative Shares of World Manufacturing Output, 1750–1900

Country	*1800*	*1830*	*1860*	*1880*	*1900*	*1913*
United Kingdom	4.3	9.5	19.9	22.9	18.5	13.6
Habsburg empire	3.2	3.2	4.2	4.4	4.7	4.4
France	4.2	5.2	7.9	7.8	6.8	6.1
German states/Germany	3.5	3.5	4.9	8.5	13.2	14.8
Russia	5.6	5.6	7.0	7.6	8.8	8.2
United States	0.8	2.4	7.2	14.7	23.6	32.0
Japan	3.5	2.8	2.6	2.4	2.4	—
Italian states/Italy	2.5	2.3	2.5	2.5	2.5	2.4

Table 2 Iron and Steel Production of the Powers, 1890–1913 (millions of tons; pig-iron production for 1890, steel therafter)

Country	*1890*	*1900*	*1910*	*1913*
United States	9.3	10.3	26.5	31.8
Britain	8.0	5.0	6.5	7.7
Germany	4.1	6.3	13.6	17.6
France	1.9	1.5	3.4	4.6
Austria-Hungary	0.97	1.1	2.1	2.6
Russia	0.95	2.2	3.5	4.8
Japan	0.02	—	0.16	0.25
Italy	0.01	0.11	0.73	0.93

Table 3 National Income, Population and per capita Income of the Powers in 1914

Country	*National income (US$ billion)*	*Population (million)*	*Per capita income (US$)*
United States	37	98	377
Britain	11	45	244
France	6	39	153
Japan	2	55	36
Germany	12	65	184
Russia	7	171	41
Austria-Hungary	3	52	57
Italy	4	37	108

Source: P. Kennedy, The Rise and Fall of the Great Powers, *1988, pp. 190, 257, 259*

It is significant that in 1913 Italy's share of world manufacturing output was almost exactly the same as in *1750* and that only in the area of per capita income did Italy do better than any other European power, thanks to massive emigrant remittances. Another striking characteristic of Italian economic growth between 1861 and 1915 was the important role played by the state, especially in the development of industry. In the first place, growth was encouraged by the mere fact of the emergence of a unified Italian state which created a 'single market' in the Italian peninsula by sweeping away the customs barriers between the old states, and by standardising the currency, weights and measures and commercial law. Given its financial condition, the state could do little thereafter except promote, and sometimes subsidise, railway construction to create an integrated network. In the 1880s, however, the state increasingly gave preferential treatment to those industries connected with national defence – shipbuilding, iron and steel and munitions, to the point of subsidising the construction of a steel works at Terni in Central Italy. Also in the 1880s, the government began to give tariff protection to heavy industry and to the wheat growers.

These trends had an important long-term political consequence: they helped create close links between politicians and both industrialists and the banks on which much manufacturing industry was dependent for capital. Parliament in the last decades of the nineteenth century and the early years of the twentieth century became vulnerable to pressure from these economic blocs and the newspapers which they controlled, the effects being felt during both the lead up to the Libyan War and the debate over Italian intervention in the First World War.

Economic development in Liberal Italy was not only spasmodic and limited, it was highly localised.

Document 1.4 Italian Industry on the Eve of the First World War

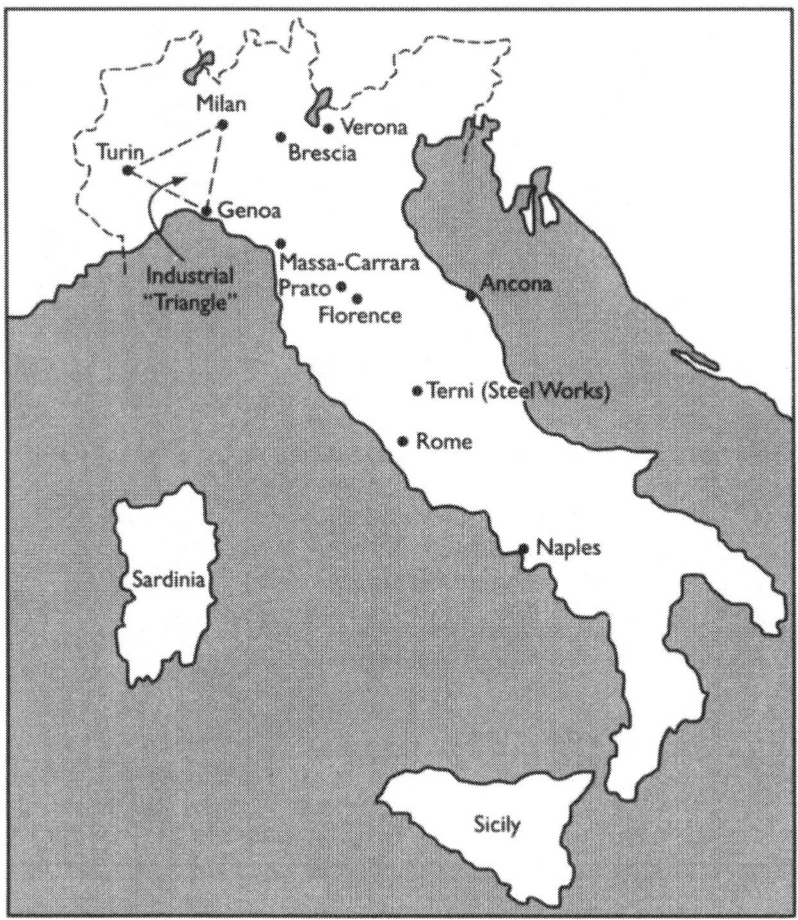

Italy's industrial base before 1915 was essentially located in the north-west of the country, in the 'industrial triangle' of Milan, Turin and Genoa. Nearness to the developing economies of other European countries meant availability of markets and sources of capital and technical know-how. In addition, the Po Valley was the country's most fertile region and seat of its most improving agriculture. Outside of the triangle, small industrial areas were to be found in a few provincial towns of Northern Italy, such as Brescia and Verona, and also of the Centre, especially Florence, Ancona and Prato.

The South, apart from the great port of Naples, was almost bereft of industry on any scale. Indeed, manufacturing in the South had been one of the casualties of unification, which had exposed it to the full blast of competition from the North.

The South, and some of the central regions such as the Marches and Umbria, remained overwhelmingly rural and agrarian, and despite some government initiatives, the pressure of population on the land led to mass migration: from the late 1890s until the mid-1900s, 600,000 Italians a year would leave Italy for the Americas, Australia and North-West Europe, mainly from the South.

As well as the great North–South divide, the Italian economy at the end of its first major stage of industrialisation was characterised by other forms of dualism: the coexistence of a modern industrial sector alongside 'backward' forms of production, that is, the artisan sector and rural 'cottage' industries; and in the agricultural sector between small-scale subsistence farming virtually everywhere in Italy and large-scale, capitalist production, especially in the Po Valley and, exceptionally, in parts of Apulia in the South.

The crucial social outcome of economic development in Liberal Italy was the emergence of a small but growing urban proletariat composed of factory, transport and other workers. Alongside these groups, a large artisan class continued to exist. Of equal if not greater importance was the emergence of a rural, agrarian proletariat in the Po Valley, Tuscany, Umbria and a part of Apulia, consisting of large numbers of *braccianti* (day labourers), *salariati* (labourers with more stable employment) and *mezzadri* (sharecroppers whose standard of living was often as precarious as that of the *braccianti*). In addition, rural society was further fragmented by a bewildering variety of small tenant farmers, leaseholders and small landholders. Embryonic working-class organisations emerged in Italy in the 1860s, under the initial tutelage of Mazzini, who saw them as an instrument in his continuing battle against the liberal-conservative monarchical state. After his rejection of socialism in 1871, following the Paris Commune, and his death in 1882, republican influences continued to play a part in working-class groups in the Romagna and the Marches. An even more powerful influence on the early Italian working-class movement was the anarchist leader Bakunin, who operated in Italy in the late 1870s and early 1880s, and whose influence was to survive in the form of anarcho-syndicalism in such places as Pisa, Livorno and the Carrara marble quarries.

The Italian working-class movement truly took off in the 1890s with the establishment of trade unions, cooperatives and peasant leagues. The latter were so successful that the strength of Italian 'agrarian socialism' was almost unique in Europe – only in parts of Spain was there any real parallel. In 1892 the Italian Socialist Party (P.S.I.) was founded under Marxist inspiration. But the fragmented nature of the Italian working class was reflected in the movement itself, which was highly prone to ideological splits. On the extreme left, and effectively outside the party, were the revolutionary syndicalists, who believed in imminent revolution to be fostered by constant use of the strike weapon, culminating in a great, insurrectionary general strike. Mainstream Marxists inside the party divided into Reformists and Maximalists, the latter taking a position of opposition to the 'capitalist-bourgeois state' that was almost as intransigent as that of the revolutionary syndicalists.

In response to the Socialist challenge, and under the inspiration of Pope Leo XIII's encyclical *Rerum Novarum* (1891), which was the founding charter of European 'social Catholicism', the Catholic movement established rival trade unions, cooperatives, peasant leagues and mutual credit institutions. By 1914 the network of Catholic economic and social organisations, though not as extensive or as well supported as those of the Socialists, could rely on the loyalty of large sections of Italy's poorer classes, especially small peasant farmers and women workers. The Italian Catholic movement acquired a grass-roots dimension which was especially strong in Northern and Eastern Italy.

The End of Century Crisis

The emergence of the working-class and Catholic subcultures was also of great significance during the decade of economic, social and political crisis which Italy was to experience in the 1890s: the 'End of Century Crisis'. World economic recession, bad harvests, Francesco Crispi's 'tariff war' with France and high taxation due to heavy military spending on colonial ventures all contributed to a worsening of the economic conditions of 'real' Italy and consequently to recurrent outbursts of violence on the part of both peasants and urban workers. The response of the political class to this unrest was, as usual, repressive. A succession of governments used more or less the same methods to put down rioting and unrest in Sicily (1892–3), in the Carrara marble quarries (1897) and a popular insurrection in Milan (1898) as they had employed in suppressing Southern brigandage in the 1860s. This time the alarm of the political class was compounded by their fear of the activities and influence of the working-class movement, and to a lesser extent the Catholic movement. As a result peasant leagues, trade unions, the Socialist Party and some organisations of the Catholic movement were dissolved, their newspapers closed down and their leaders put on trial for sedition. In 1893–4 the electoral rolls were purged of 'undesirables', and between 1898 and 1900 a concerted effort was made to restrict political debate and civil liberties.

This serious attempt to put the constitutional clock back and to refashion Italy's political system in the image of Bismarck's Germany, an authoritarian model close to the hearts of reactionary politicians such as Crispi, was ultimately a failure. But it does clearly demonstrate the fragility of the Liberal state and the reactionary instincts of some of its political class. Italy was to be less fortunate during the second crisis of the Liberal state in the early 1920s. Then, reaction was to be triumphant in the shape of a Fascist takeover. Indeed, Fascism was to be the agent of reaction on behalf of a grouping of forces which had been at work in the End of Century Crisis. The later Fascist 'block of consensus' was to contain new elements, such as the Church, but it continued to represent essentially the same forces as before – the monarchy, the armed forces and some industrial and agrarian interests. There is also a remarkable similarity between the policies of reactionary governments in the 1890s and those of the Fascist regime in the 1920s and 1930s. Mussolini's policy of colonial expansion, for example, was not so different in its objectives to that of Crispi; both were conceived as a means of achieving international prestige for Italy and at the same time intended to resolve her nagging economic and social problems. And Mussolini's conciliatory policy towards the Church was different in only one major respect from that of Crispi – it was successful.

Even the political structures of Fascist Italy bear some resemblance to the authoritarian ideas of late nineteenth century reactionary politicians. In 1898, at the height of the 'End of Century Crisis', Sidney Sonnino suggested an end to 'parliamentarism' and a return to the letter of the Italian Constitution, as a solution to what he regarded as the moral and political crisis of the state.

Document 1.5 Sidney Sonnino, 'Let Us Return to the Statute', 1898

The King embodies in himself the State, in all of its most essential and characteristic powers and in the guardianship of those powers he has an active, and not merely passive, role to play. It is the King who represents the tradition of government, the activities of the State, the permanence of its laws: in a word, he expresses the general interest of the Fatherland not only in the present, but also in the future. And he is the only institution to whom these functions have been entrusted by our laws.

Source: N. Valeri, Da Giolitti a Mussolini, *1966, p. 158*

Sonnino was right: as can be seen in the extract from the *Statuto*, the constitution invested enormous powers in the King. It could be said that the concentration of executive power in Mussolini's hands as 'Head of the Government' in 1925 was but the realisation of Sonnino's dream of a return to the original, more monarchical interpretation of the *Statuto*.

Italy in the Age of Giolitti

After the turbulence of the 1890s, the fifteen years which followed were relatively tranquil, thanks to improving economic conditions and to Giovanni Giolitti, who dominated politics in these years. Giolitti was the leading political representative of the more enlightened and progressive sections of the Italian ruling class whose parliamentary opposition had brought to a halt the repressive measures of the End of Century Crisis. That opposition had also included the fledgling parliamentary P.S.I. and it was Giolitti's attitude to the Socialists, and the working classes which they represented, which formed the basis of the strategy which we call 'Giolittianism'. Under Giolitti, the first serious attempt was made to reconcile 'real' and 'legal' Italy, to meet the just demands of the working masses by reform rather than repression and, in a broader sense, to bring the masses into the political system.

Seeking the support of reformist Socialist Deputies, Giolitti laid down a new policy of state impartiality in labour disputes, coupled with reform of working conditions, the introduction of some elements of social insurance, and electoral reform that gave the vote to the overwhelming majority of the adult male population in 1912.

Giolitti's policies were successful while Italy enjoyed the fruits of the unprecedented prosperity which resulted from the burst of industrial development that the country experienced in the early 1900s. By 1909 that prosperity was beginning to come to an end and social and political turmoil almost inevitably followed. Giolitti must also take some of the blame for the failure of his own strategy. His decision to embark on a colonial war in Libya in 1911, while it was justified by the exigencies of Italy's diplomatic situation at that time, destroyed the delicate relationship which he had built up with the Socialists. The war was denounced by the Maximalists as an act of militaristic and imperialistic barbarism and at the Socialist Party Congress in 1912 they triumphed over their Reformist colleagues, who had hitherto provided the link between the party and Giolitti. The 1912 congress was a turning point in the history of Italian Socialism, for not only did it bring to the fore a revolutionary firebrand by the name of Benito Mussolini, it fixed Socialist political strategy for the next ten years. Henceforth, the Deputies of the Socialist Party were forbidden to cooperate in any way with the representatives of the 'capitalist-bourgeois' parties in parliament. This intransigent opposition to the parliamentary system was to have tragic consequences during the rise of Fascism in the 1920s.

The Nationalist Challenge

The Libyan War had also failed to satisfy extremists of the right, particularly the Nationalists whose growing political influence and restlessness Giolitti had hoped to check by means of his North African adventure. The Nationalists were a tiny minority movement, but a vocal and influential one in the circles of 'high politics'. Their chief ideologue was Enrico Corradini, who represented those who regretted the failure of Crispi's colonial adventures in Africa in the 1880s and 1890s, who were ashamed that Italy's economic weakness obliged millions of her sons and daughters to seek a living elsewhere and who thus felt a deep national inferiority complex. The following passage demonstrates very clearly the dissatisfaction of Corradini and his followers with 'Italietta', the 'little Italy' as they saw it of the Giolittian period.

Document 1.6 Enrico Corradini, The Proletarian Nations and Nationalism, 1911

We must seek rather to discover the causes for Italy not possessing any developed national awareness and start straight away by recognising that she does not possess one because she cannot.

And here are the reasons why she cannot:

First of all, gentlemen, until quite recently Italy had in fact never been a nation.
Secondly, Italy has never had and still does not have a national language, except in literature.
Thirdly, she was created after little fighting and little revolution.
Fourthly, Italy was created as a result of the efforts of too many people, often in conflict among themselves: an official aristocratic and middle-class monarchy, popular Garibaldinianism, cosmopolitan Mazzinianism; and these conflicts persisted and still persist.
Fifthly, Italy was created as a result of diplomatic intrigues and by foreign arms.
Sixthly, Italy too quickly declined into the class struggle and the initial formation of her self-awareness was inhibited.
Seventh, and lastly, Italy – and this could not be otherwise because of the slightness of the revolution that created her – Italy fell into the hands of politicians whom I have already described more closely above: the dregs of traditions, methods and people already decadent and decaying under a regime of tiny, timorous government.

Source: A. Lyttelton (ed.), Italian Fascisms: From Pareto to Gentile, *1973, pp. 148–51*

This critique of the struggles for independence and unity during the Risorgimento, and of the men who led those struggles, is close to the revisionist interpretation of the Risorgimento. All it lacks as an explanation of Italy's weakness on the international plane, her role as 'the Least of the Great Powers', is an analysis of her economic backwardness. In point six Corradini points the finger at the main Nationalist enemy and bugbear – international socialism. Socialism, with its emphasis on class consciousness and its theory and practice of class struggle, undermined the creation of a strong national consciousness as a preparation of the Italian people for struggle on the international plane. Point seven reveals the essence of the Nationalist critique, both of the Italian political system – parliamentary government – and the politicians who ran it, chief of whom was Giolitti, who in Nationalist eyes embodied all the weaknesses and failings of politicians.

Corradini's cure for the ills of 'Italietta' was the application of Marx's idea of class struggle to the relations between nations, as set out in this speech which he made in 1910.

Document 1.7 The Principles of Nationalism

We must start by recognising that there are proletarian nations as well as proletarian classes; that is to say there are nations whose living conditions are subject to great disadvantage, to the way of life of other nations, just as classes are. Once this is realised, nationalism must, above all, insist firmly on this truth: Italy is, materially and morally, a proletarian nation. What is more, she is proletarian at a period before her recovery. That is to say, before she is organised, at a period when she is still groping and weak. And being subjected to other nations, she is weak not in the strength of her people but in her strength as a nation. Exactly like the proletariat before socialism came to its aid . . . [and] . . . just as socialism taught the proletariat the value of the class struggle, we must teach Italy the value of the international class struggle.

But international class struggle means war.

Well, let it be war! And let nationalism arouse in Italy the will to win a war.

Source: A. Lyttelton (ed.), Italian Fascisms: From Pareto to Gentile, *1973, pp. 146–7*

The international class struggle of the proletarian Italian nation would, of course, be directed against the 'plutocratic' powers, that is Britain and France principally, because the logic of Italian imperialism demanded that, apart from Ethiopia, colonies could only be acquired from the empires of those powers. And this logic was reinforced by the emphasis of Corradini and the Nationalists on the inspiring myth of Rome, the need to recreate the Roman Empire in the Mediterranean and North Africa. Conversely, Italy needed to strengthen her links with her friends in the Triple Alliance, Germany and Austria-Hungary, with the result that one of the most cherished aspirations of the Nationalists, irredentism (from the Italian *terre irredente*, 'unredeemed lands'), the desire to liberate the Italian-speaking territories inside the Habsburg empire, would have to be put on ice.

The nationalism of Corradini, and others such as Alfredo Rocco who first advocated a corporatist solution to the problems of relations between classes, was only a part of a much larger revolt against the prevailing political class and its rational, liberal-conservative ideas and policies in the period leading up to the First World War. This revolt took a largely cultural form; it was carried on, for example, in the columns of numerous literary reviews, such as Corradini's own journal, *Il Regno*, and in the literature of the period. Gabriele D'Annunzio, while remaining politically aloof, shared many of Corradini's ideas, and often in a more extreme form. D'Annunzio's poetry and prose contained lyrical exaltations of patriotism and war, all couched in religious imagery. But as Adrian Lyttelton has pointed out, 'the ethic of D'Annunzio was "Nietzschean" and "Darwinian", not Christian. "The dictates of the 'heroic will' are the highest law, and conflict is the essence of civilisation"' (Lyttelton, 1973, p. 180).

An even more radical rejection of existing values was offered by the most avantgardist of all cultural movements in Italy before the First World War, the Futurists. What the Futurists proposed was nothing less than a cultural revolution – 'Heap up the fires to the shelves of the libraries! Divert the canals to flood the cellars of the museums!' As the following extract shows, they were violently infatuated with action, speed and war.

Document 1.8 Manifesto of Futurism

1 We want to sing of the love of danger, the habit of energy and rashness.
2 The essential elements of our poetry will be courage, audacity and revolt.
3 Literature has up to now magnified pensive immobility, ecstasy and slumber. We want to exhalt movements of aggression, feverish sleeplessness, the double march, the perilous leap, the slap and the blow with the fist.
4 We declare that the splendour of the world has been enriched by a new beauty: the beauty of speed. A racing automobile with its bonnet adorned with great tubes like serpents with explosive breath . . . a roaring motor car which seems to run on machine-gun fire, is more beautiful that the Victory of Samothrace.
5 We want to sing the man at the wheel, the ideal axis of which crosses the earth, itself hurled along its orbit.
6 The poet must spend himself with warmth, glamour and prodigality to increase the enthusiastic fervour of the primordial elements.
7 Beauty only exists in struggle. There is no masterpiece that has not an aggressive character. Poetry must be a violent assault on the forces of the unknown, to force them to bow before man.
8 We are on the extreme promontory of the centuries! What is the use of looking at the moment when we must open the mysterious shutters of the impossible? Time and Space died yesterday. We are already living in the absolute, since we have already created eternal, omnipresent speed.
9 We want to glorify war – the only cure for the world – militarism, patriotism, the destructive gesture of the anarchists, the beautiful ideas that kill, and contempt for woman.

Source: A. Lyttelton (ed.), Italian Fascisms: From Parento to Gentile, *1973, pp. 211–12*

Here we see the very disturbing common elements between D'Annunzio and the Futurists, the cult of irrationalism, un-trammelled (male) egoism, the cult of violence and war and aggressive misogyny, all of which would form key parts of the peculiar 'psyche' of post-war Fascism.

The Nationalists, Futurists and the others in revolt against 'Italietta' had one other thing in common, they feared the social and political revolution which was already in train in Italy, the emergence of the working-class movement and mass politics, and they blamed Giolitti and his democratic tendencies for encouraging these developments. In the final analysis, much of their rhetoric reflected a profound sense of class insecurity.

The Nationalists may be placed on the 'right' of the Italian political spectrum at this time. D'Annunzio and the Futurists, however, would have rejected such a collocation. But there were others, also in revolt, the revolutionary socialists, including Mussolini, and the revolutionary syndicalists who are definitely to be placed on the extreme left. They shared the common opposition to Giolitti and all he stood for. They increasingly found themselves in disagreement with their more orthodox Marxist comrades, both Maximalists and Reformists, inside the working-class movement, on the question of revolution and the use of violence to achieve it. The Intervention Crisis of 1915 and the Italian experience of the First World War that followed would show that many of them had much more in common with the extremists of the right than they could have imagined.

The cultural and political movements described here were to have a profound impact on Italian society and politics. In the short term they influenced a whole generation of educated, especially university-educated, Italian youth in a nationalistic direction, predisposing them, as it were, to Fascist ideas and propaganda in the 1920s. In the medium term their ideas were to provide the basis for much of the ideology and policy of Fascism.

The Failure of Giolittianism

In 1929 the Communist Party leader Palmiro Togliatti wrote this about Giolittianism: 'Between 1901 and 1915 there took place in Italy the most serious attempt to reform the Liberal state, that is to consolidate and broaden the basis of bourgeois political hegemony' (Togliati, 1970, p. 147).

But as he also points out, the experiment was a failure. Giolitti did not succeed in broadening the base of the Liberal state. Despite all his reformist efforts, he failed to 'tame' the working-class movement, to 'absorb' it into the Italian state. On the contrary, the working-class movement as a whole was more hostile to the state at the end of the Giolittian 'experiment' than it had been at the beginning, as is demonstrated by the general elections of 1913, the first under the extended franchise. Only the massive mobilisation of the Catholic vote, freed now from the restrictions of the 'Non Expedit', saved Giolitti's liberal parliamentary majority from the Socialist 'wave'. The alienation of the masses from the state was demonstrated even more dramatically when Northern and Central Italy was convulsed by rioting during 'Red Week' in June 1914.

To make matters worse, as we have seen, he also failed to appease the Nationalist right. They exploited dissatisfaction over the outcome of the Libyan War and managed to enter parliament for the first time in 1913, winning six seats. And Italian politics generally took a turn to the right when Giolitti resigned in March 1914 and the government was taken over by his conservative critics Antonio Salandra and Sidney Sonnino. Italian politics was now polarising around an extreme left and an extreme right, and as Paul Corner has argued:

> of particular importance was the fact that (at least as far as the nationalists and Socialists were concerned) the forces which had been released remained extra-parliamentary in their attitudes and further weakened, rather than strengthened, the institutional structure of the country.
>
> **(Corner, 1986, p. 17)**

And he goes on to show what the ultimate consequences of Giolitti's failure would be.

> The Giolittian period was possibly the moment in which radical changes, representing a fundamentally new strategy towards social protest, might have occurred and been incorporated in the political framework of liberalism. That they were not ultimately destroyed the central feature of that framework – parliamentary democracy, however limited.
>
> **(Corner, 1986, p. 17)**

It is no exaggeration to say that Giolitti's failure to launch Italy on the path of a representative, mass democracy in the pre-war years helped open the way for Mussolini and Fascism in the post-war period.

2 The crisis of the Liberal state and the rise of Fascism

Fascism was a European phenomenon, in large part the result of the disturbed economic, social and political conditions which were created by the destruction and dislocation of the First World War. Italian Fascism was no exception to this; indeed, it was very much a 'child' of war, and it has frequently been claimed that without the war there would have been no (Italian) Fascism. While the crisis of the Liberal state in post-war Italy was in part a continuation of the pre-war situation, the war greatly exacerbated the problems of the earlier period, and this provided the essential conditions for the rise of Fascism.

The Intervention Crisis and the First World War

At the outbreak of the First World War in August 1914 the Italian government decided to remain neutral. In the circumstances, this was the only course of action open to the Italians. Even though she was the third partner in the Triple Alliance with Germany and Austria-Hungary, Italy had nothing to gain by going to war on the side of her allies. The attempt by the government of Salandra and Sonnino to persuade Vienna to sacrifice Trieste and Trento (the two Italian-speaking territories still under Habsburg control) as the price of Italian military support failed. Vienna believed that a cession of territory on the principle of nationality would undermine the whole basis of the empire. The presence of the British and French navies in the Mediterranean was a further disincentive to hostilities with the Entente. In any case, there was little support from Italian public opinion for entering the war on the side of Germany and Austria-Hungary; only the Nationalists were in favour of this option.

Eight months later the Italians had abandoned neutrality and in the secret Treaty of London agreed to enter the war on the side of Britain, France and Russia.

Document 2.1 The Treaty of London, 1915

Article 2 On her part, Italy undertakes to use her entire resources for the purpose of waging war jointly with France, Great Britain and Russia against all their enemies . . .
Article 4 Under the Treaty of Peace, Italy shall obtain the Trentino, Cisalpine Tyrol with its geographical and natural frontier [the Brenner

frontier], as well as Trieste, the counties of Gorizia and Gradisca, all Istria as far as the Quarnero and including Volosca and the Istrian islands of Cherso and Lussini . . .
Article 5 Italy shall also be given the province of Dalmatia within its present administrative boundaries . . .
Article 9 . . . in the event of the total or partial partition of Turkey in Asia, she [Italy] ought to obtain a just share of the Mediterranean region adjacent to the province of Adalia, where Italy has already acquired rights . . .
Article 13 In the event of France and Great Britain increasing their colonial territories in Africa at the expense of Germany, those powers agree that Italy may claim an equitable compensation . . .
Article 15 France, Great Britain and Russia shall support any such opposition as Italy shall make to any proposal in the direction of introducing a representative of the Holy See [the Papacy] in any peace negotiations or negotiations for the settlement of questions raised by the present war.

Source: J.A.S. Grenville, The Major International Treaties, 1914–1945. A History and Guide with Texts, *1987, pp. 24–7*

These terms demonstrate that the primary motivation for intervening in the war was to complete the unification process by acquiring the 'unredeemed lands' and securing a more defensible north-eastern frontier. This 'sacred egoism' justified Italy's ditching of her allies of thirty-five years' standing. Italy was made some promises in relation to future colonial gains as well, and her fears regarding the 'Roman Question' were quietened by Article 15. Another factor influencing Salandra and Sonnino in their decision to go to war was the belief that participation in a successful war would solve Italy's domestic problems, by generating national unity and restoring the authority of the political class which had been seriously damaged, so they believed, by Giolitti's compromises with the Socialists and political Catholics.

Italy's adherence to the Treaty of London had been made on the basis of royal prerogative: parliamentary approval for a declaration of war was required if national support for the war effort was to be mobilised. But parliament was still effectively controlled by Giolitti, who had steadfastly opposed Italian intervention since August 1914. On the other hand, there had been a swing away from neutralism in certain important political quarters. Like a small faction of the revolutionary syndicalists, Mussolini and a handful of his Socialist comrades had come to the conclusion that war offered an unrepeatable opportunity for the Italian working-class movement. War, he believed, would weaken the whole capitalist bourgeois system and open the way forward to revolution. His thinking on the situation could be summed up in the words used by the revolutionary syndicalist leader, Labriola, about the Libyan War three years earlier, 'A people that does not know how to make a war, will never be able to make a revolution' (quoted in Seton-Watson, 1967, p. 371).

The Nationalists and Futurists also wanted war and their influence was growing. More surprisingly perhaps, the cry for war was taken up by a motley collection of Reformist Socialists, Radicals, Republicans, Liberal Democrats and even Catholic politicians. What all of these groups had in common was a belief that intervention would break the power of the old political elite, above all Giolitti, and open the way to change. Interventionism was, therefore, a revolt against Giolitti.

However influential the interventionist groups were, they constituted a small minority of public opinion as a whole. Parliament's neutralist majority represented majority opinion in the country: Giolitti's electoral supporters, the bulk of Catholic politicians and their peasant supporters and the Socialists and their followers among the urban and rural proletariat. In addition, the Vatican was opposed to intervention, fearing the defeat of its only great power ally, Austria-Hungary, or alternatively social and political breakdown in Italy. Yet the interventionists won the day. The influence exerted by the press, the King, the armed forces and the mass demonstrations in the piazzas orchestrated by D'Annunzio and others were successful in imposing the will of Salandra and Sonnino on parliament. Giolitti was unwilling to oppose intervention vigorously for fear of precipitating the abdication of the King, who had personally committed himself to intervention. So Italy declared war on Austria-Hungary on 24 May 1915.

The events of May 1915, the 'Intervention Crisis' as they are known, bear a strong resemblance to events over seven years later, the so-called 'March on Rome' of October 1922 when the Fascists, supported by elements of the establishment, brought Mussolini to power. Indeed, the Intervention Crisis might be described as a dress rehearsal for the March on Rome. Certainly, there were lessons to be learnt from the events of 1915 for budding putschists. In both cases, the wishes of parliament and the Italian people were overridden by a small, vociferous, largely extra-parliamentary minority, while the passive role of Giolitti and the assertiveness of the King were crucial in this process. The Intervention Crisis of 1915 was to have further important significance: out of these events was born the myth of 'the glorious days of May', when allegedly Italian national spirit was reborn. This myth was to be used by the Fascists as a rallying cry throughout the 1920s, 1930s and into the 1940s.

Italy and the First World War

The First World War was a painful experience for Italy, revealing its economic weakness, the shortcomings of the political class and the incompetence of the military elite. Admittedly, Italy was literally fighting an uphill struggle, from a strategically disadvantaged position on the plains and foothills of Northern Italy against the Austrians ensconced in the mountains, as can be seen from this map.

Document 2.2 Italy during the First World War

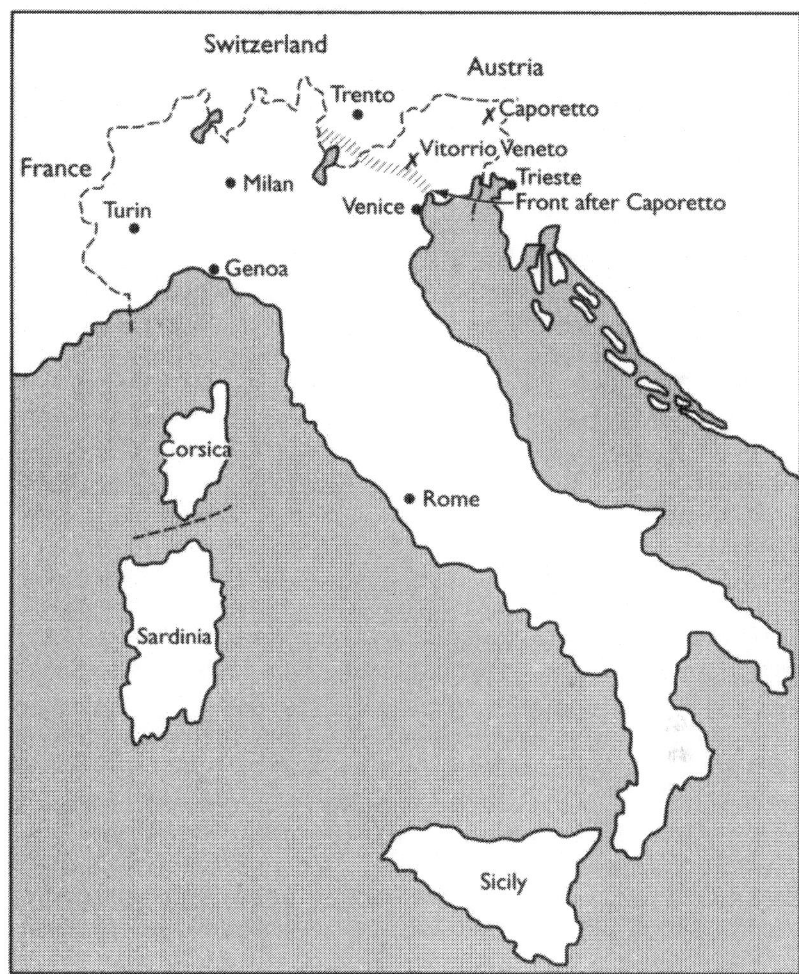

Italy's difficulties were exacerbated by the poor leadership provided by the political class, and the appalling incompetence of the High Command, hence the catastrophic defeat at Caporetto in October 1917. The officer class managed to cover up their mistakes by blaming Caporetto on the defeatism and treachery of the Socialists, whose continuing neutralist stance was summed up in the slogan 'Neither support nor sabotage', and to a lesser extent on the Pope and Catholic clergy. So the army survived the war with its honour and prestige intact, as did other elite institutions such as the monarchy. Indeed, that institution had never been so popular in its history as after the First World War. Victor Emmanuel III thus became, for the upper and middle classes at least, 'the victorious King'. But the authority of the political class led by Salandra and Sonnino was seriously undermined by its conduct of the war, as was parliament. Even more than in other democratic countries such as Britain and France, for the duration of hostilities parliament was largely ignored in the decision-making process which consequently passed into the hands of a few politicians, the High Command and the war industries lobby. On the economic front, labour, wages and price controls, the effective repression of the trade unions and the close relationship between government and the business community foreshadowed the corporate state that would be created by Fascism.

The First World War had another important effect on the Italian political situation: it radicalised a large part of a previously politically illiterate and inert mass electorate. A number of different factors were responsible for this: President Wilson's demand, encapsulated in his famous 'Fourteen Points', for a more democratic future; the promises made by wartime leaders in order to rally support for the war effort, for example, 'Save Italy and she is yours', which was specifically interpreted as a promise of land reform; the impact of the Bolshevik revolution of October 1917; and the remarkable process of informal political 'education' which took place in the trenches as peasant soldiers from remote regions rubbed shoulders with more politically sophisticated comrades from urban areas.

The radical mood created in the trenches transferred itself to civilian, peacetime society and was manifested most obviously in a general demand for radical economic, social and political change. Almost all political movements in 1919 – most especially the two newest political groupings, the Partito Popolare Italiano (henceforth the P.P.I. or Popolari) of Catholic priest Luigi Sturzo and the Fasci of Mussolini – represented this demand in their programmes. The radical mood was also reflected in the direct involvement of many ex-servicemen in politics through established parties, in veterans' associations acting as political pressure groups and through the founding of new political formations such as the Fasci and Sardinian Action Party. And due to the aggressive impatience of millions of ex-servicemen, Italian politics in the post-First World War period was inevitably rougher and more violent than in the past, an experience shared by other European countries.

The Birth of Fascism

Fascism began its life on 23 March 1919 in Milan, the industrial, commercial and cultural capital of Italy, when an assortment of Futurists, ex-revolutionary syndicalists, ex-revolutionary socialists and ex-servicemen led primarily by Mussolini founded the Fascio di Combattimento. The name was chosen with care: the word *fascio*, simply meaning group, was selected in preference to the word 'party' to demonstrate that the new political movement wished to have nothing to do with the old, 'corrupt' parties of the existing political system. From *fascio* came *fascismo*, meaning the movement and its ideology, and *fascista/i* for its followers. The word *combattimento* was meant to convey the idea that Fascism was a movement of struggle and action, and it reflected the crucial formative influence of the war on the movement and its leaders.

Indeed, the Fascists, or 'blackshirts' as they were known from their most typical garment, assumed a paramilitary character and appearance from the start, thanks to the presence of so many ex-servicemen and the adoption by the movement of the rhetoric of interventionism, the wearing of uniforms and the carrying of weapons. But ex-servicemen, however warmly they were welcomed by Mussolini, were not the only target of his propaganda. The future Duce of Fascism envisaged his movement offering a patriotic alternative to the Socialist Party.

This choice of strategy is explained by Mussolini's early political career. Born the son of a radical father in the Romagna, notoriously Italy's most revolutionary region, after a fairly chequered educational career and a not too successful period as a teacher, Mussolini found his political home, and an outlet for his literary talents, in the Socialist Party. Despite his doubtful Marxist orthodoxy, Mussolini's rise inside the party hierarchy was meteoric. Profiting from the sharp swing to the left which followed the Libyan War, Mussolini was elected editor of *Avanti!* the party newspaper, in 1912. From this vantage point he was able to exert an enormous influence on the highest counsels of the working-class movement.

But Mussolini's popularity with his fellow Socialists was to be shortlived. Though he began by vociferously denouncing the idea of Italian intervention in the war in August 1914, his doubts about Italy's continued neutrality left him out of step with majority opinion in the party. Thus support for intervention took Mussolini outside of the mainstream of the Italian working-class movement, for in October 1914 he was expelled from the Socialist Party as a traitor to its neutralist policy, an experience he neither forgot nor forgave, though he did try, unsuccessfully, to re-establish his socialist credentials as late as 1944. On the other hand, he quickly found new backers for his journalistic talents among leading war industrialists both at home and abroad who financed the start of a new daily paper *Il Popolo d'Italia*. His experience of war was fairly uneventful, apart from being invalided out after an accident in 1917. But in the trenches Mussolini had not neglected either his newspaper or his position as the leader of the revolutionary interventionist cause: in December 1917 he set up the Fascio Rivoluzionario di Intervento to add to the political pressure for a more effective prosecution of the war effort in the wake of the defeat at Caporetto. He also took note of the significance of the Bolshevik revolution of October 1917. This confirmed him in his belief that his political future still lay on the left, along a revolutionary path in association with the working masses. And this left-wing position is clearly reflected in the programme of the first *fascio*.

Document 2.3 The Manifesto of the First *Fascio*, 1919

For the social problem: WE INSIST UPON: a) Prompt promulgation of a state law that makes compulsory for all workers an eight-hour day. b) Minimum wage scales. c) Participation of workers' representatives in the technical management of industry). Transfer to such proletarian organisations as are morally and technically qualified for it the responsibility for operating industries and public services. For the financial problem: WE INSIST UPON: a) A heavy and progressive tax on capital which would take the form of a meaningful PARTIAL EXPROPRIATION of all kinds of wealth. b) Confiscation of all properties belonging to religious congregations and abolition of all the revenues of episcopal sees, which at present constitute an enormous burden on the nation while serving as a prerogative for a few privileged persons. c) Revision of all contracts supplying war *matériel*, and confiscation of 85 per cent of war profits.

For the political problem: a) Universal suffrage with a system of regional voting by list, with proportional representation, and woman suffrage and eligibility for office. b) Reduction of the age of voters to eighteen years; and that eligibility for membership of the Chamber of Deputies to twenty-five years. c) Abolition of the Senate. d) Convocation of a National Assembly to sit for three years, its primary task to be the establishment of a new contitutional structure for the state.

Source: C.F. Delzell (ed.), Mediterranean Fascism 1919–1945, *1970, pp. 12–14*

Radical though this programme may be, it is clearly not a Marxist-Socialist platform, advocating the overthrow of the capitalist bourgeois class. Again, the idea of workers' control is more national-syndicalist than Socialist. The call for the expropriation of ecclesiastical property is evidence of the anti-clericalism common to most interventionists and the demand for a tax on war profits, a reflection of the deeply felt grievances of ex-servicemen that they had been exploited by the munitions industry. These political demands firmly set the new Fascist movement in the context of the spirit of the post-war Italy – *Dicianovismo* – literally 'nineteen-nineteenism'. In other words, it was making the same kinds of demands for democratisation as all the democratic parties, the Socialists, the Catholic Popolari and the Republicans, on behalf of the politicised masses. The Fascist programme was built around an 'unholy trinity' of anti-capitalism, anti-clericalism and republicanism; though the latter was not explicit, it can be discerned in the call for 'a new constitutional structure' and in the following document.

Document 2.4 Fascist Republicanism, 1919

[The Constituent Assembly] will have to choose between a republic and a monarchy; and we who have always been inclined towards a republic say here and now that we favour a republic.

Source: E. Susmel and D. Susmel (eds), Opera Omnia di Benito Mussolini *(henceforth cited as* Opera Omnia*), XII, p. 321*

Fascism was to have little success in its chosen political setting or with the working classes: they remained overwhelmingly loyal to the Socialist Party. Instead, as it developed in 1919 and 1920, Fascism drew its support from middle- and lower-class elements – students, journalists and unemployed professionals, mostly veterans of the war. The results of the November 1919 general elections were a humiliating defeat for the Fascist movement which gained no seats. Mussolini and his fellow Fascist candidates won only 5,000 out of the 270,000 votes cast in the Milan constituency. His Socialist opponents jubilantly paraded with a coffin outside of the premises of *Il Popolo D'Italia* (the sole Fascist daily newspaper) and it seemed that his political career was over. Yet Fascism survived this setback, and grew slowly through the winter and spring of 1919/20. By the summer, thirty-six *fasci*, or branches of the movement, with a total of roughly 20,000 members, had been established, mainly in the great cities of Northern and Central Italy – Milan, Turin, Genoa and Venice. Indeed, at this stage of its development, Fascism was an almost entirely urban or even metropolitan phenomenon.

The Crisis of the Liberal State: Parliamentary Paralysis

The emergence of the Fascist movement took place against the background of an acute multiple crisis – economic, social and political – which beset the Liberal state in the post-war period. Ironically, the parliamentary dimension of the crisis was exacerbated, rather than ameliorated, by the efforts of part of its political class to meet the demands for change, for greater democracy. Francesco Nitti, the first truly post-war prime minister, carried out an electoral reform which enfranchised remaining categories of adult males and introduced proportional representation. Despite the opposition of more conservative elements, including Salandra and Giolitti, the reforms were passed in time for the general election of November 1919. Thanks to the new electoral arrangements, and to Nitti's principled refusal to use the patronage resources traditionally available to an Italian prime minister at election time, the Liberal political class effectively committed political suicide. The result was an electoral 'Caporetto' for the Liberals, who lost the parliamentary dominance they had enjoyed since unification.

This year marked the triumph, albeit temporarily, of mass politics in Italy because the victors were the two mass parties, the Socialists (who gained 150 seats and thus became the largest party and the Catholic P.P.I. (which won a quarter of the votes and seats). There were many reasons for the defeat of the Liberal notables: the radicalisation of the masses; the almost universal desire for change; and the discrediting of the old political class during the course of the war. Another was the massive transfer of Catholic votes which in the pre-war period had tended to go to Liberal candidates, but went to the P.P.I. in 1919. The emergence of the P.P.I. probably also denied the Socialist Party an outright victory in the election.

These changes were to produce a situation of political stalemate which eventually led to the paralysis of the system of parliamentary government. On the one hand, the Socialist Deputies, led by Filippo Turati, true to the directives of the

1912 party congress which forbade collaboration with the 'bourgeois parties', refused to accept the responsibilities of parliamentary government and during the King's speech at the opening of the new session they withdrew from the chamber shouting, 'Down with parliament'. On the other hand, this left the P.P.I., a brand-new, entirely inexperienced and extremely heterogeneous party, to carry burdens of government for which it was not prepared. With an effective leader, Don Luigi Sturzo, who could not lead from inside parliament because of his priestly status, and a parliamentary leader, Filippo Meda, who would not shoulder the responsibilities of the premiership when called upon to do so, the P.P.I. was condemned to play the role of junior but essential partner in a succession of short-lived coalition governments led by Liberal notables – Nitti, Giolitti, Bonomi and Facta – which ruled Italy between November 1919 and October 1922. The possibility of a broad, reformist alliance of the two mass parties was ruled out by the yawning ideological gulf between them.

The intransigence of the P.P.I., and especially Sturzo, has often been held responsible for the weakness and instability of these governments (Molony, 1977, p. 106), but the Liberal leaders were equally if not more to blame. They were unwilling to accept the reality of radically changed political circumstances, to recognise that the tactics of transformism would not work in a new era of mass politics and therefore to treat the P.P.I. as an independent, autonomous political entity. The May 1915 crisis, which had split the Liberal political class into Interventionists and Neutralists, did not help: it made it virtually impossible for supporters of Salandra and supporters of Giolitti to cooperate in government.

Whoever was to blame, the weak and unstable governments in the post-war period proved quite incapable of resolving the grave problems which Italy faced, and in their desire for effective government many Italians began to turn to Mussolini and the Fascists.

The 'Mutilated Victory'

One major problem lay in the realm of foreign policy, the so-called 'Mutilated Victory'. Italian public opinion was deeply dissatisfied with the Versailles Peace Settlement of 1919. Italy did win most of the territorial gains promised by the Treaty of London. In fact, she did rather well out of the Peace Settlement, achieving both the natural and defensible boundaries along the Eastern Alps and the 'unredeemed lands'. But Orlando (the Italian Prime Minister) failed to persuade the 'Big Three' at the Paris talks to give Italy a share of the German and Turkish empires. The aspect of the Peace which most outraged Italians was the award of the town of Fiume, which was 50 per cent Italian speaking, to the new state of Yugoslavia. The Nationalists and Fascists were able to claim that Italy had been cheated of her due reward for the war effort, that her victory had been 'mutilated' and they blamed Orlando and weak parliamentary government for this. In September 1919, despite the fact that Fiume had not been promised to Italy by the Treaty of London, Gabriele D'Annunzio and his shock troops, the *arditi*, seized the city by force and held it until 'Bloody Christmas' 1920, when Giolitti sent in the Italian army to oust him. The reluctance and slowness of Italian governments to crush this rebellion damaged their credibility, suggesting that they were unable or unwilling to prevent right-wing violence and illegal actions, a lesson that was not lost on Mussolini.

Economic and Social Problems

In common with other European countries at this time, Italy experienced severe economic problems in the aftermath of the war. The sudden switch from war to a peacetime economy was especially painful for Italy as government orders ceased, foreign markets dried up and a massive trade deficit emerged. To add to the government's difficulties, the massive budget deficit was worsened by the cutting off of foreign loans. The value of the lira continued to slide on the foreign exchanges while inflation, after a fourfold increase in the cost of living during the war, continued to rise thereafter. The groups most at risk from inflation were the middle classes and all those who had rather less bargaining power than the unionised working classes; hence their growing dissatisfaction with government policy in this period.

Unemployment was rather less of a problem immediately after the war, as a result of losses at the front and also the toll exacted by the influenza epidemic. But it began to rise very quickly in line with the rundown in production until it reached a figure of 2 million by the end of 1920. Unemployment among the educated and professional classes was a particularly severe problem, though not one of the direct economic effects of the war as such, but rather a consequence of graduate 'overproduction'. Yet another group felt aggrieved and under-represented in the political system and therefore ultimately became susceptible to the appeal of Fascism. Demobilisation was probably more rapid in Italy than elsewhere in Europe and the importance of the psychological problems facing the millions of men trying to adjust to civilian life should not be underestimated. Thousands of discontented and disillusioned ex-combatants, officers and men, were to play a key role in the development of the Fascist movement, and in the formation of the paramilitary squads in particular.

'The Red Two Years'

One of the sharpest forms which post-war political radicalism took was the militancy of the working masses, such that 1918 to 1920 have been dubbed 'the red two years'. The expansion of manufacturing industry during the war, the consequent growth of the industrial working class and the political radicalisation of sections of the peasantry all helped to reinforce the working-class movement in the post-war period. Its new strength was manifested by the increase in membership of working-class organisations, in the increased support won by the Socialist Party in the 1919 general election and the 1920 local government elections and in widespread militancy at the rank and file level of the trade unions, peasant leagues and so on, which were now freed from wartime restrictions. Significantly, a similar, though less violent, militancy is also observable among members of the Catholic peasant leagues and trade unions at this time.

In the red two years Italy was racked by numerous strikes, protests against rises in the cost of living, occupations of the factories and land (the latter often led by ex-servicemen) and some systematic violence against the opponents of socialism. But if there was a militant, not to say revolutionary, mood among the rank and file, then it is clear that the leadership of the working-class movement had not elaborated a revolutionary strategy. In particular, some of the leading figures in the Socialist Party preached revolution but had no practical plans to bring it about. A famous headline in the party newspaper, *Avanti!*, of November 1919 epitomises their attitude: 'All we have to do is wait.'

This passivity is best exemplified by the policy of the party during the Occupation of the Factories in the summer of 1920. After the failure of negotiations between the employers and the unions in the engineering and car industries, on 30 August the workers occupied the factories in Turin in order to forestall a lockout. Very quickly the occupations spread to other cities in Northern Italy, and arms were stockpiled in some factories. At this point the working-class movement, or at least some sections of it, came close to a revolutionary situation. In Turin, for example, Antonio Gramsci, a future leader of the Italian Communist Party, established a factory organisation along the lines of the Russian soviets. But by the middle of September the revolutionary potential of the situation had dissipated. On the one hand, the Socialist Party leadership declared the occupations to be an essentially economic struggle, handing over their direction to the moderate leadership of its union wing, the General Confederation of Labour. On the other hand, Prime Minister Giolitti adhered to his long-held policy of not using military or police forces in industrial disputes, precisely in order to avoid precipitating a revolutionary outcome to the dispute.

Though the solution which was eventually negotiated made some concessions to the workers, in the longer term the Occupation of the Factories was a serious defeat for the working-class movement. Members of the unions were disillusioned and demoralised, a feeling which quickly showed itself in the decline in trade union membership. The industrialists were also dissatisfied. They blamed Giolitti for what they considered to be the humiliation which they had suffered, and their confidence in his government consequently wilted. In broader terms, the factory occupations and other forms of working-class militancy, taken against the background of Bolshevik revolts and soviet-style governments in Eastern and Central Europe, gave rise to deep fears on the part of the middle and upper classes of the danger of revolution in Italy. As the anarchist leader, Errico Malatesta observed at the time: 'We shall pay with tears of blood for this fright we have given the bourgeoisie' (quoted in Seton-Watson, 1967, p. 525).

The Growth of the Fascist Movement, 1920–1

Mussolini had watched with acute interest and anxiety as the events of the red two years moved towards their climax in the Occupation of the Factories. Though some Fascist squads had already begun to take sides, by participating in strike-breaking activities, Mussolini himself played a waiting game, careful not to burn his boats, so as to be able to profit from the outcome, whoever won. In view of the wave of Bolshevik activity throughout Central and Eastern Europe at this time, it was the only prudent thing to do. But Mussolini was among the first to perceive the implications of that outcome: that though on paper the workers were the victors, in reality they had been defeated. The real victors were the industrialists who now thirsted for revenge on the workers who had held them to ransom for so long.

It is ironic, therefore, that the first major backlash against the militancy of the working-class movement took place not in the towns but in the countryside, not in an industrial but rather an agrarian context. The timing and location of this backlash, which we may conveniently call 'agrarian Fascism', are explained by the fact that successive rounds of local government elections in 1920 resulted in further advances for the Socialists (and to a lesser extent the Popolari) , who won control of the cities of Milan and Bologna, and most of Emilia and Tuscany regions, with a total of twenty-five of the provincial councils and nearly 2,200 of the district councils (Seton-Watson, 1967, pp. 567–8). In consequence, to many people in those areas it seemed as if the revolution was already taking place around them and the local ruling elites, especially the larger landowners, were ousted from the positions of power which they and their forebears had enjoyed for centuries.

After two years of strikes and land occupations led by the peasant leagues, in both cases often accompanied by violence, the landed classes had now suffered a loss of local political power and with it a loss of control over the agrarian labour market, for the local labour exchange organisation was a branch of the municipal administration. All that landowners could look forward to was an intensification of labour disputes with the peasant leagues, Catholic and Socialist, who now clearly had the upper hand. They could expect no help from a government which followed a policy of non-intervention in major industrial disputes and a succession of Popolare ministers of agriculture put forward legislation aimed at bringing about a measure of land redistribution, as well as the general improvement of the contracts of both sharecroppers and landless labourers.

As Martin Clark has argued, the absence of adequate government protection for the interests of local elites has always been the essential precondition for squadrism in Italy, the use of gangs of Fascist bully boys to repress the threat from the left (Clark, 1987, p. 25). In fact, initially, the landowners took the law into their own hands and formed vigilante groups, the first of these being the The Civil Defence Association of Bologna, to resist the peasant leagues. From the vigilante organisations it was a short step to enlisting the help of existing *fasci* in the provincial towns. While not even a majority of the new *fasci* were led by the local landowners, it is clear that the latter's moral and material support was crucial to the development of squadrism and thus the spread of agrarian Fascism.

In the winter of 1920 and the spring of 1921 agrarian Fascism swept across Northern and Central Italy with the speed and force of a prairie fire. Agrarian Fascism established strongholds in Emilia, Tuscany, Umbria and the lower parts of Lombardy and Venetia, and even spread into the Marches. But as late as October 1922 Fascism was a little-known force in the South of Italy precisely because the phenomenon against which it was largely a reaction – agrarian socialism – was almost entirely absent from among a peasantry that was effectively held in check by permanent forces of land 'guards' working on behalf of the landowners. The major exception to this situation was the Tavoliere district of Apulia region. Here bitter conflict between organised peasant unions and large-scale capitalistic farmers or farm managers created the ideal conditions for squadrism.

While the efforts of the landowners were crucial to the development of agrarian Fascism, by themselves they would not have been able to make it into the mass movement it became. Where did the thousands, and hundreds of thousands come from? Initially, they emerged from the other rural groups which felt threatened and offended by the Socialist victory in the provincial towns and cities – salaried employees of the landowners, shopkeepers and small businessmen and local professional people. A further group included small peasant proprietors and tenant farmers, leaseholders and even sharecroppers. Some of the latter felt threatened by the unprecedented dominance enjoyed by the Socialist-controlled councils and peasant leagues, which for them meant taking on labour they did not want and at wage rates they could not afford. And a factor which should not be discounted in the swelling of the ranks of agrarian Fascism was the 'Sword of Damocles' perceived in the Socialist pledge to collectivise the land. Before the war, collectivisation had been a largely empty formula in the programme and rhetoric of the working-class movement, but after the war, when the Socialists appeared to be making advances on every front, it assumed real substance as a threat to all those who held land, even miserable sharecroppers, who had been among the staunchest supporters of agrarian socialism. It has been calculated that over a half a million people acquired some land, many for the first time, in the period immediately following the war (Farneti, 1978, pp. 14–57). If this is true, then too many people had too much to lose from a victory of socialism in Italy.

Until January 1921 Fascism possessed no clear policy on agrarian matters. One had to be quickly put together to provide a policy framework which could satisfy the very diverse and sometimes conflicting interests of the various elements of rural society of which agrarian Fascism was composed, as this extract demonstrates.

Document 2.5 The Fascist Agrarian Programme, 1921

1 The Land for him who works it can be a superficial, demagogic and harmful formula if promises are made to apply it with the accompaniment

of beating drums. In reality, the question is complex and the application of this principle requires very careful preparation. Let us begin with the *latifondo* . . . the proper utilisation of lands in the *latifondi* must be a slow, gradual, and expensive process. If it were done tumultuously it would be disastrous.
2 Large-scale farming. Generally speaking, large-scale industrial enterprises are healthy. Only ignorance could confuse them with the *latifondo* . . .
3 Breaking up of estates. Not only is a system of *latifondi* harmful to the nation, so too is the breaking up of estates.

Source: C.F. Delzell (ed.), Mediterranean Fascism, 1919–1945 *1971, pp. 18–22*

The programme was cautious, gradualistic and not radically innovative, going less far than the Popolari, for example, had gone in the direction of land reform and land improvement. Its major concern was not to alienate its major backers, the large landowners in the Northern or Central regions, or in the South.

As the campaign of squadrist violence and intimidation intensified, it progressively destroyed many peasant leagues, Catholic and Socialist, between 1920 and 1922.

Document 2.6 Squadrist Violence in the Province of Bologna

Must report to your Excellency the very grave situation which has been created in the town of Budrio. Terrorised by an unpunished Fascist band using clubs, revolvers etc. Union organisers and municipal administrators forced to leave for fear of death. Workers forced to lock themselves at home because of continuous beatings and threats of beatings. Unions and socialist club ordered to dissolve themselves within 48 hours or face physical destruction. Life of the town is paralysed, authorities impotent. Mass of the workers request energetic measures to protect their freedom of association and personal safety.

Source: Central State Archives, Rome (henceforth ACS), Prime Minister's Office, Bologna Public Security file, 1921, telegram of local Deputy, Luigi Fabbri, to Bonomi, Prime Minister and Minister of the Interior, 1 October 1921

This is but one of dozens of protests, and demands for action, against Fascist violence from areas of Northern and Central Italy to be found in the Bonomi files of this period. Examination of the files also reveals that Fascist violence was often aimed at workers' and peasants' cooperatives, and that a number of former members of unions, leagues and cooperatives, especially landless labourers, were drawn into the alternative Fascist unions set up by local bosses such as Italo Balbo of Ferrara, or even into the squads. Their reward was often a job or a piece of land which the leaders of the *fasci* had little difficulty in extracting from their patrons, the local landowners.

Document 2.7 Agrarian Fascism

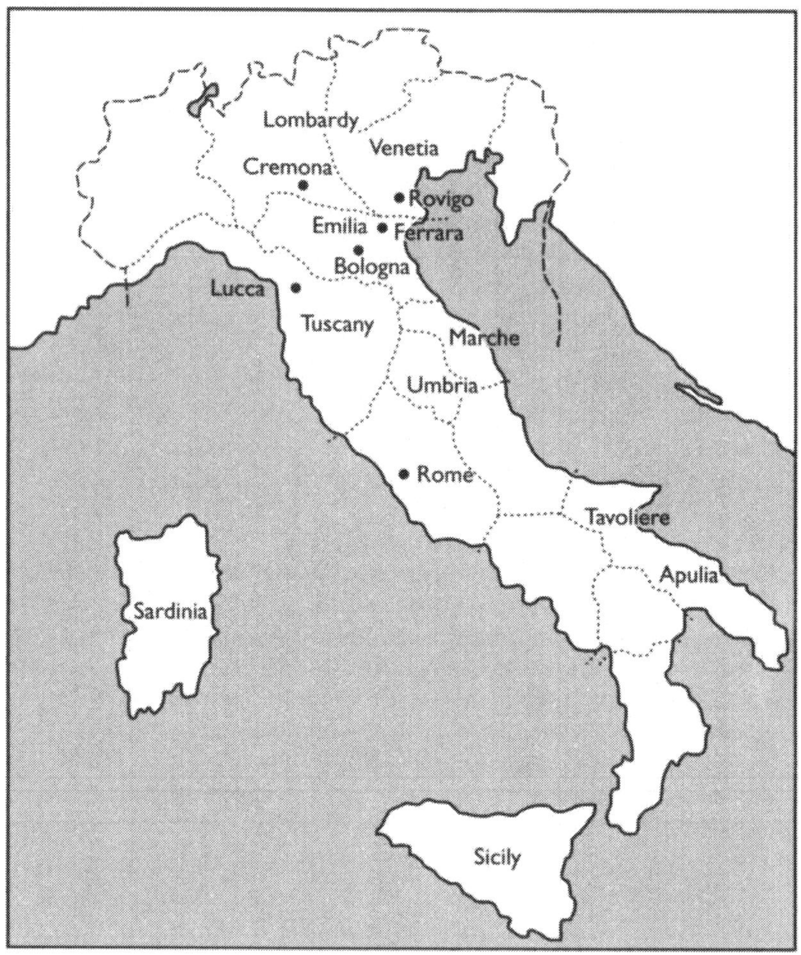

The growth of agrarian Fascism in 1920 and 1921 was sudden, spectacular and largely unexpected. Perhaps the most surprised of all observers was Mussolini who had once stated categorically that Fascism seemed destined to remain an urban phenomenon. The spontaneity and autonomy with which agrarian Fascism developed posed serious problems for the movement as a whole because, in reality, agrarian Fascism was a series of separate, independent provincial 'Fascisms' ruled by the bosses or *ras* – men such as Italo Balbo in Ferrara, Roberto Farinacci in Cremona and Carlo Scorza in Lucca. These men were virtually outside the control of Mussolini and the national leadership of the movement. It took all of Mussolini's powers of leadership, his oratical skills and his ownership of *Il Popolo d'Italia* to impose some semblance of direction on the *ras*. In some really important matters, such as the pact of pacification with the Socialists in 1921 (see Chapter 3, p. 43), the local bosses got their way and resumed their attacks on the enemy. Mussolini temporarily resigned and was only able to recover some of his authority over the bosses by founding the National Fascist Party (P.N.F.) in November 1921. But it was not until some years after he came to power in 1922 that he was finally able to establish his undisputed power over the Fascist movement. Another problem for Mussolini was the inevitable accusation that agrarian Fascism was an essentially reactionary, class movement, a belief held even by some Fascists in the towns, rather than an expression of progressive ideals. Try as he might, Mussolini would never be able to refute such claims successfully.

Support for the Fascist Movement

In the study of the Nazi movement in Germany a whole literature has developed in recent years around the question, 'Who voted for Hitler?' Unfortunately, such a line of enquiry is not feasible with the Fascist movement in Italy, because the elections prior to Fascism's assumption of power, in 1919 and 1921, and those following the March on Rome, in 1924, are not reliable guides to the development of support for the movement. In 1919 the newly born movement got a derisory share of the vote in those constituencies in which it put up candidates. In 1921 Mussolini and the thirty-five other Fascist Deputies were elected on the coat-tails of Giolitti, in his National Bloc of candidates. (Given the nature of the proportional representation voting system, it is difficult to distinguish support for the Fascists from that for other candidates.) And in 1924, imitating Giolitti's example, Mussolini created an electoral 'Big list' of Fascists, Nationalists, defectors from the Catholic P.P.I. and liberal-conservative notables, the latter especially in the South. Once again it is difficult to distinguish between the outright Fascist candidates and their 'hangers-on'. In any case, the systematic use of bribery, corruption and intimidation hopelessly distorted the outcome of the 1924 elections. Historians are, therefore, obliged to concentrate instead on sources of evidence for the *membership* of the Fascist movement as it developed between 1919 and 1922 in their efforts to decide who supported Mussolini.

Document 2.8 P.N.F. Membership Statistics*, November 1921

Profession	*Number*	*Percentage*
Industrialists	4,269	2.8
Agrarians (large, medium and small landowners)	18,094	12.1
Free professions	9,981	6.6
Tradesmen and artisans	13,979	9.3
Private employees	14,989	9.8
Public employees	7,209	4.8
Teachers	1,668	1.2
Students	19,783	13.2
Workers	23,410	15.6
Agricultural workers	36,874	24.6
Totals	150,256	100.0

Note: *Data related to half the total sample.

Source: Il Partito Nazionale Fascista, *Rome, 1935, p. 26*

Even allowing for the inevitable tendency to exaggeration on the part of the Fascists, it is clear that support for their movement had increased enormously since the summer of 1920. It is also evident that Fascism was essentially the political expression of disgruntled middle- and lower-middle-class elements. Foremost were shopkeepers, artisans and small businessmen who felt threatened by 'big business' but also by the other 'big battalions' – the working-class movement organised in Socialist councils (which had forcibly reduced prices) and in government-subsidised workers' cooperatives (which competed at an advantage to many private firms). Professional people, white-collar workers and state employees, whose savings and standard of living had been affected by inflation but who lacked the organisational clout of strong trade unions to protect their interests, also featured strongly. People engaged in farming of every status and degree felt threatened by the peasant leagues' commitment to collectivisation; it needs to be understood that the category 'agricultural workers' includes many small tenant farmers and sharecroppers. There were ex-servicemen in all of these groups, especially officers and N.C.O.s who were angered by the Socialists' lack of patriotism and respect for their sacrifices, and who had difficulty adjusting to civilian life and above all in finding jobs. In their fear, anger and frustration members of all these groups turned to Fascism.

Thus, even allowing for both upper-middle-class elements at one end of the spectrum and industrial workers at the other, Fascism was, as Luigi Salvatorelli, one of the earliest historians of Fascism described it: '. . . the class struggle of the petty bourgeoisie that was wedged between capitalism and the proletariat, as the third combatant between the others' (Salvatorelli and Mira, 1952, p. 13). Historians since Salvatorelli have not departed very much from his view. Even Renzo De Felice's interpretation differs only in emphasis from that of Salvatorelli:

> Fascism as a movement was the idealisation, the desire of an emerging middle class. Here lies the point on which I differ from many scholars of these problems: an emerging middle class that tends to activate its desires in the first person.
>
> **(De Felice, 1977, p. 56)**

For De Felice Fascism was a movement of 'rising' social forces rather than losers or failures. Certainly, the party statistics of 1921 suggest that Fascism was attracting more than its fair share of the two fastest-growing elements in Italian society after the First World War – state employees and small farmers – as well as a disproportionately large share of lawyers, journalists and army officers. With the further support of the landowners, Fascism became a movement of agrarian counter-revolution, or as Lauro Fabbri termed it, 'a preventive counter-revolution' (quoted in De Felice, 1977, p. 118).

The revolution did not, of course, take place, but this did not prevent Mussolini and the Fascists from boldly claiming that they had saved Italy from the horrors of Bolshevik revolution in the 1920s. A very convincing case has also been made by Marxist historians such as Toby Abse that Fascism in some urban contexts was also essentially counter-revolutionary, a function of the bitter class struggles between capital and labour, and this is borne out by the extensive strike-breaking activities of urban *fasci*, and the close connections of some leading manufacturers, especially those in heavy industry and the munitions sector, with the movement (Abse, 1983, pp. 52–83). In other urban contexts, most notably Trento and Trieste, the key factor was not class but ethnicity: in these newly annexed provinces of North-eastern Italy the presence of two ethnic/linguistic minorities, the Germans of the South Tyrol and the Slovenes and Croats in the hinterlands of Trieste, was a strong recruiting factor for the *fasci* from among the local Italian populations. Other statistics demonstrate the localisation of the Fascist movement's development.

Document 2.9 Support for Fascism by Geographical Area

Region	*March 1921*	*December 1921*	*May 1922*
Piedmont	2,411	9,618	14,526
Lombardy	13,968	37,939	79,329
Liguria	2,479	7,405	8,841
Venetia	23,549	44,740	46,708
North Italy	42,677	99,702	148,774
Emilia	17,652	35,647	51,637
Tuscany	2,600	17,768	51,372
North Central Italy	20,252	23,415	103,009
Umbria	485	4,000	5,41
Marches	814	2,072	2,311

Region	*March 1921*	*December 1921*	*May 1922*
Latium	1,480	4,163	9,474
Abruzzi	1,626	6,166	4,763
South Central Italy	4,405	16,401	22,231
Campania	3,550	13,423	13,944
Apulia/Lucania	4,211	19,619	20,683
Calabria	712	2,406	2,066
Sicily	3,569	10,110	9,546
Sardinia	1,100	3,372	2,057
Southern Italy	13,142	48,930	48,296
Total	80,476	218,448	332,310

Source: R. De Felice, Mussolini il Fascista: L'organizzazione della stato fascista 1925–1929, vol. IV, *1966, pp. 8–11*

Outside the major cities of Northern Italy Fascism spread into the countryside and small towns of a specifically defined area. It never managed to move beyond this 'ghetto' until after the March on Rome when seizure of the centralised Italian system of government gave Mussolini and the Fascists control over local government too. Through the prefects, Fascism was able to impose itself on local councils in many areas outside its classic heartlands, especially in the South. Thus Fascism, like Northern Liberalism before it in 1860, and Christian Democracy after it in the late 1940s, effectively 'conquered' the South.

Another strong characteristic of the Fascist movement was its youthfulness. Not for nothing was the official marching song of first D'Annunzio's *arditi*, and then the Fascist squads, entitled 'Giovinezza' ('Youth'). The figures for student support of Fascism in Document 2.8 are striking evidence of this phenomenon, as is this description of the types of people who belonged to the squads of agrarian Fascism.

Document 2.10 The Composition of a Fascist Squad

These squads consisted of young men from the bourgeoisie and petty bourgeoisie of the countryside and of provincial towns. Many were students, but some were socially humbler and there were working-class youngsters among them as well: a mixture of idealists, spoilt brats, misfits and hooligans. Some were demobilised officers or else sons or younger brothers of demobilised officers. They were all young, some very young, proud of their youth and of the war they had fought in or merely dreamed about, and in their violence they employed methods used by the shock troops in the war. The life and dignity of others mattered little to them; indeed it might even seem right and creditable to humiliate them.

Source: G. Carocci, Italian Fascism, 1972, p. 19)

What is also interesting about Carocci's description is the emphasis on the experience of war, or in many cases the vicarious experience of it. War was an essential element of (male) bonding for those who had experienced it, and an inspiring myth for those members of the squads who had not. The class war replaced the First World War as both the field of, and the legitimacy for, violent action; hatred of the working-class movement and this 'enemy within' replaced hatred of the national enemy, the Austrians. The chief pyschological factors in bringing together the disparate groups involved in agrarian Fascism were national pride and pride in the victory of 1918: they were an essential ideological cement to bind together young and old, town- and country-dweller and Italians of different classes.

3 The conquest and consolidation of power

Introduction

Fascism's rise to power was extremely rapid, it took Mussolini just over two and a half years from the founding of his new political movement to become Prime Minister of Italy. In another three years he was its effective master. The Fascists maintained that he achieved this remarkable feat by 'revolution', thus, in 1932, they celebrated their arrival in power ten years earlier with an 'Exhibition of the Fascist Revolution'. The title of the major study in English by Adrian Lyttelton of the rise of Fascism also suggests that it was a 'seizure of power'. On the other hand, it was clearly not an outright, forcible seizure of power in the manner of the Bolshevik revolution of 1917. Nor was the Italian Fascist Party in 1922, in contrast to the Nazi Party in Germany in 1933, an obvious choice to form a government by virtue of widespread electoral support. This suggests that, in some sense, Mussolini was 'given' power. If this is true then we need to know who gave it to him and why.

Having come to power, it took Italian Fascism a relatively long time to consolidate itself and establish its dictatorship – at least seven years. German Nazism, on the other hand, effected its *Gleichschaltung* in just over eighteen months from Hitler's appointment as Chancellor in January 1933. Perhaps the difference here was that the Nazis had come to power after fourteen long, hard years of struggle during which they had built up mass electoral support and also a complex and sophisticated party apparatus which would later enable them to take over the institutions of the German state with relative ease. The Fascist movement, by contrast, was a primitive, disorganised political instrument – indeed, it was to pose as much of a problem to Mussolini as the anti-Fascist opposition parties or the conservative forces during his attempts to consolidate power. Perhaps what Fascism lacked above all was a blueprint, a clear plan of action for government.

The Approach to Power: Fascism enters Parliament, 1921

At the beginning of 1921, Fascism was an essentially violent, extra-parliamentary movement. It was certainly growing rapidly and attracting sympathy and support across a wide spectrum of opinion, but as yet it lacked the crucial prerequisite for an approach to power in the Italian political system – representation in parliament. Mussolini was given his chance to remedy this defect by Giovanni Giolitti in the elections of that year. After notching up considerable successes during his months in office – economic recovery, restoration of the authority of the state in relation to the Fiume question and a peaceful outcome to the Occupation of the Factories – Giolitti now sought to bring back some stability to Italian politics by creating a broad alliance of centre and right-wing forces for electoral purposes, in order to defeat the Socialists, but he failed. The Popolari refused to enter his 'National Bloc' and though the Nationalists, the Fascists and large numbers of liberal conservatives did join forces with him, the bloc failed to win an outright parliamentary majority.

Document 3.1 Italian General Election Results, 1919 and 1921

	Number of seats	
Party/Bloc	*1919*	*1921*
Right		
Fascists*	–	35
Dissident Fascists	–	2
Nationalists*	–	10
Centre		
Conservative Liberals	41	43
Giolittian Liberals*	168	60
Democrats and Radicals	43	–
Popolari	100	108
Centre-left		
Democrats and Republicans	–	130
Extreme Left		
Socialists	156	123
Communists	–	15
Slavs and Germans		9
Total	508	535

Note: *Members of the National Bloc

Source: Compendio di Statistica Elettorale, *II, 1939, pp. 130–1*

As can be seen in the figures, despite divisions in the working-class movement, which now presented itself to the electorate under two banners – the Socialist Party and the Communist Party (founded in January 1921) – their combined representation was only slightly smaller than in 1919. And the independence of the Popolari paid off; they increased their share of the vote. The liberal-conservative and liberal-democrat elements in parliament were, however, more fragmented than ever and the mix between the modern, mass parties and the old clique-based parties of notables was worse than in 1919. After this setback, Giolitti resigned and the jockeying to form a government began all over again. But the 1921 general election was a great success for Mussolini and the Fascists who won thirty-five seats in parliament, a feat which would have been impossible without Giolitti's endorsement. By including Fascist candidates in his electoral bloc, Giolitti had hoped to 'transform' or tame them. He did not understand the real nature of Fascism, but nor did many other conservatives at the time, who tended to dismiss the systematic violence of the squads as an adolescent disorder. As important as the entry into parliament was the fact that inclusion in the National Bloc had given Fascism a respectable, parliamentary face, providing prefects, police and other state authorities in the provinces with an excuse to turn a blind eye to Fascist excesses. Even worse, it encouraged some police to cooperate with the Fascists, as is illustrated by these documents.

Document 3.2 Police Collusion with the Fascists

Deputy Chief of Police G. Carducci and deputy Superintendents Caputo and Mirabella who dealt with inquiries into the events of 30 December 1920 showed considerable sympathy for the Fascist movement.

Source: ACS, Prime Minister's Office, Public Order (1921–22), busta 2, file 31

And in the same file is to be found another letter from the chief of police of Bologna province informing Rome that on 19 October 1921 elements of the local police force had participated in a Fascist punitive expedition at the town of Minerbio. In other cases, where the authorities did not side openly with the Fascists, they were slow to oppose their violence and illegality, as is illustrated by the following document.

Document 3.3 Complaint about the Failure of the Police to Deal with Squadrism, Bologna, 14 January 1922

On the morning of the 2nd . . . action squads from Ferrara, Bologna and Reggio, led by the members of the Bologna *fascio* and Fascist Workers Union, took over control of the area blocking all roads and [thus preventing] **workers from reaching the** [Renana] **estate. Even though the authorities were kept constantly informed of the grave situation which developed, they refused to take any measures to protect the right to work.**

Source: ACS, Prime Minister's Office, Public Order (1921–22), busta 3, file 31

The interesting and, ironical, situation here is that the Fascists, unusually, were not engaged in strike-breaking but, on the contrary, were actually trying to support their union in a dispute with an agricultural cooperative controlled by the 'Reds'. The document also demonstrates the ease and regularity with which the Fascists could mobilise support from over a wide area in their battles against the Socialists.

It was not only the police who connived at squadrist violence; the local magistrates often dealt leniently with Fascists while coming down hard on left-wingers brought before the courts, and army commanders frequently supplied transport, weapons and even men to the Fascist squads for their 'punitive' expeditions, thus making possible the rapid rise to power of the Fascists in parts of Northern and Central Italy. Without the semi-official collaboration, it is hard to see how agrarian Fascism could have spread so far and so fast in 1921 and 1922. The authorities in Rome tried to control their subordinates in the localities – in August 1921, for example, Prime Minister Bonomi ordered the police to suppress all punitive expeditions and to confiscate arms, and in October a decree law forbade the carrying of arms of all kinds – but the problem was enforcing such measures when many of the provinces of Northern and Central Italy were in a state of virtual civil war.

Mussolini's 'Carrot and Stick' Policy

Mussolini exploited the new-found respectability of the Fascist movement with consummate skill, without, however, entirely repudiating the violent tactics of provincial Fascism. Indeed, his political strategy from May 1921 onwards can be likened to that of the 'carrot and the stick': a clever combination of parliamentary manoeuvring with extra-parliamentary pressure in order to gain power at a national level. On the one hand, Mussolini worked hard to consolidate the sympathy and the support which Fascism had won in conservative and Catholic circles by progressively abandoning the radical features of the programme of the first *fascio*, its strident anti-clericalism, anti-capitalism and republicanism.

Document 3.4 Mussolini's Maiden Speech in Parliament, 21 June 1921

Fascism neither practises nor preaches anti-clericalism . . . I believe and affirm that the Latin and Imperial traditions of Rome are today represented by Catholicism . . . and that the sole universal idea that exists in Rome is that which radiates from the Vatican.

Source: Atti Parlamentari *(Italian verbatim parliamentary transcription),* Camera dei Deputati, *XI Legislatura, I Sessione, Discussioni del 21 Giugno 1921, pp. 89–98*

This was an extraordinary about-turn for a man who, as late as November 1919, was writing in his newspaper, 'there is only one possible revision of the Law of Guarantees [the law regulating Church and state relations] and that is its abolition, followed by a firm invitation to his Holiness to quit Rome' (*Il Popolo d'Italia*, 18 November 1919).

The softening of the attitude towards the Church was followed a few months later by more systematic overtures to the employers in the programme of the newly founded National Fascist Party.

Document 3.5 Fascist Party Programme of November 1921

The State should be reduced to its essential function of preserving the political and juridical order. The National Fascist Party will take steps:
a) To discipline the disorderly struggles between classes and occupational interests.

Source: C.F. Delzell (ed.), Mediterranean Fascism, 1919–1945, *1971, pp. 27–34*

While the programme justified the right of the state to intervene in the economy, this statement was clearly intended to reassure the business community that Fascism had no nationalisation plans; on the contrary, it also laid down a programme of what would now be described as 'privatisation', of the railways, telephones and life insurance. The commitment to the regulation of industrial relations demonstrated just how far to the right Fascism had moved. The last remaining institution that needed to be 'squared' was the monarchy, and Mussolini accomplished this only a few weeks before the Fascist bid for power.

Document 3.6 Mussolini's Speech in Udine, 20 September 1922

Now I really believe that the regime can be profoundly altered without touching the monarchy . . . it represents the historical tradition of the Nation . . . Therefore we shall not make the monarchy part of our campaign. I am basically of the opinion that the monarchy has no reason whatsoever to oppose what one must already call the Fascist revolution. It has nothing to gain, for by doing so it would become a target, and if it became a target, it is certain that we would surely not be able to spare it.

Source: Il Popolo d'Italia, *20 September 1922*

It should be noted how blandishments are here combined with the threat of the stick.

Mussolini's main claim to the support of the establishment was that he and the Fascists were the only force capable of taking on and defeating working-class militancy and the only one capable of reversing the breakdown of law and order in the provinces, a breakdown, it has to be said, for which the Fascists were, of course, largely responsible. Alternatively, he would warn that only he could control the squads and that 'normalisation' would only be achieved at the price of concessions to Fascism.

Paradoxically, for Mussolini at least, by the summer of 1921 the violence of agrarian Fascism had become too successful. As violence and anarchy spread, he feared its consequences: a violent reaction on the part of certain sections of the working-class movement, which in the form of the *arditi del popolo* (literally, 'the People's Commandos') were beginning to put up an effective resistance to squadrism, as the 'battle' of Sarzana in Liguria in July 1921 shows; and the risk of a conservative backlash that would blame Fascism for the general breakdown in law and order. Such a development would have entirely derailed his strategy. These anxieties led Mussolini to attempt to impose the 'pact of pacification' on the Fascist squads in July 1921. Though his attempt failed, and the tempo of Fascist violence did not slacken, the pact provides clear evidence that at this stage Mussolini would have preferred a less risky strategy, perhaps an entirely parliamentary road to power. In fact, Mussolini was left with no option after the failure of the pact revealed the precariousness of his hold over the bosses of agrarian Fascism. Though Mussolini was to gain more control over the Fascist movement as a result of its transformation into a more tightly organised party – the National Fascist Party (henceforth P.N.F.) in November 1921 – both the strategy and the tactics of the Fascist bid for power were dictated by the provincial *ras*.

The Deepening Parliamentary Crisis

In any case, Mussolini's judgement turned out to be wrong. As the Fascist squads continued their rise to local power by force, the process sapped the authority of the state and created a situation of near civil war, which was the necesssary prelude to the seizure of power in the capital. Indeed, squadrist activities in the North and Centre of Italy were beginning to have an impact on government at a national level by 1922, making it more and more difficult to sustain coalition, parliamentary government. In particular, Fascist violence in Cremona in June and July, and the failure of the government to stop it, induced the Popolari to pull out of the coalition, thus provoking the longest-running ministerial crisis in the history of the Liberal state. In August the Labour Alliance, a broad grouping of those unions which had survived the batterings of Fascism, resorted to a general strike as a protest against Fascist violence. This so-called 'legalitarian general strike' was a fiasco as only a small percentage of trade unionists responded to the call. Worse still, the strikers gave Mussolini and the Fascists a propaganda coup. The latter could once more present themselves as the defenders of law and order against Bolshevism. At the same time the Fascists resurrected the spectre of revolution and through their strike-breaking activities persuaded many members of the public that they were the only force able to defeat it. In the days that followed the strike the Fascist takeovers of Trento, Bolzano, Trieste and other North Italian towns left the government looking completely impotent.

Fascist violence had negative effects on the unity of the major anti-Fascist parties. By the beginning of October 1922 the democratic, parliamentary parties were in disarray and incapable of impeding the Fascist rise to power. The working-class movement had virtually disintegrated as an effective political force. The Socialist Party had already split in January 1921, giving birth to the Italian Communist Party (P.C.I.). By the autumn of 1922 the rump of the party was deeply divided over how to deal with Fascism. The 'legalitarian' general strike split the Socialists further with the result that in October the Reformists seceded to create the P.S.U., committed to collaboration with other democratic parties against Fascism. In any case, the Maximalist leadership of the original Socialist Party was incapable of taking action against Fascism because of its blinkered ideological perspective. The same was true of the Communists. The unity of the Popolari was also beginning to crumble as rumblings of dissent came from elements on the centre-right of the party, most notably the party's senatorial contingent:

Document 3.7 Letter of Popolare Senators, 18 September 1922

In view of the fact that the National Council [of the P.P.I.] is about to meet and discuss the grave situation in the country and the issues arising out of it, it appears to the Popolare senators an opportune moment to make their feelings known . . .

While we understand that it is not possible within the parliamentary arena, which is so diverse and volatile, to close and immobilise *ourselves* in an exaggerated form of isolationism . . . Nevertheless, it is worth repeating that certain alliances, which are repugnant to the most sacred and necessary principles . . . are not acceptable . . . we repeat that to seek out allies who have not in any way changed the substance of their pernicious doctrines, to flirt with them or virtually court them . . . is not advisable.

Source: S. Jacini, Storia del PPI, *1971, pp. 359–61*

Under all this elaborate and long-winded coding was a very clear message, that the senators, and the Vatican, disapproved of any parliamentary alliance, however tactical and temporary, with the Left, thus making it impossible for the Popolari to enter into a coalition government with Turati's Reformist Socialists to block Mussolini's rise to power. Indeed, both the Vatican and the right-wingers were strongly in favour of the idea of including the Catholic party in a government of 'National Concentration' to save Italy from its problems.

This belief in the desirability of a compromise with Fascism, in the urgent need to include the Fascists in a new government, was also strong among the leading liberal-conservative politicians – Salandra, Orlando and Giolitti. The last, the political rival whom Mussolini feared the most because of his past record as the master of the parliamentary, political game, was already indicating his willingness to preside over a cabinet that would include some Fascist ministers. The only other political figure who had the potential to scupper Mussolini's chances of coming to power at this point was Gabriele D'Annunzio. After the Fiume episode D'Annunzio was still able to command support on the nationalist right, and from some parts of the trade union movement, like the seamen's and dockworkers' unions. This is borne out by the fact that Luigi Facta, the incumbent prime minister, went out of his way to court D'Annunzio. The latter was eventually neutralised by Mussolini's intrigues, but it is doubtful whether the old nationalist poet could have played a significant role in the October 1922 crisis given his political naivety and inexperience.

The March on Rome

It was in this situation of crisis, of the near-collapse of parliamentary government, that Mussolini was emboldened to lay down his challenge: after the Naples congress of his party, on 28 October, he warned that if the Fascists were not given power, they would seize it by force. This was not an entirely empty threat: having seized power by force in many localities of Northern and Central Italy, Mussolini's lieutenants, Grandi, De Vecchi, Bianchi and De Bono, were preparing an armed insurrection, the so-called 'March on Rome' by columns of Fascist *squadristi*. Yet Mussolini, even at this late stage, does not appear to have been entirely convinced of the feasibility of this strategy. As the quadumvirs prepared to lead the Fascist legions in their march on the capital, he insisted on staying behind at Fascist heaquarters in Milan, which would permit him a quick get-away across the nearby Swiss border if things went wrong. The decision to stay behind in Milan had other advantages: Mussolini was able to keep his distance from his followers, the King and the leading liberal-conservative politicians who were thus forced to negotiate with the Duce of Fascism by telephone and specially despatched envoys. This undoubtedly strengthened Mussolini's bargaining position, so much so that by the end of the month he was no longer simply asking for Fascist participation in government but nothing less than the prime ministership for himself.

All that stood against him were Facta's weak, caretaker government and the King. Facta was desperately temporising in the hope that his political patron, Giovanni Giolitti, would succeed in forming a government and thus take the poisoned chalice of ministerial respnsibility from his lips. Both the King and Facta appeared resolved to resist Mussolini by force: Facta had ready a decree of martial law and the commander of the Rome garrison had stationed his forces accordingly in defence of the city. Then, suddenly, the King lost his nerve, refused to sign the decree and instead summoned Mussolini to Rome to form a government. There remains much speculation about the motives for the King's volte-face. It could be argued, for example, that in view of the fragmented parliamentary situation, there was no serious alternative to some sort of government with Fascist participation; and there is clear evidence that the King was afraid of civil war and the subsequent loss of the throne to his more glamorous cousin, the Duke of Aosta. He also feared that the army would not obey him against the Fascists. In fact, the one thing which Mussolini could not afford to risk was a confrontation with the army, for it would have totally destroyed Fascism's credibility as a patriotic, nationalistic force. Luckily for him, Mussolini's bluff worked. Had there been a showdown between the army and the Fascist 'legions', it is clear that the former would have won.

Document 3.8 The March on Rome

Source: Storia fotographica del fascismo, ***Plates 84 and 85, Renzo De Felice and Luigi Goglia, Editori Laterza, 1981***

Whatever the reasons for the King's decision, some clear facts emerge from the events of October 1922. First, Mussolini did not actually seize power by force, the Fascist squads arrived in Rome *after* he was appointed Prime Minister; on the other hand, the *threat* of force undoubtedly played a role in persuading the King to offer him the premiership. Second, Mussolini was given power, by the King and with the backing of leading liberal-conservative politicians, Salandra, Orlando and Giolitti who had all sought an accommodation with Fascism. Cassels is not far wrong when he says, 'By 1922 there was hardly any segment of the Italian establishment that was not ready to collaborate with Fascism either for nationalistic or anti-Bolshevik reasons, or both' (Cassels, 1985, pp. 32–3)

It is also clear that Mussolini was given power legally and constitutionally – that he had only thirty-four parliamentary supporters was no barrier to office, given the fluid nature of the Italian party 'system'. Many previous prime ministers, including Giovanni Giolitti, had had fewer committed parliamentary supporters. And the administration which Mussolini eventually formed, comprising Fascists, Nationalists, Liberals and this time even the Popolari, was not very different from previous coalitions. What was unusual was the extra-parliamentary pressure which had brought it about and the granting of emergency powers for a year. It should also be taken into account that by October 1922 Mussolini and the Fascists undoubtedly represented a larger slice of the electorate than their existing thirty-five seats in parliament suggested. As Farneti has argued, Fascism 'represented the unrepresented' (Farneti, 1978, p. 16), great swathes of the middle classes which felt unrepresented by the other political parties, and unprotected by the parliamentary system. These groups shared the perception of many in the establishment that the Bolshevik threat had by no means abated in Italy and that Fascism was their only sure defence against it.

The Consolidation of Power – from the March on Rome to the Matteotti Crisis (October 1922 to June 1924)

Despite the bullying and bluster with which Mussolini greeted parliament after his appointment, despite the huge votes of confidence in his government in both chambers and despite the special powers that these majorities voted him for a year, what Mussolini lacked in November 1922 was a solid, reliable base of parliamentary support. Indeed, the very breadth of parliamentary support for Mussolini was exactly its weakest point: it left him at the mercy of non-Fascist forces. This was revealed in the spring of 1923 when the P.P.I. (which had only very reluctantly, and against Sturzo's better judgement, decided to go along with the experiment of a Fascist government) voted at its party congress for only 'conditional collaboration' with the Fascists in future. As a result, Mussolini dismissed the Popolare ministers from his government and declared war on their party.

The extraordinary powers granted him in December 1922 gave him a breathing space in which he could consolidate Fascism's power base within the parliamentary system. To strengthen his hold on government Mussolini appointed Fascists to key positions: they were nominated under-secretaries to most of the ministries; a Fascist, De Stefani, was put in charge of Finance; and Mussolini took for himself the Foreign and Interior ministries. The combination of the prime ministership with the Ministry of the Interior was the normal practice of 'strong' liberal-conservative prime ministers – Giolitti being the most obvious example – but Mussolini went further than this by placing Fascist henchmen in key positions in the ministry: Michele Bianchi as secretary-general, Aldo Finzi as under-secretary of state and Emilio De Bono as chief of police. The choice of a politician to fill the latter post was unprecedented and clearly indicates the intention of Mussolini to use the prefects and the police ruthlessly in the interests of Fascism. And in order to underline the Fascist takeover of government, he also instituted a 'Grand Council of Fascism', that is, an assembly of leading Fascist bosses, as the supreme directing organ of rule over and above the cabinet.

The support which Fascism had received from industrial and financial circles was amply rewarded by the policies pursued by De Stefani at the Ministry of Finance (see Chapter 5, p. 76), and the continuing sympathy of the Vatican was assured by a package of legislative measures announced in November 1922 – the reintroduction of religious teaching into primary schools, increased payments for parish priests and the restoration of the crucifix to public buildings. After all the Church–state conflict since unification, the latter was a powerfully symbolic gesture for Italian Catholics.

Two other measures were adopted to reassure his conservative backers, the first being the merger between the P.N.F. and the Nationalists in January 1923. This brought the benefits of a formed ideology, close links with the establishment and intellectual heavyweights such as Federzoni and Rocco who were later to play important roles in the construction of the Fascist dictatorship. The second consisted of implementing the long-promised 'normalisation' process by forming the squads into a militia – the M.V.S.N. – regulated by law and financed by the state. The creation of the militia further served Mussolini's purposes: it provided him with a counter force should the army turn against him and reduced the power of the local Fascist bosses by obliging the members of the squads to swear an oath of loyalty to himself as Duce of Fascism. Mussolini was to use other methods to strengthen his authority over the Fascist movement, the selection of candidates for the 1924 general election being one of them, but it cannot be said that squadrist violence was significantly reduced. It was too useful a means to intimidate his opponents to be discarded at this stage. As a further weapon against the anti-Fascist opposition, Mussolini obtained from parliament powers to censor and even suspend or close down the press.

The main weapon which Mussolini was to use against his enemies, however, was reform of the electoral system which became law in July 1923 and was intended to provide the Fascists with a solid parliamentary majority. The 'Acerbo

Law', as this reform is known, stipulated that the party or alliance of parties which obtained the largest number of votes in excess of a quarter plus one would receive two-thirds of the seats. The remaining seats would then be distributed on the proportional representation principle. Mussolini's success in pushing this radical change through parliament can be attributed to a combination of factors. Many liberal-conservatives, including Giolitti, had never liked proportional representation, blaming it for the emergence of the 'mass' parties in 1919, for the Liberals' subsequent loss of control over parliament and for the chronic political instability of the post-war years. Some opponents of the bill, especially the Socialists, were intimidated by threats of Fascist violence against them and the more vague threat that Fascism would, if necessary, use force to stay in power. The most important role in the debates over the law was played by the P.P.I. The party had always been one of the strongest advocates of proportional representation, but deprived of the leadership of Sturzo, who had been forced by the Vatican to resign in order to appease Mussolini, it split, the bulk of its Deputies abstaining but a rightist faction of sixteen voting for. As Santarelli has pointed out, If the P.P.I. had not split, proportional representation would not have been abandoned and Mussolini might not have been able to use the lists of 'national concentration' which in the elections of 1924 permitted him to consolidate his power (Santarelli, 1967, p. 359).

The 1924 General Election

The most remarkable feature of the 1924 general election was the fact that the Fascists not only won two-thirds of the seats, they won two-thirds of the *votes*. Much of this success can be ascribed to the composition of the 'Big List', Fascism's electoral alliance, and in particular to the presence within it of thirteen clerico-Fascist defectors from the P.P.I. and eighty liberal-conservative candidates. These candidates attracted many votes which would not otherwise have gone to the Fascists. Thus the spectacular triumph of the 'Big List' in the South, where Fascism had been largely unknown before October 1922, was due to the support of liberal-conservative notables such as Orlando who were instrumental in securing 80 per cent of the vote.

There was also a genuine feeling among sections of the middle classes that Mussolini's government had brought political stability and that the improvement in Italy's economic position, which was due to a general upturn in the world economy, was the result of the policies of De Stefani. It is ironical, therefore, that this economic development should have helped Fascism to consolidate its power in Italy, whereas it was also partly responsible for stabilising Weimar democracy in Germany.

While the employment by the Fascists of violence, intimidation and fraud on an unprecedented scale, especially in the rural areas of Northern and Central Italy, was instrumental in demoralising anti-Fascist candidates and discouraging anti-Fascist voters from going to the polls, an important contribution to Mussolini's electoral victory was also made by the opposition parties who failed to provide a united front against Fascism. Their most serious weakness lay in the hopelessly divided state of the the working-class movement which presented itself under the banners of *three* separate, rival parties – the original P.S.I., the Reformist P.S.U. of Turati and Matteotti and the P.C.I. led by Gramsci and Bordigha. United, the working-class parties might have robbed Mussolini of his victory.

The Matteotti Crisis (June 1924–January 1925)

Mussolini's strong, seemingly impregnable position on the morrow of the general election was suddenly destroyed, swept away within a few days of the first meeting of the new parliament in June. The Italian press and public opinion turned sharply, and almost unanimously, against Mussolini's government. He was deserted by many of his liberal-conservative supporters and even by some Fascist followers; as he later admitted, in those June days he felt alone and abandoned, he was ready to resign had anyone insisted that he do so. This sudden and dramatic change in the fortunes of Fascism was caused by the abduction by Fascist thugs on 10 June of Giacomo Matteotti, one of Mussolini's most implacable parliamentary opponents, who ten days earlier had made a blistering attack on the fraud and violence practised by the Fascists during the election campaign.

In view of the countless acts of violence committed by the Fascists against their opponents, including the beatings of national leaders and the murders of local politicians, it is perhaps surprising that the abduction and, as it eventually turned out, the murder should have created such a furore and precipitated a political crisis that nearly led to the overthrow of Mussolini's government. However, Matteotti was attacked while in the discharge of his parliamentary duties. In this sense the abduction was seen by many Italians as an attack on the constitutional system itself. Another important consideration was that the Prime Minister was alleged to be in some way implicated in the crime (the car used by Matteotti's abductors was traced back to Mussolini's private office). This shocked Italian public opinion. It is difficult to know the extent of Mussolini's involvement in the affair and there is even a certain plausibility in his counter-suggestion that the murder was instigated by more intransigent Fascist elements to embarrass him.

A.D. Thompson offers an interesting, alternative explanation of why the abduction led to a political crisis. He argues that the results of the 1924 general election did not represent the overwhelming political triumph which Mussolini desired. Out of a total electorate of over 12 million, only 7.25 million voted, and of these only 4.5 million, one-third of the total electorate, actually voted for the Fascist 'Big List'. Even then, many of these votes were only obtained as a result of the presence in the list of non-Fascist candidates: the clerico-Fascists and the liberal-conservative supporters of Fascism. The response to Matteotti's abduction thus revealed the real strength of opposition to Fascism (Thompson, 1979, pp. 15–16).

It also presented the opposition parties with an opportunity to overthrow Fascism. Three days after the abduction the Communists, the two Socialist parties, the Popolari and an assortment of republicans and liberal-democrats led by Giovanni Amendola withdrew from parliament and formed themselves into the 'Aventine Secession'. The Aventine was very effective as a short-term tactic, a moral protest against Mussolini, but as a long-term political strategy, it was disastrous. In a parliamentary system of government the only place in which a prime minister and government can be overthrown is, logically, parliament. The Aventine also provided the King with the excuse for doing nothing, and adversely affected the relations of the opposition with Giolitti, who was the only politician with the authority to replace Mussolini, and who insisted on staying in parliament. Worse still, it allowed Mussolini to seize the 'moral high ground': he now posed as the defender of parliamentary legitimacy and claimed that it was the opposition who were behaving in a subversive and unconstitutional manner. The opposition remained ineffectual and divided, with almost all the other parties suspicious of the Communists, but perhaps as important as the failure of the opposition was the passivity of the establishment. Not the King, the armed forces or, indeed, the economic interest groups were prepared to abandon Mussolini's Fascist government, and the Vatican effectively sabotaged the only serious alternative to it by forbidding a governmental alliance between the Catholic Popolari and the Socialists. The underlying motivation was, as always, fear of Communism.

Thanks to the failure of opposition attempts to dislodge him, Mussolini had begun to recover his nerve and he set about restoring confidence in his administration by reshuffling his cabinet. He dropped Finzi and De Bono, the two most compromised Interior Ministry officials and brought in ex-Nationalist, clerico-Fascist and liberal-conservative ministers to re-establish his government's respectability. Within the Fascist Party, confidence also began to revive. Thus, when more damning evidence against Mussolini was published in the 'Rossi memorandum' in December 1924, Mussolini was in a position to ignore it. By this time, the patience of the Fascist leadership was exhausted. On New Year's Eve, the consuls or commanders of the Fascist militia called upon Mussolini to deal with the anti-Fascist opposition once and for all, or make way for someone who would. The so-called 'Consuls' Revolt' may have had some influence on Mussolini but it is probable that he was already moving towards a resolution of the crisis. In the new year he took drastic action.

Document 3.9 Mussolini's Speech to the Chamber, 3 January 1925

First of all there was the Aventine Secession, an unconstitutional secession that was clearly subversive (lively approval). Then there followed a press campaign that lasted through June, July and August; a filthy and disgraceful campaign that dishonoured us for three months (vigorous, prolonged applause) . . . Very well, I now declare before this assembly and before the entire Italian people that I assume, I alone, political, moral and historical responsibility for all that has happened (very vigorous and repeated applause. Many voices shouting, 'We are with you! all with you!') . . . If Fascism has been nothing more than castor oil and the truncheon, instead of being a proud passion of the best part of Italian youth, then I am to blame (applause). If Fascism has been a criminal association, then I am the chief of this criminal association! (vigorous applause) . . . If all the violence has been the result of a particular historical, political and moral climate, then responsibility for this is mine, because I have created this climate with a propaganda that has lasted from the Intervention Crisis until today.

Gentlemen, Italy wants peace, tranquillity, calm in which to work. We shall give her this tranquillity by means of love if possible but by force if necessary (lively applause).

You may be sure that within twenty-four hours after this speech, the situation will be clarified in its every aspect.

Source: Il Popolo d'Italia, *3 January 1925*

This speech was probably one of Mussolini's greatest oratorical triumphs. While he had magnanimously accepted moral responsibility for *all* Fascist violence, he side-stepped the specific issue of responsibility for the murder of Matteotti. In doing so, Mussolini also took a greater credit for the achievements of Fascism than he was entitled, given his doubts and hesitations. But the speech's greatest success was in reuniting the Fascist Party under his leadership. The Duce of Fascism had crossed the Rubicon. There was no going back: Fascism was embarked upon the creation of a dictatorship and what eventually would be called a 'totalitarian' state.

The Elimination of the Opposition

Though the subsequent construction of the Fascist dictatorship did not proceed according to a prearranged timetable and plan, and this is borne out by the fact that action against opposition individuals, groups and publications in the wake of the speech of 3 January took the form of ad hoc police measures, by the middle of 1925 both the Ministry of the Interior and the Ministry of Justice were working on substantial packages of repressive legislation. While the various attempts on Mussolini's life between November 1925 and November 1926 were used to create a climate of tension, and as a propaganda excuse, in which to introduce these measures, the effect of the assassination attempts was to accelerate rather than inaugurate this process.

The parliamentary representation of the anti-Fascist groups was eliminated by two measures: when the Deputies of the Aventine Secession tried to resume their seats in the Chamber in November 1925, they were violently ejected by a group of Fascists with Farinacci at their head; and a year later the electoral mandates of all active anti-Fascists were declared to have 'expired'. On the dissolution of parliament in 1929 only the Fascists, the clerico-Fascists and a few Liberal Deputies (not including Giolitti who had died in 1927) remained from those elected in 1924. As Mussolini tightened the screw on opposition activity in 1925 and 1926, other anti-Fascist leaders and supporters followed the example of Sturzo and went into exile. Turati and Nenni of the Socialists, Amendola, Nitti and Gobetti of the Liberal Democrats and Togliatti of the Communists all managed to escape. Alcide De Gasperi, Sturzo's successor as leader of the P.P.I., was caught fleeing the country, tried, imprisoned and eventually released into the 'custody' of the Vatican which had to vouch for his good behaviour henceforth. The Communist intellectual, Antonio Gramsci, was sent to jail, where he died of tuberculosis in 1936. Despite his early death he had managed to map out the post-Fascist strategy of his party in his *Prison Notebooks*.

Parliament passed legislation outlawing all anti-Fascist political organisations, and forbidding their reconstitution. By the end of 1926 all the opposition parties had either been dissolved by the prefects or had dissolved themselves. The Fascists quickly muzzled another major focus of opposition, the press. For this purpose the decrees on the press of 1923 and 1925 were converted into 'full' laws by parliament. Thus the prefects were able confiscate whole editions of an offending newspaper, journal or magazine, suspend publication, replace editors or, in the cases of specifically party newspapers like the Partito Popolare's, the Socialists' *Avanti!* and the Communists' *L'Unita*, close them down altogether. Further squadrist violence after the assassination attempts, and the simple device of buying out recalcitrant owners, completed the process of bringing the press to heel. After 1928, only a few Catholic newspapers, remained and they, controlled either by diocesan bishops or Catholic Action, rarely entered into confrontation with the authorities. The incorporation of all journalists into a Fascist union, which controlled access to the profession and promotion within it, provided a cast-iron safeguard of the political reliability of the press in the future.

By 1927, the Catholic and Socialist trade union confederations, C.I.L. and C.G.L. respectively, had also dissolved themselves, leaving the Fascist trade unions in control of the labour field (see Chapter 5). With their dissolution a major focus of opposition to Fascism also disappeared.

The process of converting Italy into a one-party state was completed by the electoral law of 1928 which decreed that only a single list of 400 candidates, nominated by the Fascist syndical organisations and a few other associations, and endorsed by the Grand Council of Fascism, would be presented to the electorate for its approval or rejection. When the first election under this system took place in March 1929 the Fascists made it clear that they would continue in power irrespective of electoral approval. In an atmosphere of general intimidation, the list was endorsed by the electorate in a 'plebiscite' and Italian democracy was formally buried.

The Matteotti Crisis proved that though Mussolini had had no clear plan for a dictatorship when he came to power, Fascism could not coexist within even the modified framework of the Liberal parliamentary state. The anti-Liberal, anti-democratic tendencies of Fascism, however vaguely expressed, were nevertheless present in its thought and action from the beginning and they logically required that, sooner or later, the opposition would have to be silenced and a one-party, police state established, which is exactly what happened between 1925 and 1929.

4 The Fascist regime

Introduction

Until January 1925, Mussolini had sought to rule Italy through a Fascist government which operated uneasily, and sometimes illegally, within the modified framework of the Liberal parliamentary constitution. During the next four years the Fascist government was transformed into a regime. A new system of political power, a one-party, police state was created; it was dictatorial, repressive and, according to Mussolini, 'totalitarian'. Though most of the institutions of the old Liberal state – monarchy, parliament, judiciary and so on – were retained, the democratic substance was destroyed. But the 'Fascist revolution' of 1925 to 1929 involved more than constitutional reform. It attempted to transform economic and social institutions as well. In particular, it sought to create new institutions that would help to 'manufacture consensus', support for Fascism, and incorporate the masses into the state in a way that the Liberals had failed to do. Another element in this 'revolution' was the taming of the unruly Fascist movement, the subordination of the party to the state so that Mussolini could establish his own unchallenged personal power and also settle relations with the forces and institutions of the establishment, the 'block of consensus' on whose support the future of the Fascist regime would ultimately depend. In fact, according to Lyttelton, the period was dominated by Mussolini's efforts to eliminate Fascist resistance to his strategy of establishing an enduring relationship with the block of consensus (Lyttelton, 1987, p. 268).

But the regime which emerged in the late 1920s did not remain static for the rest of the Fascist period of rule. The structure of the party itself was again changed in 1932 and although, under a succession of party secretaries, this essentially endured until the collapse of Fascism in 1943, some of its collateral organisations, for example, the youth associations, went through a series of changes in the 1930s. These changes were paralleled by reforms of the educational system. The propaganda apparatus of the regime also underwent considerable development in the 1930s until a Ministry of Popular Culture was created that was virtually indistinguishable from its counterpart in Nazi Germany. Similarly, the essential structures of the corporative state were not put into place until after 1934.

The late 1930s were notable for Mussolini's attempt, under the indirect influence of the increasingly close relationship with Hitler, to launch a 'second wave' of totalitarianism. Although initially this was more concerned with social relations and customs, rather than structural changes in the economic, social and political spheres, it was geared to the overall Fascist objective of creating a new Italian, a 'Fascist man' capable of fashioning and sustaining the glorious destiny of Mussolini's Italy

Mussolini and the Institutions of the Fascist Regime

The constitutional changes wrought by Fascism in the period 1925 to 1929 had as their ultimate goal the establishment of Mussolini's unchallenged personal power over the Italian state and the perpetuation of Fascist supremacy within it. Mussolini thus became the supreme ruler of the Italian Fascist regime in his dual role as Duce (leader of Fascism) and Head of the Government. The latter title was conferred upon Mussolini by one of Rocco's major constitutional innovations, passed in 1925.

Document 4.1 Decree on the Powers of the Head of the Government, 24 December 1925

Art. I The executive power is exercised by His Majesty the King through his government. The Government consists of the Prime Minister Secretary of State and Ministers Secretaries of State. The Prime Minister is the Head of the Government.
Art. II The Head of Government, who is Prime Minister and Secretary of State, is appointed and dismissed by the King, and is responsible to the King for the general policy of the Government . . .

The Ministers Secretaries of State are appointed on the proposal of the Head of Government Prime Minister. They are responsible to the King and to the Head of Government for all the acts and measures enforced by their Ministries.
Art. IV . . . The Head of the Government may be entrusted by royal decree with the direction of one or more Ministries. In such cases, the Head of the Government by his own decree may delegate to the Undersecretaries of State a share of the responsibilities of the Minister.
Art. VI No bill or motion may be placed on the agenda of either of the two Chambers [of Parliament] without the consent of the Head of the Government.

Source: C. F. Delzell (ed.), Mediterranean Fascism, *1971, pp. 62–3*

On paper, this law realised Sonnino's turn-of-the-century dream of returning executive power to the King but, more importantly, it transformed the role of the Italian prime minister from *primus inter pares* into the effective source of all executive power, responsible not to parliament but to the King, as Sonnino had wished. Mussolini now appointed and dismissed his own ministers, who were his subordinates and not his equals. And using Article IV, he reinforced his control over government by ensuring that after 1932 he normally held seven out of the fourteen ministerial portfolios. Moreover, other ministers were increasingly mediocrities. One by one, the great figures of Italian Fascism, Rocco, Balbo, Federzoni and Grandi were edged out of high office. Rivalries between leading Fascist bosses, like that between Carlo Scorza and Renato Ricci, were also grist to the Duce's mill. Mussolini secured further control over the governmental apparatus by being his own interior minister, apart from the period between 1924 and 1927 when the post was held by the ex-Nationalist, Federzoni. He thus directly controlled the government's agents in the provinces, the prefects, and through them the security forces. As the Rome archives testify, he was kept well informed of the changing popular humour by agents of the secret police. Furthermore, as a result of the reforms of 1926 and 1928, the elective element in local government, long one of the strongholds of the opposition, was abolished. With the appointment of local councillors and mayors (renamed *podesta*) the power of the prefects, and therefore of central government, was notably increased.

Article VI, coupled with the effects of the electoral reform of 1928, brought the Chamber of Deputies under Mussolini's control. As for the the Senate, whose members were appointed for life by the King, it was an incorrigibly conservative body which had already demonstrated its acquiescence to Fascism by passing votes of confidence in Mussolini with large majorities at the height of the Matteotti Crisis. Eventually, Fascist parliamentary reform went well beyond Sonnino's proposals because the Liberal statesman had never intended that parliament should lose its representative nature and become a mere rubber stamp for the policies of the executive. Parliamentary 'reform' was taken a stage further in 1939 when the lower house was transformed into a 'Chamber of Fasces and Corporations' selected from the Fascist corporations by the Grand Council of Fascism. Not even the pretence of a democratic electoral process – the 'plebiscites' of 1929 and 1934 – was retained. Curiously, despite the Fascist contempt for parliamentary institutions, Mussolini stuck to its forms by insisting on being a member of the Chamber (National Councillor), and his ministers and deputy ministers continued to be drawn from one or other branch of parliament.

Even the continued existence of the Grand Council of Fascism, which included all of the other *gerarchi*, did not diminish the power of Mussolini. As time passed, Mussolini, in contrast to Hitler, shared less and less power with the men who came to power with him. The Grand Council, which was made a fully constitutional organ of the state in 1928, was supposed to be the supreme coordinating body of the regime with the right to discuss matters of great national importance, such as constitutional changes, the succession to the Crown, the selection of members of both Chambers and international relations. But the Duce had the sole right to summon the Council and set its agenda. He also appointed all of its members with the exception of the quadumvirs of the March on Rome. It is significant that Mussolini did not consult the Council before making the following decisions: the signing of the Lateran Pacts with the Vatican in 1929; the invasion of Ethiopia in 1935 and the entry into the Second World War in 1940. The Grand Council had its 'revenge' for this neglect by voting what was in effect a motion of no-confidence in Mussolini in July 1943 and thereby precipitating the final crisis of the regime.

The Cult of the Duce

It would be no exaggeration to say that Mussolini was the first modern dictator, on whom many other would-be dictators, including Oswald Mosley in Britain, Peron in Argentina, the Croatian Fascist Pavelić and even Adolf Hitler sought to model themselves. The nature of Mussolini's leadership, and above all the quality of his political judgement, has been hotly debated among historians. Though Mussolini had undoubted charisma and political intelligence with which to maintain his power over Fascism and the Italian people, Denis Mack Smith has tended to see his talents as lying chiefly in the areas of acting and propaganda (Mack Smith, 1981, pp. 111–14). The press, radio and the cinema played an increasingly important role in projecting his image as the omniscient, omnipotent and indispensable ruler of Italy.

Document 4.2 (Pictures of Mussolini)

[see illustrations on pages 60 and 61]

As these photographs show, however, the image projected by Mussolini was multifaceted: Mussolini as 'Renaissance Man', Mussolini as the very epitome of virile, military virtue, and Mussolini as the common man, shirt stripped off, side by side with the peasants. The last of these was crucial in the Italian cultural context. By contrast, it was inconceivable that Hitler would have been portrayed in such a pose. In this regard, Mussolini was much closer to Stalin in presenting himself as a man of the people. In the 1930s Mussolini became synonymous with Italian Fascism. Indeed, for many Italians, and most foreigners, Fascism was simply 'Mussolinianism'. 'Mussolini is always right' was a slogan used to glorify the Duce (graffiti with this message can still be seen on walls in Italy), and all the triumphs of the regime were attributed to him. But having taken virtually sole power, Mussolini was forced to take sole responsibility for the succession of military disasters which overtook Italy in the Second World War.

The Party and the State

Charles Delzell, writing of the Law on the Grand Council of Fascism of December 1928, states, 'By this legislation, therefore, Italy became a one-party state, the P.N.F. structure being superimposed upon that of the State' (Delzell, 1971, p. 742). While it is obviously true that Fascist Italy was a one-party state, the role of the Fascist Party was carefully circumscribed. Indeed, as Edward Tannenbaum has argued, 'Beginning in the late 1920s, the party became the servant of the State rather than its ruler' (Tannenbaum, 1973, p. 73). On the whole, this is an accurate assessment.

Between 1921 and 1925, the Fascist movement frequently proved to be an embarrassment to Mussolini, frightening members of the Italian establishment with whom he was trying to do deals. On the other hand, it is equally clear that without the movement Mussolini would never have come to power, or at least not in the way that he did. But once in power he played down the role of the party and stressed his own, charismatic leadership. And though pressure from within the party was partially responsible for prompting Mussolini to seek a radical solution to the Matteotti Crisis, the methods which he used to suppress the opposition – legislation and police action – meant a strengthening of his position against that of the party. The violence of the squads which accompanied the end of the Matteotti Crisis in 1925 was but a swansong, a last guttering of the candle flame before the party was brought under control.

The Defeat of the Party

The subordination of the Fascist Party to Mussolini and the new state, and its effective depoliticisation, was achieved through successive purges of the old guard by the National Party secretaries – Farinacci, Augusto Turati and Giuriati. Many of the *ras* were removed from their provincial power bases, usually 'kicked upstairs', given safe ministerial, colonial or diplomatic offices, and only rarely sent to prison or banished. A bloody purge of dangerous rivals, on the lines of the Nazis' 'Night of the Long Knives' of 1934, did not prove necessary in Fascist Italy. As the Central Archives in Rome demonstrate, the old guard rank and file was swamped by massive influxes into the party in the mid-1920s of opportunists and those for whom a party card became essential to their employment. Indeed, one of the favourite jokes about Fascism in the 1930s was that the initials of the Party, P.N.F., stood for '*Per Necessita Familiare*' – for family necessity. In January 1927 the Ministry of the Interior was able to announce that, after years of Fascist anarchy, the prefects were once more the supreme representatives of the state in the provinces. Indeed, from now on the prefect was the master and arbiter of provincial Fascism, often intervening to put an end to the squabbles and scandals which plagued provincial party federations in the late 1920s and early 1930s. It was also increasingly the case that the prefect was required by Mussolini to suggest candidates for the post of *federale*, the provincial party chief. Few of the original local Fascist bosses were able to maintain much influence in their old fiefdoms: there was no equivalent in Fascist Italy of the *Gauleiters*, the powerful local party bosses of Nazi Germany.

Renzo De Felice has argued that, despite the ruthless subordination of the party to the state which Mussolini carried out in the 1920s, a revolutionary element continued to live on inside the Fascist movement until its final destruction in 1945. Drawing a distinction between Fascism as regime and Fascism as movement, he further argues that the movement succeeded in preserving its vitality, dynamism and autonomy despite the defeat of the party and the suffocating conformity and increasing conservatism of the regime. He sees this revolutionary vitality

(a)

(b)

(c)

(a) 'Renaissance Man'

Source: Ideologia e arte del Fascismo, *Plate 49, Gabriele Mazzota Editore, 1973*

(b) 'Military Man'

Source: Storia fotographica, *Plate 197, Renzo De Felice and Luigi Goglia, Editori Laterza, 1981*

(c) 'Man of the People'

Source: Ideologia e arte del Fascismo, *Plate 4, Gabriele Mazzota Editore, 1973*

as expressing itself in support for the Abyssinian War, in the espousal of anti-Semitism and in the resurrection of Fascism in the Italian Social Republic from 1943 to 1945 (De Felice, 1977, pp. 43–4). De Felice may be overstating his case, but his distinction between movement and regime helps to explain some of the dissident currents of thought within the Fascist Party, especially on the question of corporatism, in the 1930s.

As party membership ballooned from roughly 300,000 in November 1921 to 5 million in 1943 (by which time all men in the fighting forces were entitled to join) so, inevitably, its real commitment to Fascism diminished and the political influence of the party declined. As the years passed, the party became increasingly middle and lower-middle class, some of the few working-class or peasant members either being expelled or abandoning the party. Working-class involvement in the party (though not in the Fascist trade unions because membership of them was effectively essential for employment) had always been small in relation to its weight in the population as a whole. The peasantry, which still constituted the largest sector of the population, was even less present in the membership of the party, particularly in the South and the Islands. On the other hand, members of the business, landed and professional classes, and, in the South and the Islands, the local notables, joined *en masse* in order to preserve their positions of influence. Fascism constantly claimed to be in the business of generating its own ruling class. In reality, it would seem that all the regime succeeded in doing was to co-opt cadres of the existing economic and bureaucratic classes: in this way, it ensured the 'consensus' of these groups.

The Role of the Party in the Fascist State

The extent of the subordination of the Fascist Party to the state becomes clearest in its statutes:

Document 4.3 The Statute of the National Fascist Party, 1932

Art. 1 The National Fascist Party is a civil militia, under the orders of the DUCE in the service of the Fascist State.
Art. 7 . . . The DUCE proposes to the King the nomination and dismissal of the Secretary of the National Fascist Party . . .
Art. 8 The members of the National Directorate of the National Fascist Party are appointed and removed by the DUCE on the proposal of the Secretary of the National Party.
Art. 11 Federal Secretaries are appointed and removed by the DUCE, on the proposal of the Secretary of the National Fascist Party.

Source: C.F. Delzell (ed.), Mediterranean Fascism 1919–1945 *1971, pp. 77–81*

There is no mention of a formal policy-making role for the members, but party officials sat on the managing boards of various state agencies and local authorities, and, theoretically at least, the decisions of the Grand Council were supposed to have an important influence on other policy-making bodies. The party was intended to be a faithful, obedient body of servants of the state, carrying out the orders of the government. To ensure this, a highly centralised, hierarchical system of authority, similar to the 'Fuhrer principle' in Nazi Germany, was established; to prevent the National Secretary accumulating too much power in his hands, Mussolini reserved key appointments for himself.

The party was also supposed to provide the training ground for a whole new ruling class, as the Communist Party did in Soviet Russia. Consequently, great emphasis was placed on, and thus much ritual surrounded, the *leva*, the graduation of young Fascists into the party. Though Mussolini and other party leaders paid lip-service to the idea of the party as the nucleus of a new ruling class and made some efforts in that direction, there was no wholesale takeover of the machinery of government by Fascist cadres, as had occurred in Nazi Germany. Apart from the insertion of small groups of Fascists into the prefectoral corps in the mid-1920s and the Foreign Ministry in the 1930s, the regime used the existing cadres of administrators, judges and bureaucrats for whom the price of promotion amounted at most to joining the party. The armed forces, with the monarchy as their shield, were the least affected of all state institutions by Mussolini's rise to power, except for the air force which, being relatively new, was strongly shaped by Italo Balbo and other Fascist enthusiasts.

Of all fields of national life, the economy was probably the only one in which a new Fascist technocratic elite emerged in the corporations and state-controlled industries and banks, but only towards the end of the 1930s. Paradoxically, strong Fascist influences remained in the administrative and military elites after 1945 (see Chapter 9, pp. 132–3).

As the party became depoliticised and bureaucratised, its functions inside the Fascist state were reduced. Its chief function was as an extension of the police and militia with a general supervisory role over its members, the annual renewal of the party card being absolutely vital to them. Otherwise the organisations under its control were largely cultural, recreational, sporting and youth groups. Under the direction of the slightly comic but humourless figure of Starace, National Secretary from 1932 to 1939, the party performed a largely decorative and propagandistic role in Fascist Italy – mobilising its members in endless parades and demonstrations of support for the policies of the Duce: the party became the 'choreographer of the regime' (Tannenbaum, 1973, p. 73).

Anti-Fascism and The Fascist Police State

Driven out of Italy by Fascist repression, the leaders of the Communist, Republican and the two Socialist parties (the latter managed to bury their differences and reunite) set up organisations in exile along with the trade union confederation,

C.G.L., while a collection of radical intellectuals set up a new political grouping Giustizia e Liberta (literally, 'Justice and Liberty'). The Popolari, however, did not succeed in setting up an effective party-in-exile. Few supporters had followed their leaders, Sturzo, Ferrari, Donati and Miglioli, into exile, and differences between those leaders weakened the Popolari. The primary cause of the party's decline, however, was the close relationship between Church and Fascism which followed the signing of the Lateran Pacts in 1929. This cut the ground from under the feet of Catholic dissidents. Most Popolare activists simply retired into an unobtrusive, private life alongside their Liberal colleagues.

The success of the anti-Fascist exiles in maintaining support in Italy itself was limited. The Communists managed to maintain a network of party cells in the factory cities of the North, despite police raids, as a result of the training provided by the Communist International in Moscow. Of the other anti-Fascist groups, only the Giustizia e Liberta organisation had comparable success, and the only period of sustained anti-Fascist activity in Italy was from 1930 to 1933 when the effects of the Great Depression provoked widespread social distress and unrest. In this period there were a number of show trials of anti-Fascist individuals and groups, including the 'Guelfs', the only serious Catholic anti-Fascist group.

The relative failure of Italian anti-Fascism can be attributed to the draconian laws introduced against 'subversive' opposition, and the enforcement of those laws by the police. In 1926–7, a succession of 'exceptional' laws and decrees suppressed freedom of expression, association and assembly, and prescribed a range of penalties for anti-Fascist activity, including the restoration of the death penalty for the most serious 'crimes against the state'.

Document 4.3 The Law on the Defence of the State, 1926

Art. 4 Whoever reconstitutes, even under a different name, any association, organisation or party that has been dissolved by order of the public authorities, is liable to imprisonment ranging from three to ten years, and moreover is subject to permanent exclusion from public office.

Whoever is a member of such associations, organisations, or parties is liable, for the mere fact of this participation, to imprisonment ranging from two to five years, and permanent exclusion from public office.

Whoever propagates by any means the doctrines, opinions, or methods of such association is liable to the same penalty.

Art. 7 The crimes referred to in this law shall be tried before a Special Tribunal, to consist of a president chosen from among the general officers of the Royal Army, the Royal Navy, the Royal Airforce, and the Voluntary Militia for National Security.

Source: C.F. Delzell (ed.), Mediterranean Fascism, 1919–1945, *1971, pp. 67–9*

The inclusion of high-ranking officers in the tribunal was a clever move ensuring that the armed forces now became, in a sense, a part of the Fascist 'establishment', co-opted into the process of anti-Fascist repression. It also meant the adoption of the procedure of military courts, in which the defence was more limited in its rights, making it easier to secure convictions.

In the following year a Fascist secret police (the O.V.R.A) was established. Fascist Italy hardly needed a new instrument with which to suppress its opponents for it had inherited from the Liberal state an already extensive and effective apparatus of repression. After the dismissal of De Bono as chief of police during the Matteotti Crisis, Mussolini relied upon professionals to run and man his security forces. Compared to the brutal terror campaigns of the Gestapo or the Stalinist secret police, the repression of the Fascist police state was mild: there were no concentration camps or mass liquidations of political opponents in Fascist Italy. Executions were few and far between within Italy (though the same cannot be said for Italian adventurism in Libya and Ethiopia), being chiefly reserved for terrorists fighting the 'Italianisation' of the Croats and the Slovenes in the new north-eastern provinces. Imprisonment, or banishment to remote areas of the South and Islands, were the usual punishments for such anti-Fascists as Carlo Levi, a leading intellectual in Turin, and other 'undesirables', including homosexuals, who suffered persecution in 1940 (Dall'Orto, 1994, p. 139). Though life was no joke for dissidents in Fascist Italy, it was eminently preferable to their fate in the other two totalitarian states.

Conformity and Consensus in the Fascist Regime

The Fascist regime equipped itself with powerful instruments to coerce dissidents and extract obedience to its dictatorship, but it also used more subtle methods to ensure conformity with its policies and even create popular support for them. Renzo De Felice, in the fourth volume of his biography of Mussolini, argues that Fascism, in the early 1930s at least, enjoyed widespread popularity and support in Italy (De Felice, 1965– , p. 126). When the volume was published in 1974, this claim was immediately disputed by other historians, some of whom accused De Felice of being 'pro-Fascist' and of having been taken in by his sources (see, for example, Mack Smith, 1975). In particular, De Felice's interpretation of the results of 1929 election or 'plebiscite' was at variance with the established, conventional view that the regime produced 'consensus' through police terror and propaganda. But he is undoubtedly right in suggesting that large numbers of Italians genuinely supported Fascism in 1929 out of gratitude for the economic and political stability which Italy was enjoying at the time, as well as for Mussolini's conclusion of peace with the Catholic Church. Nevertheless, De Felice does minimise the role which coercion played in the achievement of the 90 per cent vote for Fascism.

The years that have passed since De Felice first made his claims have seen an interesting development of the debate. Few writers would now seriously dispute that Mussolini enjoyed considerable support, or 'consensus', from large sections of the population during the lifetime of the regime. What has now become much clearer, however, is how this support fluctuated over time, and the contingent circumstances which influenced those fluctuations. It was obviously at a low during the initial stages of the Matteotti Crisis in June/July 1924; it reached a 'high' in 1929, thanks to the Conciliazione ('Conciliation') with the Catholic Church; only to dip between 1930 and 1933 when the police archives tell us that there was widespread discontent due to the effects of the Great Depression. In May 1936, with the capture by Italian troops of the Ethiopian capital Addis Ababa, support for the regime, and Mussolini's personal popularity, reached an unrepeatable high, only to decline in the late 1930s as resentment and fear of the implications of the tightening relationship with Nazi Germany became widespread; finally, as a result of disastrous military defeats, culminating in the Allied invasion of Italy itself in July 1943, support for Fascism had almost completely evaporated when the regime collapsed.

Much progress also has been made since De Felice opened the debate in analysing the groups which gave most consistent support to Fascism and why, and the different means which Fascism used to 'manufacture' consensus and how successful they were. In regard to the latter, Philip Cannistraro has ably demonstrated how Fascism sought to manufacture consensus through the manipulation of the media (Cannistraro, 1972 and 1975). The Fascist exploitation of the media was aimed at mobilising support for Mussolini's policies, controlling all aspects of life in Fascist Italy and creating a 'new' Italian who, in his/her thought and actions would be thoroughly Fascist. Thus the press by the 1930s had become standardised and staid as a result of the detailed directives issued by the Ministry of Popular Culture on what news to include and how to handle it. With such control of the press, and above all as a result of the deliberate editing out of 'bad news' – natural disasters and economic difficulties in the 1930s, and military defeats in the 1940s – it was difficult for the majority of Italians to hold any views other than those propagated by the regime.

The ministry also controlled radio and cinema. Radio became an important propaganda weapon in a country where a sizeable minority of the population was still illiterate. Though private ownership of radio sets was not as extensive as in more developed countries such as Britain and the U.S.A., by the mid-1930s radio apparatus had been installed in public squares and workplaces so that the voice of the Duce could be heard by all. Radio had its limitations as a medium of propaganda but cinema offered more possibilities, especially after the introduction of 'talkies'. Though the Fascists were quick to grasp its propaganda value, they never fully exploited its potential, despite the influence of Goebbels and Nazi manipulation of propaganda in the mid-1930s. They did set up the state-run Istituto Luce (literally, 'Institute of Light') to produce propaganda films, but the classic Fascist propaganda film, *The 17th Year*, produced in 1939 to extol the achievements of the regime, is much less technically sophisticated than such Nazi films as *The Triumph of the Will*. And even though controls and quotas were imposed on the import of foreign films, filmmakers were generally left undisturbed while they kept their productions to imitations of the Hollywood 'dream factory'.

Artists and intellectuals were not as rigidly regimented as in Nazi Germany or Stalin's Russia, even though Fascism sought to control all existing cultural institutions and promote new ones – such as the Royal Academy of Italy. For most intellectuals and artists, as for other professional and middle-class groups, the price of peace and a successful career was a gesture of public support for the regime, a party card or the Fascist oath. Some, like the scientist Marconi or the composer Mascagni, accepted Fascism willingly; others, like the physicist Fermi, the painter and writer Levi and the historian Salvemini, chose exile or banishment rather than submission. By 1930 many of Italy's most famous intellectuals had emigrated, and at home Benedetto Croce, the great philosopher and historian, and a few others maintained a lonely anti-Fascist vigil.

Art and architecture were obviously of special importance in presenting the image of the regime.

Document 4.4 Art and Ideology in Fascist Italy

Although Mussolini had started out as a socialist . . . and his early regime was not centred upon middle-class ideals, by the mid-1930s it was clear that Italian Fascism had become the party of the bourgeoisie. This had strong implications for design since the twin values of nationalism and traditionalism became increasingly prominent in the 1930s, and needed a style to represent them. They found this in the *Novecento* [Nineteen hundreds] movement, which evolved a new style based on a pared-down reworking of the classical idiom.

Source: P. Sparke, Italian Design: 1870 to the Present, *1988, p. 62*

As Sparke also points out, and as the photograph on page 68 demonstrates, the 'official' Fascist architectural style was essentially a synthesis of neo-classical and modern forms, with the former predominating over the latter: the architectural visions of Futurism and Rationalism found few outlets in Fascist Italy.

Document 4.5 Fascist Architecture

The Piazza della Vittoria, Brescia, between the wars

Source: Italian Design: 1870 to the Present, *Penny Sparke, Thames & Hudson, 1988*

[see illustration on page 68]

There was no such thing as a 'Fascist culture', even less a cultural revolution in Italy. What Fascist Italy lacked was a clear cultural programme and strategy, and above all someone indisputably in charge of cultural policy; perhaps the most important factor was that Mussolini, unlike Hitler, was not an artist with a fanatical artistic vision.

Document 4.5 Fascist Architecture

Fascism and Youth

Young people were the particular target of Fascist propaganda. If many of the older generation were too cynical or too sceptical to be converted to Fascism, then through the reform of the educational system and through the national network of its youth organisations the regime sought to ensure that the rising generations would be thoroughly indoctrinated with the Fascist spirit, and that in this way the future would be safe for Fascism.

The educational reforms of Giovanni Gentile in 1923–4 were not especially Fascist in inspiration, serving only to accentuate the highly elitist and anti-scientific bias of the Italian educational system. Successive Fascist ministers of education abandoned many of Gentile's changes, being more concerned with 'Fascistising' the schools and universities. This intention was especially symbolised by the change of name of the ministry from 'Public Instruction' to 'National Education' in 1929, the difference in Italian being that the word 'education' has a wider meaning than its English counterpart, embracing all aspects of the upbringing and instruction of the child, intellectual, moral, physical, spiritual and political. In pursuit of the goal of a Fascist and 'totalitarian' educational system, anti-Fascist teachers had already been purged from the schools in the 1920s, and in the 1930s it became necessary for teachers to belong to the party and for university professors to take the Fascist oath. The school curriculum was also changed, with a heavy emphasis on national history, physical education and pre-military training in secondary schools and universities. Textbooks were standardised and 'Fascistised'; even arithmetic became a source of Fascist propaganda, as the following example demonstrates.

Document 4.6 Fascist Textbooks for the Elementary Schools

The study of mathematics, not quite as readily adapted to the propaganda needs of the regime, still showed Fascist influence. Third-graders learned their numbers by writing, 'The Duce proclaimed the Empire after 174 days of economic siege by 52 states against Italy.' Elementary calculations were taught using problems like this: 'The glorious war in Africa lasted seven months. How many days is this?

Source: T. Koon, Believe, Obey and Fight: Political Socialisation of Youth in Fascist Italy, 1922–1943, *1985, pp. 80–2*

The indoctrination and regimentation of youth was not confined to the schools. Through its youth organisations the regime intended to monopolise the free time of schoolchildren as well, especially on Saturdays, the 'Fascist Sabbath'. In 1926 the Fascist youth organisation, the Balilla, was officially recognised and funded by the state. All rival organisations, with the exception of some Catholic youth organisations, were dissolved. In 1929, the Balilla was brought under the control of the Ministry of Education, and increasing pressure was applied to parents to enrol their children in its groups. When Starace became Party Secretary in 1932, membership became compulsory for all Italian children. In 1937 the youth organisations were again reshuffled and university students and Young Fascists were brought into the Gioventu del Littorio. With their smart uniforms and parades, the Fascist youth organisations were very attractive to many children in the 1930s and 1940s.

Document 4.7 Fascist Youth

Source: Storia fotographica del fascismo, *Plate 111, Gabriele Mazzota Editore, 1973*

Many Italians still have very fond memories of their experiences, if only because the Fascist youth organisations offered a number of 'carrots' to children, free sports facilities, free holidays at the seaside and in the mountains and special scholarships for the gifted. All were tangible benefits for lower-middle-class and working-class children

Material inducements were also important in attempts to win support from adults. The *dopolavoro*, after-work leisure-time organisations, provided subsidised canteens, theatres and cinemas and other social activities and cheap holidays for state employees and some workers in industry within a Fascist 'atmosphere'. Like the youth organisations, and the adult party groups, the *dopolavoro* were intended to replace equivalent organisations of the Marxist and Catholic subcultures which had been largely destroyed during the process of 'Fascistisation' in the mid- and late 1920s. The plan was to draw the masses 'into the State', giving them a nationalist, Fascist culture in contrast to the sectarian, 'anti-national' cultures of the Marxists and Catholics.

All these attempts to create consensus by socialising and 'nationalising' Italians had their limitations, as Vicki De Grazia has demonstrated for the *dopolavoro* (De Grazia, 1982, pp. 124–6). Fascist organisations were, on the whole, more successful in urban rather than rural areas, in Northern and Central rather than Southern Italy, among middle and lower-middle classes than the working-classes or peasantry. Despite the huge commitment to these organisations, including the Massaie, the 2 million-strong rural women's movement, the Fascist regime failed to break down the barriers between town and country and 'real' and 'legal' Italy. Deep-rooted peasant cynicism and fatalism, and a profound mistrust of the state and its agents, militated against associationalism of any kind, especially in the rural South, as is poignantly illustrated by Carlo Levi's description of his experiences there.

Document 4.8 The Peasantry and the Proclamation of the Ethiopian War

The gentry were all Party members, even the few like Dr Millo who were dissenters. The Party stood for Power, as vested in the Government and the State, and they felt entitled to a share of it. For exactly the same reason none of the peasants were members; indeed, it was unlikely that they should belong to any party . . . Such matters had nothing to do with them; they belonged to another world. What had the peasants to do with Power, Government and the State? The State, whatever form it might take, meant 'the fellows in Rome' . . . They make us kill our goats, they carry off our furniture, and now they are going to send us away to the wars. Such is life! The third of October, which marked the official opening of the war, was a miserable sort of day. Twenty or twenty-five peasants roped in by the *carabinieri* and the Fascist Scouts stood woodenly in the square to listen to the historic pronouncement that came over the radio . . . the war so light-heartedly set in motion from Rome was greeted in Gagliano with stony indifference. Mayor Don Luigi spoke from the balcony of the town hall. He enlarged upon the eternal grandeur of Rome, the seven hills, the wolf that suckled Romulus and Remus, Caesar's legions, Roman civilisation, and the Roman Empire that was about to be revived . . . Huddled against the wall below, the peasants listened in silence, shielding their eyes with their hands from the sun and looking as dark and gloomy as bats in their black suits.

Source: J. Whittam, Fascist Italy, *1995, pp. 153–5*

The passage confirms all the archival evidence that the Fascist Party in the South had inevitably been taken over by the local elites for their own advantage, and not on the whole out of ideological commitment. It is equally no surprise that the announcement of the start of the Ethiopian War elicited no enthusiasm from the peasantry.

The Block of Consensus and the 'Totalitarian' Regime

However successful or unsuccessful the regime was in 'manufacturing consensus', it could always rely upon the forces and institutions which constituted what Alberto Aquarone has described as the 'block of consensus' (Aquarone, 1965, p. 15). This comprised the monarchy and with it the armed forces, the Church and the landed and business elites, in other words those elements of the Italian establishment which had welcomed and, in part at least, helped Fascism to come to power. As long, that is, as its policies were in harmony with the interests they represented. The major survivor from the Liberal constitutional order was the monarchy. Mussolini, with his tactical abandonment of his republicanism in 1922, recognised that monarchism was the essential prerequisite for any compromise with the establishment. Behind the monarchy stood the civil service, the judiciary and the armed forces, the latter linked through particularly close bonds of loyalty to the King. The monarchy was also able to provide Fascism with historical continuity and legitimacy; it would have been foolish to have attempted to overthrow the King at this stage given his post-war popularity.

The relationship between King and Duce was not an especially cordial one, but it worked. The King never openly challenged Fascism in the 1920s and 1930s, and would never have dreamt of doing so. In any case, Fascism brought him new titles and dominions: Emperor of Ethiopia in 1936 and King of Albania in 1939. On the other hand, the King was forced to suffer in silence the diminution of prerogative imposed by Fascism, such as the transfer to the Grand Council of the power to fix the line of succession and the transfer to Mussolini of the King's supreme command of the armed forces in time of war.

Mussolini found the survival of the monarchy an irritant, especially in the late 1930s when the contrast between himself and Hitler was starkly revealed by the latter's state visit to Rome. Hitler was head of both government and state and therefore drove with Victor Emmanuel in the first carriage; Mussolini, as only head of government, drove in the second. The Duce increasingly inveighed, in private, against the monarchy and threatened to 'settle accounts' with it after his successful war. His unhappiness with the survival of the monarchy was well motivated: the monarch possessed the power to appoint and dismiss the head of government, and retained the support of the armed forces, thus constituting a brake on the totalitarian ambitions of Fascism and ultimately its Achilles heel.

Fascism and the Church

The other major institutional and social force with which Mussolini had to come to terms between 1925 and 1929 was the Catholic Church. Despite the benevolence which it had displayed towards Fascism and its leader in the preceding period, there were still serious problems to be resolved before a stable relationship could be established between them. Starting in 1926, representatives of the Vatican and Italy negotiated to achieve a full and definitive settlement of the 'Roman

Question', spurred on, as far as the Vatican was concerned, by the continuing process of 'Fascistisation' which was demolishing many of the economic and social organisations of the Catholic subculture and which now threatened its youth organisations.

A final reconciliation between the Papacy and Italy was brought about in the Lateran Pacts, signed on 11 February 1929. The pacts consisted of the Treaty, which re-established a tiny portion of the papal 'Temporal Power', in the form of the sovereign 'State of the Vatican City', the Financial Convention and the Concordat, which regulated certain matters between Church and state inside Italy, including Church property, marriage and education. The Pacts undoubtedly represent one of the greatest achievements of Fascism and laid the foundations for a 'marriage of convenience' between the Vatican and Italian Fascism which was to last for nearly a decade. In this period the Catholic Church saw eye to eye with Fascism on a number of issues – Communism, social stability, the superiority of rural over urban society, the role of women, the encouragement of childbirth and so on. As a result, the Church gave its support to Fascism in the elections of 1929 and 1934, and rather more guarded support for Fascist corporatism and imperialism, thereby helping to consolidate the consensus on which the regime was built in the 1930s. Despite the euphoria in both camps, the 'marriage' was not without its conflicts. Both sides had unrealistic expectations of the benefits they were going to derive from the Conciliation of 1929. The original anti-clericalism of the early days lived on to some extent in the Fascist movement. Mussolini, therefore, sought to reassure his followers that the Conciliation was not a victory of the Church over the state.

Document 4.8 Mussolini's Speech to the Chamber on the Lateran Pacts, 13 May 1929

I wish to take up a formula with which the Hon. Solmi concluded his speech on Saturday. He said, 'A free and sovereign Church; a free and sovereign state.' [This] will lead to a misunderstanding which it is important to clear up. . . inside the State the Church is neither sovereign nor free . . .

We have not resurrected the temporal power of the popes, we have buried it . . .

Italy has the singular privilege . . . to be the only European nation which is the seat of a universal religion. This religion was born in Palestine but it became Catholic and universal in Rome. If it had stayed in Palestine it would probably have remained just another of the . . . sects, like the Essenes and the Therapeutis, and very probably would have died out leaving no trace.

Source: Atti Parlamentari, *1929, vol. 1, Camera, Discussioni, p. 152*

The remarks about the origins of Catholicism were in effect a denial of the divine nature of the Catholic Church and the Papacy and naturally caused outrage in the Vatican, while reasserting Fascism's essentially instrumentalist attitude towards religion.

Elements of anti-Fascism, as well as *afascism*, an indifference to the regime, also survived among the Catholic clergy and laity, despite the official disapproval of the Vatican. These tensions surfaced in the conflicts of 1929, 1931 and 1938/9 between Mussolini and Pope Pius XI. A more fundamental cause of conflict was the fact that, despite Mussolini's totalitarian declarations, Catholicism remained a competitor with Fascism for the ultimate loyalty of the Italian people. Hence many Catholics continued to prefer Catholic organisations to the Fascist Balilla and *dopolavoro*, especially in the 'white provinces'. The major cause of the 1931 crisis, for example, was the growth and activism of Catholic Action, and especially its youth wing. An added ingredient in the 1938/9 crisis was Mussolini's introduction of the Racial Laws. Pope Pius XI denounced them as a slavish imitation of Hitler and Nazism, which the Vatican by now regarded as only a little less evil and threatening than Stalin and Communism. On the eve of the Second World War, the Catholic Church was beginning to distance itself from the regime, alienated by the increasingly close relationship that had developed between Hitler and Mussolini. The latter, for his part, was making threatening noises about the future of the Church.

By the end of the 1930s, in the new totalitarian phase induced by Nazi influence, Mussolini was finding the constraints imposed by his relationship with the various components of the block of consensus harder to bear. The business and landowning elites, no less than the Church and the monarchy, constituted insuperable barriers to the extension of the Fascist revolution into the economic and social fields, resisting land reform and genuine corporatism (see Chapter 5). In broader terms, they absolutely guaranteed that Fascism's totalitarian ambitions would never be realised. Fascism's failure to eradicate the Mafia in Sicily is further proof of the limits of totalitarian power. The man who had given birth to the concept of totalitarianism was obliged to admit that he was, 'the most disobeyed dictator in history'.

Nevertheless, despite the failure to live up to its totalitarian aspirations, it would be wrong to argue, as Hannah Arendt has, that the Fascist regime until 1938 was: 'Not totalitarian, just an ordinary, nationalist dictatorship' (Arendt, 1967, p. 257). Fascist Italy between 1922 and 1943 was more than that, something more than Franco's Spain, Salazar's Portugal or Pilsudski's Poland. Its partial success in achieving its explicit totalitarian vocation differentiates it from them and puts it into a different league, along with Hitler's Germany and Stalin's Russia, even if it fell short of the brutal, terroristic rule of those states.

Fascist economic and social policies

5

Introduction

Fascism took great pride in its economic and social policies, constantly contrasting its 'successes' in these fields with the 'failures' of the pre-Fascist, Liberal regime, and also with the economic failures of the 'plutocratic democracies', especially in the 1930s. Its greatest pride was reserved for the 'corporate state' which it proclaimed to be a unique and original Italian Fascist creation, the only effective and enduring solution to the problem of relations between capital and labour. Italian Fascism also saw itself as an innovatory and modernising force in the economic and social fields.

While Fascism did not come to power in 1922 with a clearly defined overall economic and social strategy, it did possess some economic and social policies. Just as the economic and social policies of the Fascist movement prior to 1922 were to change according to circumstances, so the policies adopted in power were to change according to contingent circumstances and, in particular, to changing demands from economic pressure groups. On the other hand, as the years passed, Fascist economic and social policies acquired coherence as they increasingly took the form of an implementation of the the pre-First World War Nationalist programme and by the mid-1930s they were essentially determined by the needs of empire and war.

The Economic and Social Policies of Fascism, 1919–22

As has been seen in Document 2.3, the Manifesto of the First *fascio* of 1919 had a strongly anti-capitalistic tone which was a reflection of the left-wing origins of many of its founders, and its urban preoccupations were such that there was no mention of agrarian problems. With the rapid spread of agrarian Fascism, in January 1921 Fascism adopted an agrarian programme with specific proposals for land reclamation and colonial resettlement of rural populations, rather than land 'reform', that is, the break up of large estates and redistribution of their land among small peasant proprietors. Fascist economic-policy thinking moved further to the right as its support crystallised around middle- and lower-middle-class elements in town and country, and saw its fullest expression in the programme of the Partito Nazionale Fascista of November 1921. The emphasis on the conditions and rights of the (urban) proletariat was replaced by a stress on the corporative structuring of the economy, on statutory regulation of industrial relations and on a call for a return to orthodoxy in the management of state finances, and in the state's management of the economy.

Fascist Economic Policy in Practice, 1922–6

The programme of the P.N.F. served as an inspiration for Fascist economic policy during the first three years in power. The new Fascist government inherited a difficult, though improving, financial situation at the end of 1922. Its most serious problems were a large excess of public expenditure over income, a growing National Debt and a balance of payments deficit. Under the direction of Alberto De Stefani as Minister of Finances, attempts were made to cut the budget deficit by privatising telephones and other public utilities, and drastically reducing state expenditure, including subsidies to industry. These deflationary measures were accompanied by deregulation of the economy and an attempt to cut protective tariffs. If this was Fascist economic policy then there was clearly nothing new about it. But De Stefani's measures did not appeal to all of Italy's economic interest groups. As was so often to be the case, the Fascist government's economic policy at this point was strongly influenced by the big economic interest groups. Italy's economic revival got out of hand as it led to a trade deficit, rising inflation and pressure on the lira in foreign markets. In these circumstances, De Stefani was unable to defend his policies against the sugar industry and the wheat growers, who demanded tariff protection.

Mussolini's Economic Battles: The 'Battle for the Lira'

Though not obvious at the time, the replacement of De Stefani as Finance Minister by Giuseppe Volpi marked a change in the direction of economic policy, from free trade to protectionism and from deregulation towards state intervention. It also marked the beginning of a more active role in economic decision making by Mussolini himself, his first major intervention in economic affairs being prompted by the crisis of the lira. Whereas the Italian currency had stood at 90 to the pound on the eve of the March on Rome, by July 1926 it had sunk to 150. Mussolini's decision to restore the lira to its 1922 value, announced in his Pesaro speech of August 1926, was bold but risky. Even Volpi believed that at this level the lira was overvalued.

Document 5.1 Mussolini's Pesaro Speech, 18 August 1926

I want to tell you that we will fight the economic battle to defend the lira with the utmost firmness and to this square and to the whole of the world I declare that I will defend the lira to my last breath, the last drop of my blood.

I will never inflict upon the marvellous people of Italy, who for four years have worked like heroes and suffered like saints, the moral and the economic disaster that would follow the collapse of the lira. The Fascist regime will resist the speculation of hostile financial forces, resolved to stamp on any domestic ones. The Fascist regime, from its leader to the lowliest follower, is determined to impose all necessary sacrifices, but our lira . . . the symbol of the nation, the sign of our prosperity, the fruit of our labours . . . of our blood, tears and sacrifices, must . . . and will be defended.

Source: G. Bonfanti, Il Fascismo, *1977, pp. 220–1*

It seems likely that Mussolini's decision was prompted by fears that without a decisive policy Italy could suffer inflation of Weimar proportions. But Italian national prestige, and that of the new regime, was also at stake. 'Quota 90', as the revaluation was called, was the first of a series of economic 'battles' that Mussolini was to wage over the years, largely, he claimed, by the power of political will. But the 'Battle for the Lira' could not be fought solely through willpower; a package of drastic deflationary measures, a forced loan, massive price reductions and corresponding wage cuts were also required. The battle had its casualties, principally the smaller savings banks, the export industries, and the workers in them who had to make the sacrifices. When the 'Great Depression' hit Italy after 1929, the country had barely recovered from the effects of 'Quota 90'.

The 'Battle for Grain'

The great advantage of the economic battles was that the Italian people could be mobilised in a cross-class, non-political way for nationalistic economic ends, a perfect application of the ideas of nationalism to the economy. Another economic battle foreshadowed by the Pesaro speech was the 'Battle for Grain'.

In order to cut Italy's massive balance of payments deficit, which was largely caused by the cost of the food import bill – at that time grain accounted for 50 per cent of Italy's imports – Mussolini set in motion a campaign to increase Italy's production of cereals. Propaganda, including pictures of a bare-chested Duce working in the fields, the mobilisation of the rural clergy, tariffs on grain imports and a battery of incentives were all employed to induce farmers to switch to cereals. While cereals output did increase enormously – by 1939 Italy was producing 75 per cent of her own needs – the campaign had its drawbacks: it encouraged farmers to abandon vital export crops such as vines, olives and citrus fruits (whose export had traditionally paid for cereals imports) and to cultivate land that was often not suitable for grains.

Land Improvement and Resettlement

The 'Battle for Grain', like all of the regime's agrarian policies, pleased Fascism's rural constituency, the large and medium-size landowners, especially the great estate owners, or *latifundisti*, in the South. On the other hand, the rural poor benefited little. In an attempt to solve the twin problems of land hunger and technical backwardness in agriculture, from the late 1920s onwards, under the direction of the agrarian expert Serpieri, the regime pursued a policy of *bonifica integrale* – that is, land reclamation and improvement schemes – in both Northern and Southern Italy. One much-publicised venture was the Pontine Marshes scheme south of Rome, where vast areas were reclaimed from marsh and malaria and whole new villages and towns were constructed. The Pontine Marshes project was used as a 'showcase' of Fascist achievement for foreign visitors. In fact, the value of the reclamation schemes as a whole was largely propagandistic. Though it notably increased the amount of cultivable land, it had only a marginal effect upon land hunger. Martin Clark, for example, claims that fewer than 10,000 people benefited from land reclamation (Clark, 1996, p. 274).

Resettlement of the unemployed/landless rural poor in Italy's colonies, an early objective of the Nationalists, was carried out in Libya after its final, brutal pacification in the early 1930s. Like the Nationalists, Mussolini disapproved of emigration to foreign countries. It was not, in any case, an option for most Italians following the closure of their doors by the U.S.A. in the early 1920s. But given the smallness of Italy's colonial empire, and the limited scope for resettlement in such 'sandboxes' as Libya, Eritrea and, after 1936, Ethiopia, the resettlement of land-hungry peasants was no more effective than land reclamation. Both policies did little but scratch the surface of rural problems.

The 'Demographic Battle'

Allied to the Battle for Grain, perversely, was a battle to increase the birth rate and, consequently, the Italian population. Mussolini first justified this 'Demographic Battle' in a speech to parliament in May 1927.

Document 5.2 Mussolini's 'Speech of the Ascension', 1927

It is therefore necessary to take great care of the future of the race, starting with measures to look after the health of mothers and infants. This is the purpose of the National Organisation for the Protection of Mothers and Children . . .

Throughout the country there exist 5,700 branches . . . for which there still is not enough money. Hence the tax on bachelors and perhaps in the future there will be a tax on childless marriages.

This tax brings in between 40 and 50 million lire: but do you really believe that this is why I introduced the tax? I have used the tax to give a demographic prod to the nation. This may surprise you and someone will ask: 'But why? Is it really necessary?'

Yes, it is really necessary . . .

I tell you that the most fundamental, essential element in the political, and therefore economic and moral, influence of a nation lies in its demographic strength.

Let us be quite clear: what are 40 million Italians compared to 90 million Germans and 200 million Slavs? What are 40 million Italians compared to 40 million Frenchmen, plus 90 million inhabitants of their colonies, or 46 million Englishmen plus 450 million people who live in their colonies?

Gentlemen!

Italy, if she is to count for anything in the world, must have a population of not less than 60 million inhabitants by the middle of this century.

Source: Il Popolo d'Italia, *26 May 1927*

Demographic/pro-natalist concerns were also to be found in other European countries at this time, most notably France in the wake of the First World War, which had decimated a whole generation of Frenchmen. And as in France, the campaign to increase Italy's birth rate was determined by fashionable military thinking, its purpose being to ensure that Mussolini could put '8 million' bayonets into the field. True to his word, Mussolini followed the bachelor tax by a tax on childless couples, accompanied by a powerful propaganda barrage, annual campaigns and a range of rewards, including family allowances and premiums, for large families.

Mussolini saw a particular obstacle to the growth in the birth rate as lying in the evils of city life.

Document 5.3 The Policy of 'Ruralisation'

There is a kind of urbanism which is destructive, which helps render the population 'sterile', and that is urban industrialism. Let us take the population figures for the large cities, those with round about half a million inhabitants or more. These are not reassuring: Turin, for example, lost 538 inhabitants in 1926. The population of Milan increased by twenty-two . . .

So do you really think that when I talk about the 'ruralisation' of Italy, that these are empty words?

Source: Il Popolo d'Italia, *26 May 1927*

The logical conclusion of 'ruralisation' was the banning of migration from the countryside to the towns. Yet, despite many legal restraints, the rural poor voted with their feet and Italian towns, especially the industrial metropolises, had considerably increased in population, predominantly as a result of migration, by the end of the 1930s. Milan, for example, the epitome of the corrupt and unhealthy metropolis, increased its population from 718,000 in 1921 to 1,114,000 in 1934 (Willson, 1996b, n. 27). Fascism brought about a major change in the countryside in terms of its social structure. As the following statistics show, the landless proletariat shrank while smallholders of all kinds increased.

Document 5.4 Agrarian Social Structure under Fascism

Occupation	*1911*	*1921*	*1936*
Owner-operators	19.0	33.6	33.5
Tenant farmers	8.1	6.8	18.6
Sharecroppers	17.5	15.6	20.4
Day labourers	55.1	43.8	27.2
Others	0.3	0.2	0.3

Source: V. Zamagni, The Economic History of Italy, 1860–1990: Recovery after Decline, *1993, p. 264*

Other Social Policies

The Demographic Battle had knock-on effects in Fascist social policy in general, the first in relation to women. The obsession with pro-natalism and 'race hygiene', which was more than just a concern for high standards of public health, helped reverse what little progress Italian women had made towards emancipation in the early twentieth century. Ironically, it was Mussolini who first gave the vote to women in Italy, for local elections in 1925, only effectively to take it away again when he abolished local elections in 1926.

The Demographic Battle required that an Italian woman be firmly locked into the role of 'producer for the nation', or, as Fascist propaganda had it, 'exemplary wife and mother'. This led to a reinforcement of the legal bans on contraception, sterilisation and abortion in the Rocco Criminal Code of 1932. Worse, the code entrenched the legal and financial power of the husband over his wife and even made adultery a punishable crime for women but not for men. There was nothing especially new or Fascist about this treatment of women – it fitted in almost perfectly with traditional Italian custom, and with Catholic teaching on women and the family which was actually reiterated by Pope Pius XI in 1930. In fact, Catholic teaching was harsher in the matter of abortion than Fascist law which allowed abortion to save the life of the woman. On the other hand, the Fascist treatment of women was indicative of a crude, chauvinist mentality common to the Fascists, which was virtually erected into an ideology.

Another effect of pro-natalism and race hygiene was to focus Fascist attention on questions of health, welfare and social security generally. Though the Fascists were not the creators of the Mother and Child Organisation, whose origins predated Mussolini's accession to power, this body flourished during the Fascist regime. It constituted the first attempt in Italian history to provide a universal and comprehensive antenatal care system and was thus one of the first steps on the road to the establishment of an Italian National Health Service. In real terms the extension of health and welfare provision under Fascism was spectacular – welfare spending rose from 7 per cent of the budget to 20 per cent between 1930 and 1940 (Clark, 1996, p. 267). But such provision was fragmented, and social insurance, for example, was usually provided on the basis of organised occupational groups, with the professions and state employees benefiting the most. This development led to a profusion under Fascism of what we would now call 'quangos' (quasi non-governmental organisations). There was also a strong element of consensus building in Fascist social welfare policies – some social groups were privileged at the expense of others and much basic poor relief was provided not by the state as of right but by the Fascist Party as charity.

The economic historian, Vera Zamagni (1993, p. 304), describes 'slow social progress under Fascism'. Certainly, if social trends under the regime are judged by its social objectives, then they largely suggest failure. As we have seen, the Italian population did not increase in line with Mussolini's expectations; indeed, the birth rate actually declined under Fascism, and migration from the countryside to towns did not cease. Fascism's attempts to imprison women in the home were less than successful: the proportion of women graduates rose under Fascism and women also took more jobs in the expanding public service sector. And when the Second World War broke out, women once more had to take the place of their menfolk in the workplace. Fascism is best remembered in the area of social change for its creation of a new 'state bourgeoisie': enormous groups of highly privileged, middling and lower-grade civil servants, and other bureaucrats in party, parastatal and corporative agencies for whom whole new residential quarters were created in Rome, and also in the larger Southern cities.

The 'Corporate State'

The years 1925–6 marked an important turning point in the regulation of industrial relations in Italy, with events taking place that laid the foundations of the Fascist 'corporate state'; this was the system of labour relations and corporative organisations (the term is also frequently used to describe the whole complex of Fascist economic and social policies). In October 1925 the Palazzo Vidoni Pact was signed between Confindustria, the industrial employers' association, and the Fascist trade union confederation.

Document 5.5 The Palazzo Vidoni Pact, 2 October 1925

On 2 October 1925, under the chairmanship of the Hon. Roberto Farinacci, the following was agreed between the Hon. Benni and Olivetti, Commander Jarach, Prof. Balella and Mr Liverani representing the General Confederation of Industry and the Hon. Cucini and the Hon. Rossini representing the Confederation of Fascist Corporations [the Fascist trade union organisation]:

1 The General Confederation of Industry recognises the Confederation of Fascist Corporations and its affiliated organisations as the sole representatives of the workers.

2 The Confederation of Fascist Corporations recognises the General Confederation of Industry and its affiliated organisations as the sole representatives of the industrialists.
3 All contractual relationships between industrialists and workers will be conducted via the two confederations.
4 Consequently, the internal factory committees are abolished and their functions transferred to the local trade union organisation.

Source: G. Bonfanti, Il Fascismo, *1977, p. 175*

The importance of the pact was enormous. With each side recognising the other's sole right to negotiate on behalf of their respective categories, the other trade union organisations were effectively excluded from the labour-relations process. Already battered by Fascist violence and weakened by the demoralisation and defection of members, the free trade union confederations, that is the Catholic C.I.L. and the Socialist/Communist C.G.L. were now deprived of their very *raison d'être*, the right to negotiate wages and working conditions on behalf of their members. They were, therefore, not in a strong position to resist the effects which 'Quota 90' had on their members after July 1926, and by the end of that year the remnants of both trade union confederations were dissolved, leaving the Fascists with a monopoly in the labour field. Henceforth this monopoly was regulated by legislation.

Document 5.6 The Labour and Anti-strike Law, 1926

Art. 1 Syndical associations of employers and of workers, both intellectual and manual, may obtain legal recognition when they can prove that they can comply with the following requirements:

1 In the case of associations of employers, that the employers who have voluntarily registered as members employ not less than one-tenth of the workers in the service of concerns of the kind for which the association has been formed . . . In the case of employees' associations, that the employees who have been voluntarily enrolled shall represent at least one-tenth of the total number of workers of the category for which the association is formed . . .

2 That the associations shall include among their aims not only the protection of the economic and moral interests of their members, but shall also aim to promote the welfare and education (especially moral and national education) of their members.

3 That the directors of the associations shall give proof of their competence, good moral behaviour, and sound national loyalty.

Art. 10 Collective labour contracts drawn up by the legally recognised associations of employers, workers, artists, and professional men are valid in respect to all employees, workers, artists and professional men belonging to

each category to which the said contract refers and which the associations represent in accordance with the provisions of Art. 5 of this law . . .
Art. 13 All disputes arising as to the regulation of collective contracts, or of other existing regulations, or the request for new conditions of labour, come within the jurisdiction of the Courts of Appeal acting as Labour Courts. The president of the court shall attempt to bring about conciliation before pronouncing his own decision.
Art. 18 The lockout and the strike are prohibited.

Source: C.F. Delzell (ed.),* Mediterranean Fascism, 1919–1945, *1971, pp. 111–12

Even though the monopoly enjoyed by the Fascist unions was only *de facto* and not legally established, these clauses ensured that the Fascist state had ample scope to exclude and disqualify any organisations outside them.

Article 18 was the real sting in the tail of Alfredo Rocco's labour legislation. Lockouts and strike action were punishable by fines and in extreme cases by imprisonment. Punishment was especially severe for civil servants involved in strikes. Trade union organisations for state employees were to be separately organised, and certain categories of state employee, including the police, teachers and the employees of the ministries of the Interior, Foreign Affairs and the Colonies were forbidden to belong to trade unions. On the other hand, Italian Fascism anticipated by decades the attempts of some democracies to regulate industrial relations though the courts.

In 1927 a 'Charter of Labour' was created setting out the rights of workers and setting laudable objectives to be reached in the fields of welfare, education and training, but much of the charter remained a dead letter.

In this system the role of the Fascist trade unions was carefully controlled and circumscribed; this was the price which Mussolini had to pay for the assured support of the industrialists. The 1926 law represented a victory of Rocco's concept of a state-regulated system of industrial relations over the national-syndicalist ideas of Edmondo Rossoni, the Fascist trade union leader. The abolition of the internal commissions reduced the influence of the trade unions on the factory floor, and Mussolini's insistence that the monolithic Fascist trade union confederation be broken up weakened their bargaining power at the national level. In this way, syndicalism, an element in the Fascist movement which was as potentially threatening to Mussolini as uncontrolled squadrism, was brought under control. The Fascist trade unions would find it increasingly difficult to defend their members' interests. In effect, the unions became an appendage of the party or a department of the state, similar to their counterparts in Nazi Germany and Stalin's Russia. As Tannenbaum has noted, 'Fascist Italy had complete control over the labour force and very little control over the nation's economic structure' (Tannenbaum, 1972, p. 100).

As a fig-leaf to this ruthless exploitation of the labour force, Mussolini constructed the vast edifice of the Corporate state. Corporate theory sounded impressive.

Document 5.7 The Corporations and the Party: *Critica Fascista*, 1934

What do we mean by the 'Fascist corporative system'? What we mean is a form of decentralised control of the economy, delegated by the political authorities in the state to the various economic categories, properly organised. Private ownership, understood as a full right of use rather than as a right to abuse, however, remains. Private enterprise, the irreplaceable and essential motor of the economy also remains.

In the corporation the power of employers and employees is balanced and reconciled . . . in this respect, the corporative regime in Italy has already achieved brilliant results, even before the institution of the corporations themselves; that is, with the introduction of collective contracts and the useful work of the labour courts . . .

But purely economic criteria will not be enough to guide the activity of the corporations: they will need to be illuminated by a political vision in the highest and fullest sense of that word. A political vision that is complete, organic, totalitarian; a vision capable of overcoming and resolving economic problems, subjecting the dull necessities of economic life to the rule of the spirit.

Source: G. Bonfanti, Il Fascismo, *1977, pp. 192–3*

Leaving aside the high-flown, and sometimes vacuous, rhetoric typical of the Fascist periodical press, what we have here is a theory of corporatism; that is, of a system of corporate institutions or councils representing employers, employees and state delegates which would settle problems of industrial relations and productivity amicably, and in the higher interests of the nation. The emphasis on private capitalism remaining the basis of the Italian economy was obviously intended as a reassurance to the industrialists.

By the end of the 1920s only one corporation, that for the arts and professions, had been created and it was not until after 1934 that corporations covering all areas of the economy and a National Council of Corporations, whose job it would be to manage the economy, had been set up. And in 1939 Mussolini transformed the lower house of parliament into a Chamber of Fasces and Corporations. The political structure of Italy, or so the Fascists claimed, had thus been reorganised on a wholly corporative, 'organic' basis, that of the occupations and professions, rather than one-man, one-vote. In reality, in the corporations and other new government agencies, Fascism had created a vast, largely useless apparatus, as Giovanni Giuriati, former Party Secretary, pointed out to Mussolini on the eve of the collapse of the regime.

Document 5.8 The Regime in Theory and Practice

The Charter of Labour. What the objects of your social legislation were supposed to be I shall not even mention. One can decide whether or not they have been achieved by a dispassionate examination of their results:

1 The Creation of a mastodontic state, parastate and syndical-corporative bureaucracy.
2 The duplication of bodies with the function of regulating individual sectors of the economy (how many offices are now responsible for cereals, alcoholic beverages etc?).
3 An increase in the number of plutocrats and in the power of the plutocracies.
4 Chaos in the provision and distribution of raw materials and basic foods (no fruit has been available in the capital for three months and frequently there are no vegetables).

Source: A. Aquarone, L'Organizzazione della Stato Totalitario, *1965, p. 612*

Even allowing for wartime conditions, this is an appalling indictment of the systemic inefficiency of the Fascist regime by one of its own leaders. The corporate state has also been condemned by historians, as a sham, an empty façade (Tannenbaum, 1973, p. 105 and Cassels, 1985, p. 58). Real power over the economy was shared between the government and major economic interest groups: the irrelevance of the corporations was revealed by the fact that they played little part in Fascism's response to the Great Depression. But the sham served its purpose for Mussolini in a variety of ways. Apart from providing yet more bureaucratic jobs for loyal supporters, the corporate state was another point of convergence between Catholics and Fascism. Some Catholic intellectuals saw in it the realisation of the ideals of Catholic social teaching, despite the fact that in his encyclical *Quadragesimo Anno* of 1931, Pope Pius XI argued that in several of its most essential aspects it emphatically was not (Pollard, 1985, pp. 138–9). Another advantage was that corporatism provided an ongoing theoretical debate within the party, a safety valve for potential intellectual dissidence. Probably the greatest benefit, however, lay in its propaganda value. In a world suffering the hardships of capitalist crisis – the Great Depression – and witnessing the horrors of socialist industrialisation in Russia, the corporate state in Fascist Italy seemed to provide an alternative to both in the harmonious collaboration of employers and employees, the much-vaunted 'third way' between capitalism and communism. And it had its admirers in France, Britain and America, and its imitators in the Austria of Dollfuss, Salazar's Portugal and Franco's Spain.

Italy and the Great Depression

For obvious reasons, there were no 'hunger marches' of the unemployed in Fascist Italy, and unemployment statistics ceased to be published after 1932. Nevertheless there is evidence that Italy was badly hit by the economic crisis, though probably not as badly as more heavily industrialised countries such as Britain, Germany and America. There is also some evidence that Italy recovered more quickly than they did. Mussolini's government was willing to use what would now be regarded as Keynesian methods to escape from the crisis: increasing rather than decreasing expenditure on public-works projects, social welfare and armaments. Italy was, after all, at war virtually continuously in some part of Africa or Europe from October 1935 onwards, and arms expenditure correspondingly leapt from 7 billion lire in 1935 to nearly double that a year later. The impact of the Great Depression and, in particular, the difficulties which the banks found themselves in as a result of business failures stimulated the creation of two institutions – I.M.I., a business credit bank founded in 1931 and I.R.I., the Industrial Reconstruction Institute, founded in 1933 – which were the most original of Fascism's policy innovations in the economic and social field. Through these agencies, the government intervened to salvage collapsing banks and manufacturing companies. I.R.I. was intended as a temporary measure, but the result was that, 'after 1936 the (Italian) state owned or controlled a proportionately larger share of industry than was the case in any other European country with the exception of the Soviet Union' (Ricossa, 1976, p. 287).

Empire and Autarky

The term autarky, meaning economic self-sufficiency, usefully describes a number of Fascist economic policies, including, of course, the 'Battle for Grain', and its origins can be traced back to that policy. In addition, there was a sustained attempt to follow a policy of import substitution for the same reasons. But autarky only became a wholesale policy of Fascism from the mid-1930s onwards, as a result of the economic sanctions imposed on Italy by the League of Nations following her invasion of Ethiopia. Some improvement was achieved in Italy's energy supply position under Fascism – including the discovery of natural gas in the Po Valley – and progress was made made in the development of textile and petro-chemical industries. But as Italy once more faced balance of payments problems in the 1930s, ministers resorted to tariff barriers, currency restrictions and other regulations to plug the gap. The result was a 'closed' economy, which did not have the capacity to import all necessities or to produce them at home or in the colonies. Autarky was not a great success, as the list of raw materials, machinery and arms which Mussolini presented to Hitler as being necessary before Italy could go to war in September 1939 shows (see Chapter 6, p. 101).

According to Zamagni (1993, p. 275), 'The Fascist period did not represent a standstill in the industrialisation process . . . nevertheless one thing is certain, and that is that Fascism failed to narrow the gap between Italy and the other industrialised countries.'

Document 5.9 Shares of World Manufacturing Output, 1929–38

	Percentage			
Country	*1929*	*1932*	*1937*	*1938*
United States	43.3	31.8	35.1	28.7
U.S.S.R.	5.0	11.5	14.1	17.6
Germany	11.1	10.6	11.4	13.2
UK	9.4	10.9	9.4	9.2
France	6.6	6.9	4.5	4.5
Japan	2.5	3.5	3.5	3.8
Italy	3.3	3.1	2.7	2.9

Source: P. Kennedy, The Rise and Fall of the Great Powers: Economic Change and Military Conflict from 1500 to 2000, *1988, p. 426*

The figures vindicate her claim, and they furnish clear evidence that A.J. Gregor's idea of Fascist Italy as a 'developmental dictatorship', similar to Stalin's in the Soviet Union, is incorrect. This is hardly surprising in view of the fact that Mussolini had categorically repudiated economic prosperity as a goal of Fascism.

Document 5.10 The Goals of Fascism

Here Fascism rejects the concept of economic 'happiness', to be realised in a socialist manner, as an inevitable, automatic element of economic development, in order to assure everyone a maximum of material well-being.

Source: Enciclopedia Italiana, *XIV, 1932, p. 848*

Though Fascism sought to develop some new industrial areas in Northern Italy, most notably Porto Marghera near Venice, Bolzano and Ferrara, it had no comprehensive economic development strategy. Most surprising of all, it had no development plan for the South, Italy's most backward and poverty-stricken region. Here, the limited development of industry in the Fascist period was the work of private rather than state initiative, but some of the potentially most important proposed changes for the South – the expropriation of absentee landlords and hydro-electric power programmes – were repeatedly rejected because of the opposition of the landowning elite. Mussolini was aware of the problems of the South, as this quotation from one of his speeches demonstrates.

Document 5.11 Mussolini and the South

I have visited the South and I have returned with very complex and contradictory impressions. Large sections of the population are marvellous, sober, instinctively and traditionally patriotic and have not been contaminated by

Nordic or Russian 'diseases'. But in some areas especially they live in conditions which I would call pre-human, prehistoric. None of the districts in Basilicata has water, not for washing, but for drinking! Only under the Fascist government will Basilicata have its aqueduct. Dozens of districts in Calabria and hundreds in Sicily have living standards that one can only describe as absolutely primitive. Sixty thousand Italian citizens in Messina are living in conditions that are a disgrace to the human race.

Source: Opera Omnia, *XX, pp. 18–19*

But the mass of the Northern and Central Italian population were ignorant of all this, and this ignorance was aggravated by the fact that eventually Mussolini forbade the media to talk about the 'Southern Problem'; only in this way was it 'solved'. In broader terms, it is doubtful whether Fascism was in any meaningful sense an agent of modernisation, despite its original commitment to fight against technological and moral backwardness, the rhetoric of Futurism and the commitment, on paper at least, 'to make way to the qualified'. A key sector in any strategy of modernisation would have to have been education. There is some evidence of progress here – the national illiteracy rate fell by 10 per cent and the regime managed to coerce almost 100 per cent of children of primary-school age into enrolling, a considerable improvement on the situation prior to Fascism coming to power. The real problem was that until the end of the 1930s, when Bottai was Minister of Education, no attempt had been made to alter the philosophy and structure of the Italian school system, which at the secondary level was overwhelmingly biased towards the humanities and against sciences and technology. His attempts to correct the balance by reinforcing technical and vocational education were too little and, because of the imminence of war, too late.

Italy's underlying economic and social problems had not been solved by Fascism: it would take the post-war democratic republic using economic policies fundamentally different from those of Fascism to bring about the economic 'miracle' of the 1950s and 1960s and thus transform Italy into a modern, industrial society.

Fascist foreign policy, 1922–39

The whole thrust of Fascist foreign policy was determined by an ideology, deriving from pre-war Nationalism, which was constructed around strong elements of imperialism and *romanita* – the myth of Rome – and social Darwinism. Mussolini endorsed Enrico Corradini's idea of 'the international class struggle of the proletarian against the plutocratic nations', and Italy was, of course, a 'proletarian nation'. Fascism, like pre-war Nationalism, believed in the necessity and virtue of war.

Document 6.1 The Fascist View of War and Peace

Above all, in general terms, as far as the future and the development of the human race is concerned, leaving aside present foreign policy considerations, Fascism does not believe in either the possibility or the desirability of permanent peace. It therefore rejects pacifism, which hides an unwillingness to fight and refusal to accept sacrifice. Only war brings to their fullest all human tensions and energies, and it alone places the seal of nobility on those peoples who have the courage to face it . . . Fascism carries this anti-pacifist attitude into the life of the individual. 'I don't give a damn' – the proud motto of the fighting squads . . . sums up a doctrine which is not merely political: it is evidence of a fighting spirit which accepts all risks. It signifies a new mode of life.

Source: Enciclopedia Italiana, *XIV, 1932, p. 849*

The circumstances of Fascism's conception and birth – the Intervention Crisis of 1915 and the 'mutilated victory' of 1919, also meant that Fascism came to power offering a strongly nationalistic foreign policy that would reassert Italy's international role and wipe out the shape of previous military and diplomatic defeats. But Italy's 'national inferiority complex', and her modest showing in international affairs prior to the First World War, stemmed from a fundamental weakness. As 'the least of the great powers', she did not possess the economic resources or, in particular, the industrial base, to compete effectively with other great powers. To offset this deficiency, Italian foreign-policy makers would always have to exercise diplomatic skills of a positively Cavourian subtlety in order to exploit the situations which presented themselves to Italy's advantage.

Document 6.2 Map of Italy's International Position after Versailles, 1919

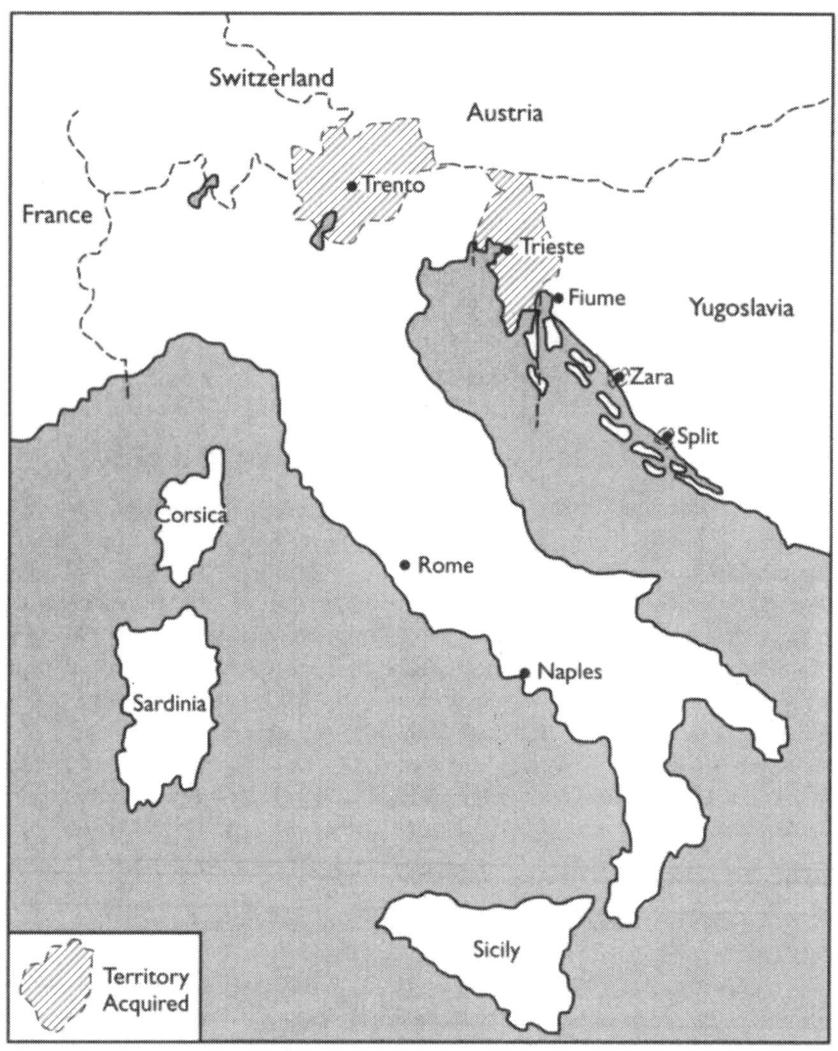

As the map shows, despite Italian complaints about a 'mutilated victory', the 1919 peace settlement fulfilled most of Italy's war aims as laid down in the Treaty of London, 1915. The defensible frontier which Italy had so long desired was provided by a new boundary along the watersheds of the Carinthian and Julian Alps. The 'unredeemed lands' of Trento, Gorizia and Trieste were at last brought within the Kingdom of Italy, at the expense of a quarter of a million

German speakers in the South Tyrol and half a million Slavs in Istria, whose rights to national self-determination were ignored. The defence of an independent Austrian buffer state against German claims now became a central element in Italian foreign policy. Indeed, Mussolini said of Austria that if she had not existed it would have been necessary to invent her. By 1934, Austria had been transformed into a docile satellite, complete with a one-party regime and corporatist institutions on the Italian model.

The Slav minorities in Istria, the unsatisfactory status of Fiume, the Italian toe-holds on the coast of Dalmatia and Italian designs on Albania, so close to the Apulian coast, reinforced Italy's traditional interest in the Adriatic and the Balkans generally. But she also remained a Mediterranean power *par excellence*, with the largest navy in the region. On the other hand, the Mediterranean was dominated by the navies of Britain and France, and it had been axiomatic to Italian foreign policy from unification onwards that she could not afford to fall out with the two dominant naval powers, especially Britain. Relations with these powers was a problem for the Italian foreign office. The extent of Italy's gains at Versailles seemed to suggest the overwhelming need to stand shoulder to shoulder with Britain and France in defence of the peace settlement against the defeated, 'revisionist' powers of Germany, Hungary and Bulgaria. But resentment over the 'mutilated victory' influenced the diplomatic establishment as well as Italian public opinion. Britain and France had blocked Italian aspirations to the ex-German colonies in Africa and ex-Ottoman territories in the Middle East. Revisionist tendencies were, therefore, present in Italian foreign policy from the start, as is proved by the Italians' interest in Palestine before Mussolini came to power.

Fascist Foreign Policy in the 1920s

Though Mussolini gave foreign affairs a central importance – he was his own foreign minister between 1922 and 1929 – Fascism's actual achievements in the foreign-policy field in the 1920s were extremely modest. Fascism retained the links with Britain and France, even if those links were rarely cordial. Mussolini even joined in the Locarno Pacts of 1925, thereby guaranteeing the Belgium–Germany and France–Germany boundaries without, however, receiving any tangible reward, such as the obvious one, a guarantee of the boundary between Austria and Germany. The Duce had once proudly boasted that Italy would give 'nothing for nothing', but this was patently not true as far as Locarno was concerned.

Nor did the Duce obtain any substantial improvement in the 'mutilated victory', except for Fiume, whose incorporation into Italy was finally accepted by Yugoslavia in 1924. 'Ten years of good behaviour', as Fascist foreign policy in the 1920s has been described, working with rather than against Britain and France, produced very meagre results: the acquisition of thin slices of territory from Britain in Africa, Jarabub, annexed to Libya, and Jubaland to Italian Somaliland. And in spite of all Mussolini's hopes, Kemal Atatürk's new, secular Turkish Republic did not disintegrate, thus preventing the realisation of the Italian dream of a colony in Asia Minor. On the other hand, Mussolini, surprisingly perhaps in view of his bluster at international gatherings, acquired a reputation for himself as a moderate and wise statesman, due partly to his role at Locarno and partly to his domestic achievements, particularly the signing of the Lateran Pacts in 1929, as the following extract demonstrates.

Document 6.3 Mussolini – the Greatest Italian Statesman since Cavour?

The resolution of the Roman Question was the result . . . of a bold stroke of statesmanship. The prestige of the Head of the Government must be greatly increased in Italy and abroad . . . Italy's prestige will . . . be greatly strengthened by the cessation of the quarrel with the pope.

Source:* The Times*, editorial, 12 February 1929

Yet it would be wrong to take the idea of a decade of good behaviour too far. In *intention* at least, Fascist foreign policy was no less aggressive, ambitious and potentially revisionist in the 1920s than in the 1930s. One of Mussolini's first steps in foreign policy took the form of a blatant adventure in 'gunboat diplomacy', the shelling and occupation of the Greek island of Corfu following the murder of an Italian general by Greek bandits 1923. And by the mid-1920s, Mussolini was already flirting with the revisionist powers, Russia, Germany and Hungary, as a means of bringing pressure to bear for an improvement in Italy's status under the Versailles Treaty. Relations with Yugoslavia deteriorated rapidly after 1924 because of Fascism's brutal attempt forcibly to 'Italianise' the Slav minorities in the new north-eastern provinces, and its thinly veiled economic penetration of Albania. By the end of the 1920s, Fascist Italy was engaged in a policy of subverting and destabilising her Yugoslav neighbour by supporting the Croat nationalist leader Pavelić and the Ustasha, a semi-Fascist terrorist movement fighting against the Belgrade government.

Mussolini also tried to undermine British power by a variety of means: in the Mediterranean by encouraging pro-Italian elements in Malta, in the Middle East generally by proclaiming his desire to protect Islam and in Palestine by briefly and unsuccessfully flirting with the Zionist movement.

What Fascist foreign policy lacked in the 1920s was not ambitious aims but the means and, above all, the opportunity to achieve them. It has been argued that Mussolini's inexperience in foreign affairs and his ignorance of the complexities and subtleties of diplomacy allowed the career diplomats in the Italian Foreign Office to hinder the execution of his more radical initiatives. But as Absalom (1984, p. 17) has demonstrated the main difference between Mussolini and the career diplomats was one of style rather than substance. Again, though Mussolini may well have been distracted by the exigencies of domestic affairs in the mid-1920s, eliminating opposition and building up the regime, the Corfu affair was just the sort of assertion of Italian power in the world that Fascism needed to consolidate its support at home.

Economic difficulties also played a part. Until the 1930s, Italy was too closely tied into the world economic system, and in particular too dependent on other powers, notably the United States and Britain, for its financial stability, to be able to indulge in military adventures. Above all, until the early 1930s, the international situation was not conducive to the success of Fascism's ambitious, expansionist foreign-policy aims. Thanks to American isolationism, the international boycott of Soviet Russia and the weakness of Weimar Germany, Britain and France ruled the international roost, dominating European affairs and effectively controlling the League of Nations; hence Mussolini's suspicion, sometimes hostility, towards that organisation. Forced to continue playing the junior partner to the Western powers, Mussolini had little room for diplomatic manoeuvre or to flex his international muscles.

Fascist Foreign Policy in the 1930s: the Attack on Ethiopia

As far as Fascist foreign policy is concerned, the 1930s began in 1932, because it was in that year, in a major cabinet reshuffle, that Mussolini reverted to being his own foreign minister. In all likelihood, Mussolini was genuinely dissatisfied with Dino Grandi's conduct of foreign affairs. Grandi, who had been in office since 1929, appeared to be too Anglophile and 'soft' on disarmament. Furthermore, Mussolini believed that Fascism demanded a spectacular foreign-policy achievement and the only one that would suffice was the conquest of Ethiopia (then known as Abyssinia). De Grand (1982, p. 99) is almost certainly correct when he says that, 'there were no compelling economic imperatives in Italy for expansion in 1934 and 1935. The worst crisis of the depression had been overcome'. But while the invasion was launched in 1935, it is clear that the decision to go to war was actually made in *1932*, when Italy was still suffering the worst effects of the slump. Thus, the traditional view that the Ethiopian adventure was almost certainly contrived, at least in part, as an alternative to social reform still has some force. The resort to colonial adventures as a way of distracting attention from domestic difficulties, and even hopefully resolving them, was an established tradition among the Italian political class before the advent of Fascism. Francesco Crispi had tried it, albeit unsuccessfully, in the 1890s, and Giovanni Giolitti used this expedient with more success in 1911–12. Ethiopia had been the traditional target of Italian colonial aspirations since the 1870s, thus Mussolini's proposed conquest had the additional attraction of offering to wipe out the humiliation of Italy's defeats by the Ethiopians at Dogali in 1887 and Adowa in 1896. In any case, by the early 1930s, Ethiopia, as one of the two surviving independent states in Africa, was the only realistic outlet for further Italian colonial expansion.

That three years should have elapsed between the decision and the deed can largely be accounted for by the change in the international situation. Hitler's accession to power in Germany dramatically transformed the power balance in Europe. By the spring of 1934, Germany had left both the disarmament conference and the League of Nations, and a year later, at the Stresa Conference, Britain and France actively sought Mussolini's support in their efforts to contain a resurgent and rearming Germany. Consequently, Italy was now more than a junior partner to Britain and France: it was Mussolini's judgement that she had, instead, become their absolutely indispensable ally. As a result, he saw his path clear to conquer Ethiopia unhindered by adverse developments in Europe, as the following document demonstrates.

Document 6.4 Mussolini on Abyssinia, 30 December 1934

Memorandum by Mussolini for Marshal Badoglio, Chief of General Staff. Directive and Plan of Action to solve the Abyssinian question.

5 . . . time is working against us. The longer we delay the solution of this problem, the more difficult the task will be and the greater the sacrifices . . .

6 I decide on this war, the object of which is nothing more than the complete destruction of the Abyssinian army and the total conquest of Abyssinia. In no other way can we build the empire . . .

One essential condition, which is in no way prejudicial to our action, is having a peaceful Europe on our hands, certainly for the period of two years 1935–36 and 1936–37, by the latter period the solution must have been completed. An examination of the position emerging at the beginning of 1935 leads to the conclusion that in the next two years war will be averted in Europe . . . Moreover it can be said of Germany that her military machine has not even approximately reached the level of efficiency which would enable her to take the initiative in starting a war . . .

No-one in Europe would raise any difficulties provided the prosecution of operations resulted rapidly in an accomplished fact. It would suffice to declare to England and France that their interests would be recognised . . .

Source: G. Rochat, Militari e politici nella preparazione della Campagna d'Etiopia: Studio e documenti, 1932–1936, *1971, p. 29)*

Mussolini considered the greatest potential threat to peace, and to Italy's interests, as being posed by Germany. Nazis in Austria, presumably with Hitler's backing, had murdered the Austrian Chancellor Dollfuss in July 1934. The attempted *putsch* by the Austrian Nazis which had accompanied the assassination attempt failed. Mussolini's response had been to send troops to Italy's Brenner frontier with Austria and to warn Hitler 'hands off Austria'. His evaluation of Germany's state of war preparedness is consistent with known data and lends credence to Robertson's (1977, p. 112) argument that Mussolini believed that he had ample time to conquer Ethiopia and be back on the Brenner to resist any further threat from Germany.

The optimism expressed in the last sentence of Document 6.4 was apparently confirmed at a meeting in January 1935 with Laval, the French foreign minister, whose remarks Mussolini interpreted as giving a 'green light' to his Ethiopian adventure. Similarly, Britain's silence on the question at the Stresa Conference he took to mean an acceptance of his claims. But Mussolini ignored British warnings about the consequences of invading Ethiopia, made in the summer and autumn of 1935, with the result that the launch of the invasion in October 1935 brought him into conflict with the League of Nations. When the British and French attempted a compromise solution by means of the Hoare–Laval Pact of December 1935, which would have effectively partitioned Ethiopia, British public opinion was outraged.

The Consequences of the Ethiopian War

Italian progress after the invasion had initially been slow, but by May 1936 the capital, Addis Ababa, had been captured and Mussolini celebrated his victory in 'Roman' style, declaring that 'the Empire has returned to the hills of Rome'. Thus the immediate consequence of the Ethiopian War was to stir the nationalistic pride of the Italian people. At last Italy had asserted herself in international affairs. Mussolini was more popular in the summer of 1936 than at any other time in the history of the regime, and this popularity was reinforced by a genuine feeling of resentment against the economic sanctions imposed by the League of Nations. Though the sanctions did not work, largely because they excluded both a ban on oil and closure of the Suez Canal, Italy's only viable line of communication with the East African fronts, they infuriated Mussolini, helped to rupture the relationship with Britain and France and showed the ineffectiveness of the latter's policy of collective security.

Fascist propaganda concentrated increasingly on Italy's 'Roman', imperial destinies, as the following song shows.

Document 6.5 'Facetta Nera' *('Little Black Face')*.

Little black girl, slave among slaves,
If you look from the plateau towards the sea,
You will see in a dream many ships,
And a tricolour waving for thee.

Little black face,
Beautiful Abyssinian,
Wait and hope,
Already Italy is close,
When we manage to reach you,
We will give you another law, another king.

Source: A.V. Savona and M.L. Straniero, Canti dell'Italia Fascista (1919–1945), *1979, p. 270*

The words of this song, which went to the top of the Italian 'hit parade' in the mid-1930s, express the sense of the civilising mission with which Fascism sought to coat its imperialism in Africa, in particular the claim to be saving the peoples of Ethiopia from slavery. Fascism even claimed that its civilising mission coincided with a Christianising mission of Catholic Italy. While this was supported in some Catholic circles in Italy, most notably by Cardinal Schuster, Archbishop of Milan, it has to be remembered that the bulk of Ethiopia's population was already Christian, albeit not in communion with Rome.

There is also evidence that the acquisition of a large tract of Africa enhanced the racial consciousness of the regime, a development which Mussolini would later cite as one of the contributory factors to his decision to introduce the laws against the Jews in 1938.

Another consequence of the conquest of Ethiopia was the reinforcement of Italy's expansionistic ambitions. Mussolini was soon reiterating his claims to a string of territories around the Mediterranean: Nice, Savoy, Corsica (all once Italian), Malta, Albania and Tunisia, and he proudly declared that the Mediterranean was an 'Italian lake'. By the end of the 1930s, Fascist megalomania was stretching even further. Mussolini began to argue that the Mediterranean had become Italy's 'prison' and cast his eyes beyond Gibraltar and Suez towards world power status for Italy. His world power pretensions were founded on a dangerous illusion, that a victory over a weak, semi-feudal African country was proof of Italy's ability to fight and win a war against the economic and military might of one of the European great powers.

The Rome–Berlin Axis and the Spanish Civil War

The major beneficiary of the rupture between Britain and France and Italy was Germany. Profiting from the breakdown of the Stresa front, Hitler remilitarised the Rhineland in March 1936 and by continuing to supply Italy with coal, he also helped Mussolini survive sanctions. The latter's gratitude knew no bounds when Nazi Germany became the first great power to recognise the Italian conquest of Ethiopia in July 1936. Mussolini's attitude towards Hitler and Nazi Germany accordingly changed. His intransigence over Austrian independence softened and from the autumn of 1936 onwards he talked about a 'Rome–Berlin Axis', around which, he argued, henceforth European affairs would revolve, as opposed to the the previous dominance of the London–Paris axis.

The Spanish Civil War, which broke out in the summer of 1936 and was to last for two and a half years, was a major factor in developing and deepening the 'Axis' relationship. Mussolini's decision to intervene on the side of Franco and the Nationalist rebels against the Republican government was motivated by immediate political considerations. His action was essentially a logical continuation of the policy of supporting right-wing and anti-Republican forces in Spain that had been initiated in 1931. Aiding Franco was also a means of striking a blow against the anti-Fascist Popular Front governments which had come to power in France and Spain in 1936, and Mussolini appears to have been genuinely concerned at the danger of a Communist takeover in Spain, a fear that seemed to be confirmed by the Soviet Union's intervention on the side of the Republic. Another factor was Mussolini's search for fresh fields of conquest and glory for the Italian armies after the victory in Ethiopia.

As the Civil War dragged on and the Italian commitment of men and materials increased, Mussolini enlarged his ambitions. Now he sought air and naval bases in the Balearic Islands as a means of strengthening his presence in the Western Mediterranean against Britain and France. He also hoped that after Franco's victory Spain would become a client state of Fascist Italy.

But the Spanish adventure brought few benefits for Mussolini. Franco refused to concede bases, and though in its laws and institutions the new Spain paid many compliments to Fascism, it did not become a satellite or even an ally. And even though Italian military supplies and assistance were essential to Franco's victory, glory eluded Mussolini's legions in Spain. In fact, at the Battle of Guadalajara in March 1937 the Italian Fascists suffered a humiliating defeat at the hands of their fellow-countrymen fighting in the International Brigade on the side of the Republic. Nazi Germany, which had contributed substantially less to the Nationalist cause in men and materials, gained far more than Italy, especially in long-term economic concessions.

On the other hand, the struggle in Spain helped to cement the relationship between Hitler and Mussolini, emphasising the ideological common ground between the two regimes. Another important stage in this process was the carefully stage-managed, and slightly comic, visit of Mussolini to the capital of the Third Reich in September 1937. Mussolini was deeply impressed by the display of totalitarian efficiency and military strength staged for his benefit and it helped convince him that only through an alliance with Hitler could he realise his dreams of Italian greatness. A further stage in the development of the relationship was reached in November 1937 when Galeazzo Ciano, Mussolini's son-in-law and foreign minister since 1936, signed the Anti-Comintern Pact (aimed against Russia) with Germany and Japan. When Germany occupied Austria in March 1938, Mussolini was already reconciled to the inevitable.

Document 6.6 Conversation between Mussolini and Ribbentrop, German Ambassador in London, 6 November 1937

Finally, Ribbentrop discusses the Austrian question . . . he points out to the Duce that in the grand policy of Rome and Berlin, Austria now represents an element of secondary importance, and that he considers that at a certain point it will become necessary to settle finally a question on which the enemies of the common Italo-German policy still speculate. The Duce replies that Austria is a German country by race, language and culture. The Austrian question must not be considered as a problem affecting Italy and

Germany, but, on the contrary, as a problem of an international order. For his part he has stated, and he repeats it now, that he is tired of mounting guard over Austrian independence . . . Italian interest today is no longer as lively as it was some years ago, for one thing because of Italy's imperialist development, which was now concentrating her interest on the Mediterranean and the Colonies.

Source: C.J. Lowe and F. Marzari,* Italian Foreign Policy, 1870–1940, *1975, pp. 408–9

It is significant that Ribbentrop viewed the diplomatic relationship between Italy and Germany as already being close, and that he saw it as being directed against Britain and France. Mussolini's comments are probably an accurate reflection of his feelings. The switch of Italian attention to the Mediterranean from Central Europe had gone hand in hand with the growth in friendship with Hitler, hence Austria was no longer a priority. But his massive commitment of fighting men and equipment to Spain had left him in such a weak military position that he would have been unable to defend Austrian independence had he wished to do so. His involvement in Spain, by bringing him into frequent clashes with Britain and France over violations of the Non-intervention Agreement, also meant that he had squandered the diplomatic support which would have been crucial to the defence of Austrian independence against Germany. And, of course, Hitler had deliberately encouraged Mussolini to increase his commitment in Spain with precisely this end in view.

Many Italians were unhappy about the way Mussolini had written off Austria. The foreign-policy about-turn over the *Anschluss* caused grave misgivings in the Vatican, at Court and even in Fascist Party circles, as did domestic manifestations of the Rome–Berlin Axis. There were murmurings against the novelties which Mussolini brought back from Germany, like the goose step which Mussolini attempted to Italianise by calling it the 'Roman step'. The introduction of the Racial Laws against Italy's Jews in the autumn of 1938 was the most blatant importation from Nazi Germany, and one that aroused opposition from the Church and little popular enthusiasm. Mussolini's foreign policy was beginning to strain the fragile and complex structure of the 'block of consensus' and even the loyalty of some good Fascists.

The most profound evidence of widespread Italian lack of enthusiasm for the Axis is to be found in the reaction of public opinion to the Munich Crisis of September 1938. Mussolini liked to fancy that the crisis was one of the high points of his diplomacy, when he acted as mediator between Hitler and the grateful Western powers over the problem of Czechoslovakia, and thus saved Europe from war. In reality, he effectively operated as Hitler's broker, manipulating Britain and France into accepting Germany's expansionism. When he returned home to Italy he indeed found himself greeted as the hero of the hour, but to Mussolini's disgust it quickly became clear that Italians were grateful for having been spared a war on the side of Nazi Germany.

Towards the Pact of Steel, May 1939

Neither this opposition nor the increasingly subordinate position which he was forced to take in the relationship with Hitler deflected Mussolini from his chosen path. When Hitler occupied the shattered rump of Czechoslovakia (partitioned in the Munich agreement of September 1938) in March 1939, Mussolini's pathetically inadequate response was to invade Albania, which had been a virtual Italian protectorate for some years. And by May 1939 Mussolini's concern was not to resist the progressive reduction of Fascist Italy to the status of a client state of the Third Reich, but to ensure that he was not abandoned by Hitler, hence his willingness to conclude a military alliance with Germany in that month. De Grand (1982, p. 181) has argued that Mussolini 'bumbled' into the Pact of Steel whereas McGregor Knox claims that it was the result of a careful design by the Italians (Knox, 1986, p. 150). Yet with no draft of his own, Galeazzo Ciano, the Italian foreign minister, was obliged to accept the German proposals.

Document 6.7 The Pact of Steel, May 1939

Art. 2 . . . should the security or other vital interests of the High Contracting Parties be threatened from without, the other High Contract Party will afford the threatened Party full political and diplomatic support in order to remove this threat.
Art. 3 If, contrary to the wishes and hopes of the High Contracting Parties, it should happen that one of them became involved in warlike complications with another Power or Powers, the other High Contracting Party would immediately come to its assistance as an ally and support with all its military forces on land, at sea and in the air.

Source: J.A.S. Grenville, The Major International Treaties, 1914–1945. A History and Guide with Texts, *1987, pp. 193–4*

The pact must be regarded as one of the most extraordinary in Italy's history. Unlike the pre-1914 Triple Alliance with Germany and Austria-Hungary which was essentially defensive in its scope, this was offensive; moreover, whereas the Triple Alliance had laid only very restricted commitments on Italy, the pact committed Mussolini go to the support of his ally in whatever circumstances. The Duce, however, consistently argued that he had signed on the understanding that there would be no major war until 1943, and the full-scale preparations for the World Fair to be held in Rome in 1942, the twentieth anniversary of the founding of the regime, suggest that this was true.

Mussolini and the Outbreak of the Second World War

In view of his interpretation of the Pact of Steel, the outbreak of war between Germany and Britain and France in September 1939, following Hitler's invasion of Poland, must have come as a shock to Mussolini. It certainly gave him food for thought. After a brief period of uncertainty he decided to opt for neutrality, or to use the euphemism which he invented, 'non-belligerence'. He had plenty of reasons for doing so. He clearly believed that Hitler had bitten off more than he could chew by provoking the hostility of Britain and France and that his chances of defeating them were extremely slim. Mussolini was also less than happy with the direction that German foreign policy had taken since the Pact of Steel. With the latter treaty minimising the possibility of a rapprochement between Mussolini and the Western powers, Hitler sought to protect his position in the East by the Non-agression Pact with Stalin, signed in August 1939. Though it opened the way to a successful invasion and defeat of Poland, it was manifestly a negation of the anti-Bolshevik stance adopted by Japan, Italy and Germany in the Anti-Comintern Pact of November 1937. Mussolini now seriously suspected German duplicity.

Italian public opinion may also have played a part in Mussolini's decision not to intervene: police sources demonstrated there was absolutely no popular support for a war on the side of Nazi Germany, and both the King and the Vatican were also opposed to it. Probably the overriding consideration, and the one used officially to justify 'non-belligerence' to the Germans, was the fact that Italy was utterly unprepared for war in September 1939. Apart from Italy's underlying economic weaknesses, the failures of autarky and the massive expenditure of military resources in Ethiopia, Spain and Albania had left the armed forces woefully ill equipped to fight a major war.

From 'Non-belligerence' to War

Mussolini's decision in September 1939 may have been a wise one, indeed the only one in the circumstances, but it was embarrassing, not to say humiliating, for an old interventionist to have to endure a rerun of Italy's neutrality at the beginning of the First World War – hence the attempt to disguise the situation. From September onwards Mussolini frequently reiterated his moral and diplomatic support for Hitler, and his intention to enter the war just as soon as circumstances would permit. As a result of Hitler's successful *blitzkriegs* in Denmark and Norway in April 1940, and Holland, Belgium and Luxembourg at the beginning of May, followed by the invasion of France on the tenth of that month, Mussolini's patience with enforced 'non-belligerence' ran out. The German army was driving all before it and unless he intervened quickly Mussolini would get no share of the spoils of victory. As he moved towards a decision to intervene on the side of Germany, the King, the Pope, President Roosevelt and the Italian High Command all sought to dissuade him, as did his foreign minister, Ciano. In his *Diary*, Ciano chronicled his unsuccessful efforts as the tide of victory seemed to flow more and more strongly in favour of Germany.

Document 6.8 Mussolini and Hitler's War, 10 May to 12 May 1940

10 May 1940 No direct news from the battle front, but from all that we hear it seems that things are going well for the Germans . . .
11 May 1940 . . . Nothing new here. Today Mussolini is less bellicose than he was yesterday, and more disposed to wait. It seems that the Italian General Staff has thrown most timely cold water on our present military prospects. Even Balbo has told me that we cannot go into the field for two months, and before we have received a definite quantity of arms and military supplies.
12 May 1940 The telegrams sent by the Pope to the rulers of the three invaded states have incensed Mussolini, who would like to curb the Vatican, and is often inclined to extremes. In these last few days he often repeats that the Papacy is a cancer which gnaws at our national life, and that he intends, if necessary, to root it out once and for all. 'The Pope need not think that he can seek an alliance with the monarchy, because I am ready to blow them both sky high at the same time.' I do not share this policy of the Duce because, if he intends to wage war on the Church . . . I believe that it is indispensable for us to avoid a clash, and for this reason I give Alfieri [Italian Ambassador to the Vatican] instructions to proceed in a manner that will not have any of the controversial character the Duce wanted to give it.

Source: Ciano's Diary, *1947, pp. 248–9*

This document confirms the widespread feeling that the Italian armed forces were not keen on a war alongside Germany and that they knew they were not prepared for it. It also suggests that the list of supplies which Mussolini sent Hitler as an excuse for not entering the war at the end of August 1939, and which prompted Ciano's comment, 'Its enough to kill a bull, if a bull could read it' (*Ciano's Diary*, 1947, p. 135), was not entirely inflated. Balbo was both a leading 'Fascist of the first hour' and largely responsible for the creation of Italy's air force. He knew what he was talking about. Mussolini's relations with the Vatican had been less than cordial since the confrontation with Pius XI over the Racial Laws (see Chapter 4, p. 74). While he had the sense to see, like Ciano, that a conflict with the Church at this juncture was out of the question, his bluster was not entirely without substance. His glimpses of the Nazi state, with its totalitarian control over German society, including the churches, aroused genuine resentment against two institutions – the Papacy and the monarchy – which impeded the realisation of such a goal in Italy.

Pius XII's earlier efforts to prevent the outbreak of war, his condemnation of the invasions of Poland and the Low Countries and his later attempts to dissuade Mussolini from war in 1940 only increased the Duce's anger. To make matters worse, the Pope and the King, the latter a notorious anti-clerical, saw eye to eye on the issue of the German alliance and war: the King's hostility to the alliance was widely known in Rome.

The Declaration of War

Mussolini's original reluctance turned into an impatience for war as Hitler's armies swept through France. He now feared that he would be unable to seize anything of value before Hitler signed an armistice. On 10 June Mussolini finally declared war on Britain and France. Ciano remarked on the Duce's speech from the balcony of Palazzo Venezia in Rome that, predictably, it did not 'arouse very much enthusiasm' (*Ciano's Diary*, 1947, p. 264).

Rosaria Quartararo claims that Mussolini did not want to go to war against Britain and France in June 1940 but that he was forced into the decision by the blunders, intransigence and hostility of British diplomacy, and she cites the British blockade of German coal exports to Italy as evidence (Quartararo, 1980, pp. 524–6). In broader terms, she argues that Mussolini was pursuing a policy of equidistance from Germany and the Western democracies, but that the British *wanted* a war with Italy and that, in any case, they were unwilling to offer the concessions to Mussolini that would make his continued neutrality worthwhile. This picture of Mussolini reluctantly forced into a war which he did not want does not fit the circumstances or the evidence, especially that to be found in Ciano's diaries. June 1940 offered Mussolini his last window of opportunity to acquire hegemony over the Mediterranean at the expense of Britain and France, and to do so in the glorious, warlike fashion required by Fascist ideology and rhetoric. This was, and always had been, the natural, logical and ultimate objective of Fascist foreign policy.

War, defeat and the fall of Fascism

7

Mussolini's war aims in 1940 were very predictable, the creation of a new Roman Empire; in other words, domination of the Mediterranean basin, and hopefully much of Africa and the Middle East as well. Beyond these fairly concrete objectives was the more nebulous goal of becoming a world power. In this plan, the main targets of Fascist aggression were, as always, the colonial empires of Britain and France. But Mussolini had a secondary agenda encapsulated in the phrase the 'parallel war'. By this he meant that Fascist Italy would conduct its military campaigns parallel to and independent of Nazi Germany, and with a clear line of demarcation between their respective spheres of interest in continental Europe and the Mediterranean. In this way he hoped to regain some of his status as the 'senior' of the two Fascist dictators and re-establish the power balance between Fascist Italy and Nazi Germany.

Mussolini's internal war aims were also clear: he intended that victory in an explicitly Fascist and 'revolutionary' war would establish him in a position of unchallenged political dominance, thus releasing him from dependence upon the conservative forces in the block of consensus. As a result, he would be able to carry forward the new phase in the construction of the totalitarian state which had begun with the introduction of the Racial Laws in 1938. Land reform would be inaugurated in the South without worrying about the objections of the landed interests, and Mussolini would strike against those institutions, especially the Church and the monarchy, which limited his power. As McGregor Knox has written, 'Mussolini's war was to be a war of internal as well as external conquest, a war of revenge against the Italian establishment' (Knox, 1986, p. 281).

The course of the war suggests that Mussolini's strategy, if it can properly be called that, was always strongly influenced by a desire to keep up with Hitler. In particular the timing of the attacks on France (June 1940) and Greece (October 1940) seemed designed as a 'parallel war' to maintain Italian military prestige and standing in the face of growing German strength and success. In fact, Mussolini does not seem to have had a very coherent or logical strategy to rival that of Hitler. Such a strategy would have pointed to the supreme necessity of capturing Malta and destroying British naval power in the Mediterranean as the first step towards establishing Italian domination in that sea and building the new Roman Empire. Instead, Mussolini, after his ill-fated attack on France in June 1940, next conquered British Somaliland in August, launched his troops in a land attack against Egypt and the Suez Canal in September and then against Greece in October. Ciano's *Diary* reveals that none of these operations was dictated by a strategic plan but rather by contingent circumstances. In the case of Egypt, Mussolini was seeking an Italian victory there before Hitler's invasion force could land in England! And the invasion of Greece was simply an attempt to repay Hitler in kind for the occupation of Romania.

Document 7.1 The Attack on Greece, October 1940

The Duce returns . . . he is indignant at the German occupation of Romania. He says that this has impressed Italian public opinion very adversely, because, in view of the decisions taken at Vienna, nobody had expected this to happen. 'Hitler always presents me with a *fait accompli*. He will find out from the newspapers that I have occupied Greece; in this way the equilibrium will be re-established.

Source: Ciano's Diary, *1947, p. 297*

But as Hitler expostulated, 'If he had wanted to pick a fight, why did he not attack Malta or Crete? It would at least make some sense in the context of war with Britain in the Mediterranean' (Collier, 1995, p. 207). Why not indeed!

In the meantime, the Royal Navy crippled the Italian fleet, sinking one battleship and badly damaging two others in a surprise attack on the southern base of Taranto in November 1940. Though the Italian navy turned the Mediterranean into 'a major theatre of war for the surface forces of the Royal Navy' (Sadkovich, 1990, p. 148), though they maintained their convoys to Italian North Africa, and indeed probably had the best war record of all the Italian forces, Taranto and the subsequent Battle of Matapan in March 1941 destroyed any hope the Italians had of winning control of the Mediterranean: even the long siege of Malta had no useful outcome.

Document 7.2 Map of Mussolini's 'Parallel War'

[see illustration on page 105]

After these fundamentally mistaken moves, the Italian war effort went from bad to worse. Between 1940 and 1943 the Italians suffered one defeat after another with few compensatory victories. The 'parallel war' had begun badly, for the treacherous attack on France bogged down in the Alps before Hitler concluded an armistice with the Paris government, and Mussolini gained little from it, except Corsica which was a long-standing Italian claim. The Greek and North African campaigns were also fiascos. Far from reasserting Italian military prestige and re-establishing an equilibrium with Nazi Germany, they forced Mussolini to call upon Hitler to pull his chestnuts out of the fire. It has even been argued that Mussolini's decision to invade Greece ultimately cost Hitler the war, by obliging

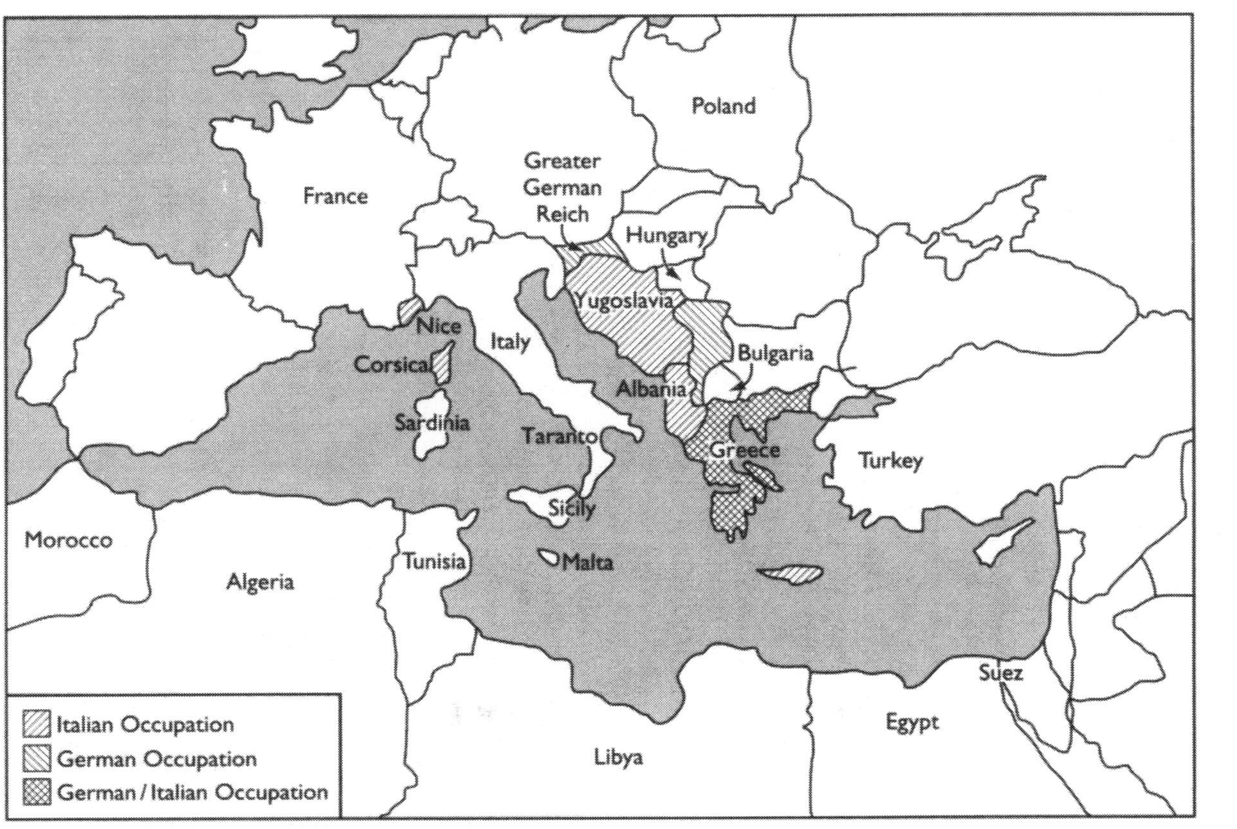
Poland
Greater German Reich
France
Hungary
Yugoslavia
Nice
Italy
Corsica
Bulgaria
Albania
Sardinia
Taranto
Greece
Turkey
Sicily
Morocco
Tunisia
Malta
Algeria
Suez
Egypt
Libya
Italian Occupation
German Occupation
German / Italian Occupation

him to intervene massively in the Balkans, thus diverting troops intended for the launch of the campaign against Russia (Collier, 1995, p. 207). And Mussolini's insistence that the Italians should be given their chance to fight Bolshevism on the Eastern Front also ended in disaster. By the end of 1941 Italy's East African empire, including Ethiopia, had been lost to a British colonial army, and in January 1943 so was Italian North Africa. In May the final Italian toe-hold in Tunisia was abandoned and two months later Anglo-American forces launched their invasion of Sicily from there.

Much of the blame for Italy's catastrophic military record in the Second World War can be legitimately laid at Mussolini's door. As supreme commander of the Armed Forces, he alone dictated strategy; but, as we have seen, Mussolini failed to establish a coherent strategy. Instead, he made unrealistic and sometimes contradictory demands on his service chiefs and the generals in the field. Furthermore, as minister for all three armed forces prior to the war, Mussolini must take some share of the blame for the fact that old-fashioned views of warfare condemned the Italian army to fighting with inadequate armour, the air force with no long-range bombers, and with fighters slower than those of the British, and the navy to a lack of a fleet air arm and aircraft carriers. Mussolini blamed the poor fighting qualities of the Italians for failure in war; in fact, when properly motivated and equipped, Italian troops fought well.

The armed forces also bear some responsibility. There had been little planning for war prior to 1940, and the whole Italian officer class, and the generals in particular, appears to have been every bit as incompetent as their predecessors twenty years before. To make matters worse, the Fascist leadership was allowed to interfere in military operations and behaved with farcical amateurishness. Ciano, for example, took time off from his duties as foreign minister to lead bombing raids on enemy targets! In the French campaign, and initially in the Greek campaign, they failed to take the war seriously, a legacy, perhaps, of squadrism, Ethiopia and Italian intervention in the Spanish Civil War.

A factor of overwhelming importance, however, was the lack of resources. Mussolini, despite his control of all three service ministries and his pursuit of autarky, failed to make good Italy's desperate deficiencies in raw materials, fuel and the other essential goods of war. In any case, much of Italy's best military equipment and her best fighting units had been used up in the wars in Ethiopia, Spain and Albania, while the continuing native resistance in the Italian colonies bottled up further divisions of Italy's forces. Toby Abse has argued that, 'Italy's war economy proved less successful in the Second World War than in the First' (Abse, 1992, p. 107). That Italy simply did not possess the economic strength to be a great military power is borne out by the statistics.

Document 7.3 Italy's Economic Preparedness for War

RELATIVE WAR POTENTIAL OF THE POWERS IN 1937

Country	*Percentage*
United States	41.7
Germany	14.4
USSR	14.0
UK	10.2
France	4.2
Japan	3.5
Italy	2.5

ARMAMENTS PRODUCTION OF THE POWERS, 1940–3

Country		*Production*	
	1940	*1941*	*1943*
		(Billions US dollars)	
Great Britain	3.5	6.5	11.1
USSR	(5.0)	8.5	13.9
United States	(1.5)	4.5	37.5
Total Allied combatants	3.5	19.5	62.5
Germany	6.0	6.0	13.8
Japan	(1.0)	2.0	4.5
Italy	0.75	1.0	—
Total Axis combatants	6.75	9.0	18.3

Source: P. Kennedy, The Rise and Fall of the Great Powers: Economic Change and Military Conflict from 1500 to 2000, *1988, pp. 430 and 458*

Clearly, Italy remained the 'least of the Great Powers' in industrial terms, and Fascist rule worsened rather than improved matters and her weakness is revealed most dramatically by the figures on 'war potential'. But Italy's weakness was even more pronounced during the years of war, when it could only raise armaments production by a third, by comparison with the enormous progress made by all the other belligerent powers. All this supports Roger Absalom's contention that Mussolini decided to intervene in the war in 1940:

> in order not to have to wage war seriously . . . [He] hoped to win the conquests he had promised the Italian people on the back of Hitler's victories. But he came too late into the war to win significant gains from France or concessions from Britain and so was forced by the 'parallel' war to progressively reveal the hollowness of his military pretensions.
>
> **(Absalom, 1984, p. 27)**

After the Allied landings in Sicily the morale of the Italian civilian population had reached an all-time low. Three years of virtually continuous military defeats, the failure of the regime to organise the 'home front' properly, including inadequate air-raid precautions, serious food shortages and the bombing of Italian cities had all taken their toll. While there is clear evidence that as many men volunteered for service in the Second World War as in the First (Scoppola, 1995, p. 12), the mass of the population showed little enthusiasm for either.

By July 1943 the Italian people were fed up with war. Italy by then had been at war in one form or another, with inevitable domestic consequences, in Ethiopia, Spain, Albania, France, North Africa, Greece and Russia for nearly eight years almost continuously. The consequent progressive alienation of the population from Mussolini and the regime was dramatically demonstrated by the strikes which took place in the Northern factory cities in March and April 1943: they seem to have been largely spontaneous protests over deteriorating economic conditions and continuation of the war. This resurgence of working-class dissent went largely unpunished for there was little that the Fascist unions or police could do, such was the internal disintegration of the regime.

The Overthrow of the Regime

The military defeats and the increasing arrogance of the Germans also brought about disenchantment with the regime on the part of those establishment forces who constituted the block of consensus. As mentioned earlier, the Vatican began to disentangle itself from the regime as far back as 1938–9, and by 1943 the major economic interest group, the industrialists, had also lost their faith in Fascism. In their case, the almost total German takeover and economic penetration of the Balkans, with a resulting loss of Italian markets, was a decisive factor in their alienation. And the King, backed by leading military figures such as Badoglio, was seeking a way out of the war and an opportunity to ditch Mussolini; he was supported in these efforts by the Vatican. As usual, the King was too timid to take the initiative in removing the Duce. He left that to others, excusing his inaction again with the lame excuse that he was a constitutional monarch. As for the anti-Fascist parties, inside and outside Italy, they were neither strong enough nor well organised enough to overthrow Fascism.

This only left the Fascist Party. While we have a less than clear picture of the attitudes of local party functionaries and members at this time, all the existing evidence suggests that these groups must have been as demoralised and disillusioned as the rest of the population, and that their continued loyalty and obedience to the regime was now largely a matter of conformism and habit. The widespread corruption in ruling circles, led by Dr Petacci, the father of Mussolini's mistress, and Mussolini's own tangible physical decay and consequent decline in prestige did not help. At the top of the party hierarchy bitter resentment against the Germans and total disillusionment with the Duce's military leadership were the dominant sentiments. Despite Mussolini's last reshuffle of his cabinet in January 1943 he could not stop the rot; on the contrary, the sacking of reasonably competent men such as Ciano simply drove them into opposition. By 24 July a determined group of leading Fascists – Bottai, Grandi, Ciano and De Bono had become convinced that Italy's salvation could only be ensured by the deposition of Mussolini.

The overthrow of Fascism when it came was essentially a 'palace revolution': as has so often been the case in modern Italian history, popular initiative played no part in this momentous event. Though the anti-Fascist forces both inside and outside Italy had been stirring themselves into life since the beginning of the year, they contributed little indirectly, and nothing directly, to the overthrow of Mussolini. The crucial initiative in this process came from *within* the party. Grandi was the prime mover. Supported by Ciano and Bottai, he requested the fateful meeting of the Grand Council on the night of 24 July and at that meeting proposed the motion which was tantamount to a vote of 'no confidence' in Mussolini's dictatorship, demanding that he hand back his extraordinary powers, including the supreme command of the armed forces, to the King.

Document 7.4 Grandi's Resolution at the Grand Council Meeting, 24–25 July 1943

The Grand Council, meeting at this hour of supreme trial . . .

Having examined the internal and international situation and the political and military conduct of the war . . . It declares that . . . it is necessary to revive forthwith the offices of the State and to assign to the Crown, the Grand Council, the Government, Parliament and the Corporations the duties and responsibilities prescribed by our statutory and constitutional laws.

It invites the Head of the Government to request His Majesty the King – towards whom the heart of the nation turns with loyalty and confidence – to assume, for the honour and the salvation of our fatherland, not only the effective command of the armed forces, on land, sea, and in the air, accordance with Article 5 of the *Statuto* of the Realm, but also that supreme power of decision which our laws ascribe to him, and which, throughout the nation's history, has ever been the glorious heritage of our august dynasty of Savoy.

Source: C.F. Delzell, Mediterranean Fascism, 1919–1945, *1971, p. 222*

It is interesting to note how the Fascists of 1943 sought to escape from a crisis situation using much the same methods suggested by Sonnino in 1898 to escape the End of Century Crisis. It is clear from Grandi's testimony that he foresaw exactly what the consequences would be if his motion were successful – the overthrow of Fascism, and not just Mussolini (Grandi, 1983, pp. 227–8). Whether his fellow conspirators fully understood this is less certain. In any case, Mussolini could easily have avoided the confrontation by simply refusing to call the meeting and, as the conspirators themselves admitted, he had the power to circumvent their plans by arresting them. That he did neither suggests just how dangerously the

Duce of Fascism was out of touch with reality. The Grand Council meeting was very tense – more than one of the Fascist leaders had concealed arms about his person in case things got too rough (Guerri, 1979, p. 587). Nevertheless, Grandi's motion attracted a substantial majority of the vote (a vote in the Grand Council was unprecedented).

The next day the King, emboldened by the outcome of the meeting, dismissed the Head of the Government and had him arrested, appointing in his stead a cabinet of 'technicians' headed by Marshal Badoglio, who promptly abolished most of the institutions of the Fascist regime, but not its tough public order legislation or the Racial Laws. The total failure of the regime, at any level, to offer even a minimum of resistance demonstrates the extent to which Fascism had crumbled from within, eaten away by corruption, cynicism, disillusionment and despair. On the other hand, there was almost universal popular rejoicing at the downfall of Fascism, with images of Mussolini and symbols of the regime ceremonially destroyed in the streets of Italy's cities. What the events of July 1943 also prove is the extent to which the Fascist regime in Italy had been dependent upon the support of the various components of the block of consensus. When they withdrew their support, the regime was doomed. They all survived the downfall of Fascism, with the exception of the monarchy, which was abolished by popular referendum in June 1946.

The Collapse of the Italian State and the Partition of Italy

Marshal Badoglio's government had been quick to assure the Germans that Italy would remain true to the Pact of Steel and fight on against the Allies, but from the moment of his appointment he sought to negotiate an armistice, which was what the Italian people overwhelmingly wanted. Unfortunately, it was not until 8 September that such an agreement was reached, blame for this delay being disputed between the Allies and Badoglio. In the meantime, Badoglio failed to prevent the rapid takeover of Italian territory by German troops, according to a contingency plan Hitler's generals had long prepared. As a result, the events which followed the armistice turned into a farcical tragedy. On the announcement of the agreement the King and the Badoglio government were forced to flee from Rome to escape capture by the Germans. Other Italians were not so lucky: hundreds of thousands of Italian soldiers in Italy, France, Yugoslavia and Greece were left without orders. Some bravely turned their arms against the Germans and were wiped out; others were surrounded, imprisoned and deported to Germany.

The overthrow of Fascism had been followed, within a few weeks, by the effective collapse of the Italian state; and the Italian peninsula, contended for by the Germans and the Allies, was a major theatre of war between September 1943 and May 1945.

Document 7.6 Italy, September 1943 to May 1945

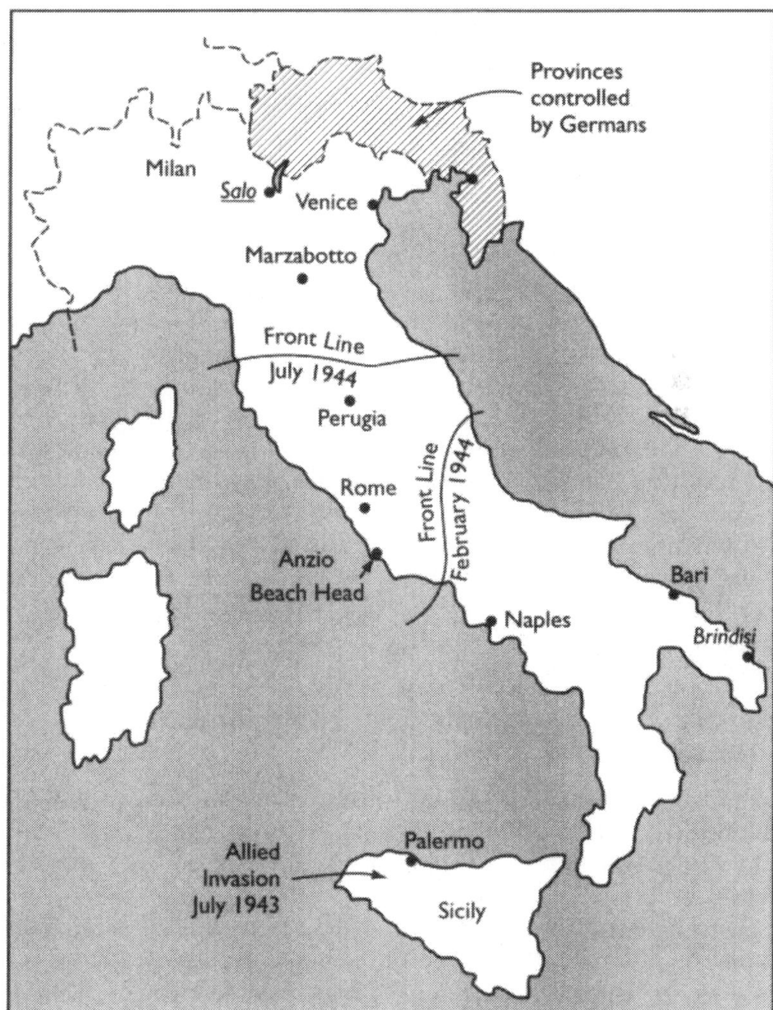

The Fascist Social Republic, 1943–5

The Germans succeeded in locating Mussolini's place of captivity and by the middle of September the former Duce had been liberated and flown to Munich. Here Hitler persuaded him that it was his duty to return to Italy at the head of a restored Fascist regime. This in reality was the last thing he wanted: he would have preferred to retire into a quiet private life. He was also doubtful about the wisdom of restoring Fascism and in this he was not alone; many of Hitler's closest military and political advisers agreed with him. The generals in particular would have preferred a straightforward military occupation, without the complication of dealing with the despised Italian Fascists. Against these counsels were the strong pressures exerted by the Fascist diehards who had taken refuge at Hitler's court – Buffarini-Guidi, Farinacci, Pavolini and Preziosi. For these men a restored regime offered the chance to take revenge on the 'traitors' of July and redeem the honour of Italian Fascism. Another consideration, and probably the determining one in Mussolini's case, was the belief that a restoration of Fascism was necessary to limit the brutality of a German occupation of Italy and to provide the Italians with some sort of independent bargaining counter in a victorious Nazi 'new order' in Europe. And to Hitler, of course, it was inconceivable that his fellow dictator would not wish to do his duty to the end. Hitler's will prevailed and on 20 September Mussolini was flown back to Northern Italy to head a new government. It was formally known as the Fascist Social Republic, to signify the break with Fascism's temporary, monarchist past. More colloquially it was given the title Republic of Salo, from the name of the little town on Lago di Garda which became Mussolini's headquarters and the republic's effective capital.

The spirit and policies of the restored Fascist regime were expressed most cogently by Mussolini in his last public speech, in Milan on 16 December 1944. The force and optimism of the speech were remarkable – it was an echo of the Mussolini of pre-war days – considering that by this date Mussolini must have known that the war was lost and the Fascist republic doomed.

Document 7.7 Mussolini's Last Public Speech, 16 December 1944

Comrades! Dear Comrades of Milan! I shall dispense with any preamble and enter immediately into the heart of the subject matter of my speech . . . Who is guilty of betrayal? Who has suffered or is suffering the consequences of this treachery? . . .

The unconditional surrender announced on 8 September was desired by the monarchy, by court circles, by the plutocratic currents of the Italian bourgeoisie, by certain clerical forces, combined for the occasion with Masonic ones, and by the General Staff which no longer believed in victory and which were headed by Badoglio . . . But . . . to get to 8 September, there first has to be 25 July – viz., the coup and the change of regime.

From the social standpoint, the program of Republican Fascism is but the logical continuation of the program of 1919 – of the achievements of the splendid years that took place between the announcement of the Labour Charter and the conquest of the empire . . .

It was necessary to build a foundation of syndical legislation and corporative bodies before we could take the subsequent step towards socialisation . . .

Through socialisation, the best elements drawn from the ranks of the workers will be able to demonstrate their talents. I am determined to continue in this direction.

Source: C.F. Delzell, Mediterranean Fascism, 1919–1945, *1971, pp. 243–51*

Here Mussolini encapsulated much of the motivating spirit of the supporters of the Fascist republic, the desire for revenge on the traitors and the compulsive need to vindicate the honour of Fascism and Italy in the eyes of the German allies. Revenge was taken in the Verona trials and executions of Ciano, De Bono and others, between November 1943 and January 1944. Of course, this all served both as an alibi for Fascism's humiliating failures in war and as a way of appeasing the Germans. The themes of revenge, redemption of honour and continuing the struggle against the Jewish–Masonic–plutocratic forces of the League of Nations alongside the German allies were to be the leitmotifs of the propaganda of the republic until the end.

Document 7.8 Blood and Honour in the Salo Republic

Ours is a ruthless battle: against the renunciatory attitudes of the Bonomi and Sforza [leading anti-Fascist politicians] kind, against all who try to destroy the Italian soul, against all coalitions within and without, against the capitalistic plutocracy and destructive Bolshevism, against anyone who tries to oppose us on our painful and bloody road towards resurrection . . . We know only too well that we have many enemies: powerful and cowardly people, learned and ignorant, rich and poor, humble and arrogant, priests and women. But what does it matter? We believe in the saying: 'The more enemies the greater the honour' and we are determined to live up to it for the sake of Italy.

Source: L'Ardimento *(Turin newspaper), 26 September 1944*

In Mussolini's speech, and in the November 1943 Verona Manifesto, the official charter of the Social Republic, corporatism, once one of the proudest achievements of Fascism, was dumped in favour of 'socialisation', a cross between nationalisation and workers' control of industry. Socialisation, and the inclusion of the word 'social' in the title of the regime, had a clear tactical purpose: it was meant to signal a deliberate shift back to the left-wing, pro-working-class elements of the original Fascist movement. The new Fascism pledged itself to a programme of wide-ranging nationalisation. Perhaps in his senile decay Mussolini hoped against hope that he could patch up his relations with the Italian working-class movement and thus create a broad base of popular support for republican Fascism. But republican Fascism's left-wing rhetoric cut no ice with the working masses of Northern Italy who returned to their original allegiance to the Socialist and Communist parties (some had never abandoned them). Many, in fact, gave their active support to Mussolini's enemies, the partisan bands of the Armed Resistance which sprang up in the hills and mountains of Northern and Central Italy from the end of 1943 onwards. Such was the concern of the Social Republic to extend its popular support that throughout its existence there was even a tendency to tolerate, and in a sense co-opt, certain non-Fascist political groups.

The new Fascist regime did not, however, return to the anti-clerical sentiments of its origins. That would have been foolhardy given the fact that it was geographically based in some of the most Catholic regions of Italy: the North and East. But the continuing support of Fascism for the Church did not earn it diplomatic recognition from the Vatican, which preserved its links with the royal government in the South and accorded the Republic of Salo only *de facto* status. Indeed, relations between the Social Republic and the local hierarchy were extremely chequered. On the other hand, the policy of anti-Semitism adopted in 1938 was strengthened, so that all Jews were stripped of their possessions and sent to internment camps. This assisted the Germans in their attempts to deport Italy's Jewish population to the concentration camps at Trieste (which was under direct German rule) and outside Italy.

The general return to the radical policies of early Fascism was also part of an attempt to win the support of the intransigent old guard of Fascists, many of whom had been disgraced or ignored by Mussolini following his rise to power. Up to a point, this strategy worked. Many of the 'Fascists of the first hour' joined the Republican Fascist Party, and what little real idealism republican Fascism possessed probably derived from these elements. But, in the main, the politics of both the new party and the regime were dominated by the fanatics. The squabbles and intrigues of Preziosi, Pavolini and Farinacci only served to reinforce German contempt for their Italian colleagues. One German official remarked that, 'The formation of the new Fascist Republican government was beset by a tragi-comedy of disgusting intrigues for office and old feuds' (Deakin, 1966b, p. 121) And Mussolini was partly to blame for this: playing off one faction against another was one way that a tired and sick man could maintain his own authority.

The fundamental weakness of the Fascist Social Republic was its failure to win the loyalty of the mass of the population in those areas of Northern and Central Italy where its writ ran. Most Italians were simply waiting for the Allies to liberate them, while they endured heavy air raids, strict food rationing and the oppressive demands of both the Germans and the Fascists. By Liberation there were at least a dozen different Italian or German military, paramilitary or civilian police forces operating in the territory of the Social Republic. The Fascists' dependence on and subservience to the German occupying authorities did not help matters. Mussolini's regime was little more than a puppet government under the surveillance and control of the Germans – German Ambassador Rahn and S.S. General Wolff were effectively Hitler's viceroys in Italy. Thus the Italian Social Republic differed little from Pétain's Vichy France, Tišo's Slovakia, Pavelić's 'Croatian Independent State' or Quisling's collaborationist government in Norway. The Germans were able to commandeer at will Italian industrial output and manpower resources for their war machine. Hundreds of thousands of Italian men were sent to Germany as forced labour (few volunteered) and the Gestapo brutally persecuted Italy's small Jewish community: it is to the credit of the Italians that many resisted the pogroms, hiding Jews and thus saving the bulk of Italy's 40,000 Jews from the gas chambers (8,000 perished). But the Fascist Social Republic collaborated in the hunt for the Jews, a far cry from the response of army officers in Italian-occupied territories prior to the armistice when faced by demands from the Germans to hand over Jews for deportation.

The crowning humiliation for Mussolini and his government was Hitler's insistence on detaching most of Italy's north-eastern provinces from the Social Republic and placing them under direct German control. These provinces were subjected to a process of 'Germanisation', with the intention of eventually incorporating them into the Greater German Reich at the end of the war.

The Armed Resistance

Given the grim conditions in which the civilian population was obliged to live between September 1943 and the Liberation in April 1945, it is hardly surprising that many of them literally 'took to the hills' and joined the partisan bands fighting against the Fascists and the Germans. One obvious motive for many young men was to avoid being conscripted either by the various competing German labour organisations or by the military/police forces of the nascent republic. In this, they were encouraged by the armed resistance movement.

Document 7.9 The Resistance Appeals to Young Conscripts

PARTISAN COMMAND, UMBRIA-MARCHES SECTOR
ITALIAN BROTHERS
Conscripts of the years 1924 and 1925:

The German oppressor and his Nazi–Fascist servants want to conscript you in order to make you share in their criminal actions against the liberty and salvation of Italy.

Do not take any notice of their promises.

Do not allow yourselves to be taken in by them.

COME

Your brothers the partisans have been fighting for five months for you and they are waiting for you amidst the immaculate snows of the mountains, untouched by the oppressor.

We are waiting for you!
Long Live Italy!
February 1994

Source: XXX Anni della Resistenza e della Liberazione: 40 documenti della Resistenza nella provincia di Perugia, *1975, pp. 23–4*

But to evade the call-up or to desert was also very dangerous, as this further document shows.

Document 7.10 The Shooting of Deserters, 1944

PREFECTURE OF PERUGIA

Following a search operation, on the 14th of this month the deserter ALPINOLO PRESENZINI, born at Deruta on 3 November 1924, and the following who failed to answer the call-up, DOMENICO CONVERSINI, born at Cornieto (province of Macerata) on 2 February 1924, and AGELIO SFASCIOTTI, born at Foligno on 23 March 1924 and ADRIANO PAOLINI, born at S. Eraclio di Foligno on 18 July 1922 were all shot. All were collaborating with the partisans.

Perugia, 16 March 1944

The Head of the Province
ROCCHI

Source: XXX Anni della Resistenza e della Liberazione: 40 documenti della Resistenza nella provincia di Perugia, *1975, pp. 23–4*

The inspiring idealism of the partisans was a patriotic desire to resist the German occupiers and destroy the last residue of Fascism. Thus the Italian armed resistance was both a patriotic war against the German invaders and a civil war against the Fascist Social Republic. The Fascist and anti-Fascist forces were almost equally balanced – at about 150,000 men – and the fighting, especially by the Fascist 'Black Bands' and Decima Mas (a military formation), was conducted with the ferocity characteristic of a civil war. There were atrocities on both sides, and also some settling of private scores.

In the present lively debate about the nature of the Italian resistance, the point is made that due to the dominant role of the Communist and Socialist parties in the leadership of the partisan bands, there was an element of *class* war as well. What is rather less plausible is the claim that the resistance was almost entirely an affair of the Communists for the ultimate purpose of bringing about revolution. Though the latter controlled a majority of the partisan formations, supporters of all the anti-Fascist parties – Socialists, Christian Democrats, the Action Party and even the liberal-monarchists – took part in the resistance. If we take into account the role played by the workers who sabotaged industrial production in the cities, the peasantry and rural clergy who gave food, shelter and information to the partisans, the Jews and escaped Allied prisoners-of-war, the large numbers of women who acted as spies and couriers, and even allowing for the opportunistic motives of some of these people, it would be correct to say that the Italian resistance was a mass, popular phenomenon. Also, non-combatant civilians frequently suffered reprisals at the hands of the German army, the most infamous examples being the massacres at Marzabotto in Emilia and the Fosse Ardeatine near Rome.

Though, as General Alexander, Allied commander in Italy, recognised, the partisans played a significant role in the struggle against the Germans – he estimated that they kept the equivalent of ten German divisions away from the front line – the final liquidation of Fascism was not brought about by them. It was Allied military success rather than the efforts of the resistance that defeated the Germans. Ironically, the fate of Mussolini and the Fascist Social Republic was sealed by German betrayal, the secret decision of General Wolff to surrender German forces to the Allies in April 1945. Betrayed by the Germans, deserted by many of his Fascist colleagues and long abandoned by the overwhelming majority of his fellow-countrymen, Mussolini attempted to flee to Switzerland with his mistress Clara Petacci. Not far from the border he was recognised, captured and shot by partisans, and his body was exposed to execration in a Milan square. The Fascist experiment ended, as it had begun, in squalid circumstances.

Conclusion

Italian Fascism failed the supreme test: war. Failure in war revealed the emptiness of Fascist rhetoric, and the bankruptcy of Mussolini's leadership. Having dragged Italy through a succession of military disasters and the hardships and horrors of war, Italian Fascism lost all credibility – except to a band of fanatical diehards. Hence its disintegration as an autonomous political movement in July 1943.

The war also exposed the fundamental contradictions of Fascism. Mussolini's foreign-policy aims required a massive, total mobilisation of existing economic and military resources combined with a modernisation of the economic and social structures of Italy. However, the Fascist political system simultaneously attempted to act as a guarantor of the powers and privileges of the conservative establishment – monarchy, Church, armed forces and industrial and agrarian elites. Mussolini's increasingly frequent and violent verbal attacks on the 'bourgeoisie', so faithfully recorded in Ciano's memoirs, should be read as an expression of his frustrated realisation that he was trapped by the compromise which he had made with various elements in the block of consensus. These compromises prevented him from fully mobilising the nation's resources. He was thus unable to win the 'revolutionary-war' which he believed would have put him in an unassailable position to neutralise the establishment and realise his dream of creating a truly totalitarian state on the Nazi German model.

8 The ideology of Italian Fascism

Introduction

Modern political movements and regimes, Fascist, democratic or Communist, need ideology, some set of ideas and myths, to inspire and motivate the ruling elite and to arouse and enthuse the masses. Material prosperity, leadership charisma, the cult of personality, even terror, are rarely sufficient to sustain them. But ideology can vary enormously from a few simple, compelling ideas and myths, easily reducible to propaganda slogans, to a complex and logically coherent system of ideas. It has often been said that Italian Fascism did not really possess an ideology, that it was essentially inspired by 'the cudgel and castor oil', or alternatively it has been argued that the ideas of Italian Fascism were almost all negative – anti-socialist, anti-liberal, anti-democratic, anti-capitalist, anti-clerical, anti-monarchist. Early Fascism was certainly characterised by all these sentiments, but it has to be stressed that Fascism, at all stages of its development, possessed ideology and that this ideology was more than just a set of negatives.

What is less certain, however, is whether Mussolini and the Fascist leadership were, 'inspired by a systematic ideological view of society or were . . . merely manipulators of power' (Sarti, 1974b, p. 53). When Bolshevism came to power in Russia in October 1917, it did so with a ready-made ideology, the writings of the philosopher Karl Marx, to which had been added those of the leader of the Bolshevik Party, Vladimir Lenin. And when the National Socialists came to power in Germany in January 1933, they brought with them a fairly clear, though not necessarily coherent, set of ideas, particularly those contained in Hitler's book *Mein Kampf* (literally, 'My Struggle'). But when the Fascists came to power in Italy in October 1922, they possessed nothing comparable to either of these systems of ideas.

The men who founded the first *fascio* in 1919 were motivated by some common ideas and feelings, but given the diversity of their political histories, those common ideas were few. The diversity can best be appreciated when one considers that Mussolini came from the Marxist P.S.I., Grandi was a former member of the Republican Party, which had a long and glorious tradition in Italy, Marinetti was a Futurist, Michele Bianchi and Edmondo Rossoni were ex-revolutionary syndicalists and Leandro Arpinati had been an anarchist. As the movement grew, lots of men of a different, more pro-Catholic, conservative and even monarchist stamp, such as Giorgio De Vecchi di Val Cismon, joined the ranks of the *fasci*. Most of these men had been brought together for the first time by the Intervention Crisis or the First World War and the lowest common denominator of their political ideas was, therefore, some form of Corradinian or D'Annunzian nationalism. And given the persistent rejection of the war by the majority of the working-class movement, anti-socialism inevitably became the natural accompaniment of this nationalism. These were the sentiments which held the Fascist movement somewhat precariously together in the early years; these and the memories and myths of the experience of trench warfare.

In addition, for Italian Fascism, as for all Fascist movements and regimes, from the beginning the most central myth was that of national rebirth, or 'palingenetic ultranationalism' as Roger Griffin describes it. This commitment to the rebirth or regeneration of Italy was a recurrent motif of Fascist propaganda throughout the existence of the regime and arguably one of the inspirations for the creation of the youth and other 'socialising' organisations, all designed to produce 'new' Italian men and women, and therefore a new Italy. Linked to the myth of 'rebirth' was the myth of 'revolution'. Italian Fascist propaganda was saturated with revolutionary rhetoric, in part at least a hangover from the leftist past of so many of the Fascist leaders. But if Fascism was revolutionary in terms of the intentions of its leaders, especially in the 1920s and late 1930s, it could hardly be said to have been so in its achievements.

Italian Fascism was to undergo a considerable process of ideological development, especially in the period after it came to power. Indeed, of all three inter-war totalitarian regimes, Italian Fascism undoubtedly went through the greatest degree of ideological development. German National Socialism could not be said to have undergone a significant process of ideological development: after 1933 Hitler's essential purpose was to translate into action an already formed ideology. In the Soviet Union, on the other hand, there was some further development of Bolshevik ideas as Stalin strove to reconcile the realities of his policy of 'Socialism in One Country' with the established tenets of Marxism–Leninism. But in the late 1920s, Mussolini coined the concept of 'totalitarianism' and in 1932, ten years after coming to power, in the *Enciclopedia Italiana*, he published his 'Doctrine of Fascism', a summary of Fascist ideas. As late as 1937–8 Fascist ideology underwent further development with the introduction of anti-Semitism. During the Salo period, Fascist ideology did not change to any great extent: there was some intensification of the commitment to racialism and a (temporary) laying aside of the ideas of corporatism in favour of a return to national syndicalism, but little else.

The reasons for this history of ideological development are multiple and complex. Mussolini's explanation for the weakness of the Fascists in the realm of political ideas was that they had had little time between the birth of their movement and their coming to power to think out and elaborate a political philosophy:

> The years which preceded the March on Rome were ones in which the overriding need for action did not allow us the possibility of profound philosophical enquiries or complete doctrinal elaborations.
>
> **(*Enciclopedia Italiana*, XIV, 1932, p. 849)**

This explanation has a certain plausibility. On the other hand, the ideological vagueness of early Fascism was probably a major 'selling point' to potential supporters: Fascism could be all things to all men. In this sense, there was an element of making virtue out of a necessity. Again, it was precisely the changes in the nature of support for Fascism that made it necessary to change or even abandon ideas – such as republicanism and anti-clericalism – before 1922. But the inspiring ideas of a movement struggling to win mass support and power are necessarily different from those of a movement in power. When Fascism did come to power the construction of new political institutions prompted the Fascists to invent underpinning ideas for these arrangements – thus the concept of totalitarianism was essentially a rationalisation of the dictatorship which the Fascists created from the mid-1920s onwards. There is, therefore, a lot of truth in Ernest Nolte's dictum that Fascist ideology was 'practice as premiss' (Nolte, 1965, p. 196).

Opportunism was also a crucial determinant of the development of Italian Fascist ideology, and this is most strongly exemplified in the introduction of anti-Semitic legislation. This episode also demonstrates that Mussolini and the Fascists drew their ideas from a very wide variety of sources, both Italian and foreign – Corradini, Rocco, Marinetti, Pareto and Gentile, Nietzsche, Le Bon and Sorel, and, in the case of racialism, primarily German National Socialism. Yet if Italian Fascism in the 1930s had developed a long way from the simplicity of its original ideas, then it has to be said that the later elaborations were usually a logical progression. In other words the later ideas were latent in the thinking of the movement from the beginning. In this respect, only the introduction of racialism can be regarded as a radical departure from the ideas of the early Fascist movement.

The Ideas of Early Fascism

In the manifesto of the first *fascio* of March 1919, the underlying influence of the German philosopher Nietzsche, author of *Man and Superman*, is clearly evident.

Document 8.1 Fascism and the Will to Power

I have the impression that the present regime in Italy is finished . . . If the present regime really is going to be superseded, we must take its place . . . it is we who have the right of succession because we are the ones who pushed the country into war and led it to victory . . .

We are strongly against all forms of dictatorship, whether they be of the sword or the cocked hat, of money or numbers. We will accept only one dictatorship, that of will and intelligence.

. . . majorities are fated to be static, whereas minorities are dynamic. We wish to be an active minority, to draw the proletariat away from the Socialist Party.

Source: Opera Omnia, *XII, pp. 326*

This is the underlying justification of the demand of the 'war generation', those who had fought, or claimed to have fought, the victorious war on Italy's behalf, to rule her in peacetime. For the Fascists, will and intelligence were the base of their moral right, coupled with the fact that they were 'the brave and strong', rather than possessors of any historical or democratic legitimacy. The idea of a dynamic, enlightened minority is implicit. Mussolini was much influenced by Vilfredo Pareto's idea of 'the circulation of elites', that is, of an inevitable historical process in which one ruling elite would rise, fall and be replaced by another, and so on. The Fascists believed that they were an elite whose time had come.

Concomitant with the idea of the 'will to power' was the legitimisation of the the political use of violence. The morality of violence as a political weapon against Fascism's enemies – especially the unpatriotic Socialists – was axiomatic to the Fascist concept of 'Action', and was hallowed and sanctified by the ideas of Sorel, the Futurists and Gabriele D'Annunzio, the latter two having glorified violence and war for their own sake. Mussolini reiterated its legitimacy in his speech of 3 January 1925: '[a] degree of violence cannot be eliminated from history. I have always said . . . that violence, to be effective, must be surgical, intelligent and chivalrous' (*Opera Omnia*, XII, p. 230).

Sorel had been the philosopher of revolutionary syndicalism, and the early documents of Fascism show other signs of his influence and that of his followers, many of whom ended up in the Fascist movement. That they should have done so is hardly surprising. Sorel had preached intransigence, violence and insurrection. Having espoused the Interventionist cause and been expelled from the Italian working-class movement, like Mussolini, some of the syndicalists inevitably moved to the right, thus creating a synthesis of their original revolutionary ideas and nationalism: 'national syndicalism'. Mussolini defined this synthesis.

Document 8.2 Fascism and National Syndicalism

If syndicalist doctrine maintains that it is possible to find among the masses men with the leadership qualities necessary for taking over the management of production, we cannot oppose this, especially if this movement takes into account two realities; the reality of the productive process and reality of the nation . . .

We want the workers to get accustomed to the responsibility of management and to learn as a result that it isn't easy to operate a business successfully.

Source: Opera Omnia, *XII, p. 325*

Mussolini had effectively adopted syndicalist ideas when he changed the title of *Il Popolo d'Italia* to the *Organ of Soldiers and Producers* in 1916, and national syndicalism ostensibly formed the ideological basis for the Fascist trade union movement that emerged in 1921 under Rossoni's leadership. It did not however, provide the framework for the development of the so-called 'corporate state', either in theory or practice.

The Doctrine of Fascism, 1932

With the publication of the *Enciclopedia Italiana* in 1932 Italian Fascism took the opportunity to present to the world a summary of its major inspiring and defining ideas. By 1932, the physiognomy of the Fascist regime had assumed a stable, permanent character and it seemed fitting to Mussolini and other Fascist leaders that they should now possess a formed ideology to go with it. But the 'Doctrine of Fascism' article which appeared was by no means comprehensive: there was little on corporatism, presumably because as yet so little of the 'corporate state' was in being, and nothing on anti-Semitism, because that particular aspect of Italian Fascist theory and practice was at least five years in the future.

The general editor of the *Enciclopedia* was the neo-idealist philosopher Giovanni Gentile, one of the first of the major Italian intellectuals to give their support to Fascism: in 1925 he organised a conference on 'Fascist Culture' and wrote the 'Manifesto of the Fascist Intellectuals' which followed it. It was Gentile who wrote the section in the 'Fascism' entry known as the 'Doctrine of Fascism'. Although protests from some of the *gerarchi* led to Mussolini being induced to rewrite large parts of the doctrine himself, it is infused with Gentile's idealism, in particular the concept of the 'ethical state'. This concept, which provided the philosophical basis for the Fascist doctrine of totalitarianism, has been defined thus: 'the state is the authority that represents the universality of all moral will and through which moral values become civil law. Self-realisation can best be fulfilled through integration into society and into the nation [the state is the legal embodiment of the nation]' (Cannistraro, 1982, p. 244).

Much of the Doctrine of Fascism is accordingly devoted to a definition and elaboration of totalitarianism.

Document 8.3 The State in Fascist Thought

The foundation of Fascist doctrine is the idea of the state: its nature, its functions and its objectives. For Fascism the state is an absolute, thus individuals and groups only have an existence in relation to it . . . Anti-individualistic, Fascist thinking is wholly committed to the state; and for the individual only in so far as his interests coincide with those of the state . . .

Fascism supports the only liberty that can be a serious thing, that is the liberty of the state and of the individual within the state. Thus, everything must be within the state, nothing can exist outside the state, let alone have value. In this sense Fascism is totalitarian, and the Fascist state, which is the synthesis and unity of all values, interprets, develops and strengthens the whole life of the people . . .

The principle that society exists solely for the well-being and liberty of the individuals who compose it does not seem to fit with the laws of nature, laws which only take the species into consideration and sacrifice the individual.

Source: Enciclopedia Italiana, *XIV, 1932, p. 847*

Here we have, in the clearest terms, a rejection of the liberal-democratic doctrine of individual, imprescriptible human rights, and its corollary, the 'mechanistic' idea of the state as a convenience, as the result of a contract between individuals to promote their common interests and nothing more. The Fascist idea of the state is organic: that is, the individual cannot 'choose' to belong to it, but belongs to it, unconditionally, by virtue of history and genealogy. By the accident of his birth he comes under the authority of a nation/state and belongs to it body and soul: he is an organic part of it. Hence, all human activity – economic, cultural, political, religious – comes into its purview. Ultimately, the individual exists for the state and not the state for the individual, and, according neo-Darwinist logic, his interests must be sacrificed in the interests of those of society. Social Darwinism also characterises the remarks on the 'Roman', imperial destiny of the Italian people. This concept of 'destiny' is also clearly influenced by Corradini's idea of the 'international class struggle of the proletarian and plutocratic nations'.

Document 8.4 The Roman, Imperial Destiny of the Italian People

The Fascist state is a will to power and empire, The Roman tradition is also an idea of power . . . For Fascism the tendency towards empire, that is, towards the expansion of nations, is a sign of vitality; the opposite, the 'stay-at-home' mentality, is a sign of decadence. Peoples who rise or rise again are imperialistic, peoples who die are weak peoples. Fascist doctrine is the one most appropriate for the tendencies and soul of a people like the Italians who are rising again after many centuries of neglect and foreign servitude

Source: Enciclopedia Italiana, *XIV, 1932, p. 848*

The Doctrine of Fascism also offers an example of the effects of Fascism's compromises with the forces of the establishment, in the following case the confusion and ambiguity surrounding its attitude towards religion.

Document 8.5 Fascism and Religion

Fascism is a religious concept in which man is seen in his immanent relationship with a superior law and an objective Will which transcends the particular individual: man is a conscious member of a spiritual association. Those who see in the religious policy of the regime only opportunistic considerations have not understood that Fascism, as well as being a system of government, is also, and above all, a system of thought . . .

The Fascist state is not indifferent to the phenomenon of religion in general and to that positive religion, Italian Catholicism, in particular. The state does not have a theology but it does have a morality.

Source: Enciclopedia Italiana, *XIV, 1932, pp. 847, 850*

The first paragraph is both a statement of what many Fascists, such as Gentile, saw to be true – Fascism was a total system of belief, and therefore a kind of religion – and an attempt to reconcile this with Mussolini's concessions to the Church in the Lateran Pacts of 1929. The second paragraph marks something of a retreat from the absoluteness of Gentile's idea of the totalitarian state, for the Catholic Church was not fully 'inside the state', rather it was a 'state within the state' in Fascist Italy. Here, too, Mussolini was forced to bow to outside criticism, in this case from the Vatican, and rewrite Gentile's original manuscript. Nevertheless, Fascism in the 1930s came increasingly close to Gentile's ideal of a state that generated and controlled the development of all aspects of the life of its people, even in the religious sphere, by effectively operating as a religion. It possessed a school of so-called 'Fascist Mysticism', demanded absolute belief in a (largely irrational) faith and conducted mass rites and rituals, what the historian Emilio Gentile has described as a certain 'sacralising' tendency (Gentile, 1993).

Corporatism

The Doctrine of Fascism said very little about corporatism. Though the real foundations of the 'corporate state' had been laid in the Palazzo Vidoni Pact, the Labour and Anti-strike Law and the Labour Charter, it was not until the Law on the Corporations was passed in 1934, setting up the system of corporations, that Mussolini set out the theory behind these new institutions in his contribution to the parliamentary discussions which accompanied the passing of the law. Mussolini boasted that the Italian corporatist model, the 'third way' between capitalism and Communism, was the way forward for all civilised nations.

Document 8.6 Mussolini on the Corporate State

. . . it can now be confidently asserted that the capitalist mode of production is superseded, and with it the theory of economic liberalism that has in reality brought about the end of free competition . . . Corporatism supersedes both socialism and liberalism . . .

Corporatism is an Italian Fascist creation . . . Fascist corporatism is an integrated, unified vision of life and of man which influences every human activity, individual and collective, and consequently also the economy.

Source: Il Popolo d'Italia, *24 February 1934, p. 3*

Having rejected liberalism as a political system, here Fascism also rejects its economic counterpart, laissez-faire capitalism, since the essence of the capitalist mode of production was never repudiated either in theory or practice in Fascist Italy. And with a certain triumphalistic confidence, Mussolini claimed to have replaced the very philosophy of liberalism with a more modern and human Fascist one.

Anti-Semitism

Until 1937, the major factor which distinguished Italian Fascism from German Nazism, and from most other European Fascist movements, like the varieties in Hungary, Romania, France and Britain, not to mention the Nazi movements in Scandinavia and the Low Countries, was the absence of a racial anti-Semitic element in its ideology and policy. In that year, the first moves were made in the direction of anti-Semitism and a year later the Racial Laws were introduced against the Jews. Until then, Italian Fascist notions of race had been essentially cultural and followed the traditional Mazzinian definition as a linguistic, cultural, historical community, usually within fixed geographical boundaries, as is clear from the following document.

Document 8.7 The Nation in the Doctrine of Fascism, 1932

All those who, by reason of nature, history and ethnicity, and who follow the same line of spiritual formation and development, with a single conscience and will, form a nation. It is not a race nor a region geographically limited but a lineage which perpetuates itself historically, a multitude united by ideas, that is the will to exist and the will to power, with a personality, a self-consciousness.

Source: Enciclopedia Italiana, *XV, 1932, pp. 845–51*

Fascism's rejection of a geographical/territorial element in the definition of race was motivated by the desire to assert the importance of the Italian emigrant communities scattered throughout the world, and thus maintain their allegiance to their 'mother country', Fascist Italy. It should also be noted that when the Fascist government set out to 'Italianise' the new north-eastern provinces in the late 1920s, by changing the place and family names and suppressing as far as possible the use of the ethnic-minority languages – German in Trentino–Alto Adige and Slovene and Serbo-Croat in Istria and Dalmatia – it was engaged in a form of 'cultural genocide'. It was seeking not to expel or physically exterminate the ethnic minorities, but to assimilate them forcibly, to transform them into something culturally superior – Italians. This sense of cultural superiority towards both Germans and Slavs was based upon an Italian consciousness of being Latin, of being the heirs of the Roman Empire. Latinity, or Romanita, was seen to be culturally superior because it was a set of fundamental, universal ideas – order, discipline, law and so on – with which some of the 'Barbarian' races had been assimilated into the Roman Empire, and on which a later Christian Europe had been constructed.

The frequent references in the late 1920s and early 1930s in the rhetoric of the demographic battle to 'the defence of the race' and 'racial hygiene' should not be misconstrued: their meaning was a world away from the theory and practice of German racialism in this period. There was no question here of racial stereotyping, anti-miscegenation laws or, even less, *Lebensborn*. They were slogans designed to raise standards of public health and ensure higher birth rates and lower death rates. Again, though the policy of ruralisation included the notion of the Italian peasantry as a sort of warrior-peasant class, it was very different in inspiration from the essentially pagan *Blut und Boden* ('blood and soil') ideas of Nazi Germany.

In 1938, Mussolini claimed that the ideas of Italian Fascism had always been intrinsically racial, and that anti-Semitism had always been a part of its conscious practice. This was a patently dishonest attempt to rewrite the history of Italian Fascism. The Fascist movement never discriminated against Italy's Jewish population; indeed, it is a measure of how integrated Italian Jews were that out of a total population of 40,000, 5,000 became Fascists in the early 1920s (Zucotti, 1987, p. 27). One of the leaders of early Fascism, Aldo Finzi, was a Jew, as was Mussolini's minister of finances in the 1930s, Guido Jung, and his mistress, Margherita Sarfatti. There were certainly some notorious anti-Semites inside the Fascist Party – such as Roberto Farinacci and Giuseppe Preziosi – but they were notable precisely because they were so rare. And when Mussolini placed his proposals before the Grand Council of Fascism he met opposition from Italo Balbo who hailed from Ferrara, which had one of Italy's largest Jewish communities.

Outside the party, there was a general lack of enthusiasm for the laws which were seen to be unnecessary, 'un-Italian' and, above all, a foreign, German, import. There was no counterpart in Italian history after unification of the discrimination and persecution experienced by Jews in Eastern and Central Europe and in France. Ironically, the extent of the integration of the Italian Jews after 1861 is revealed by the large numbers who qualified for slightly more favourable treatment under the Racial Laws on the grounds that they had served in war or had been members of the party, or were related to those who had.

Mussolini argued that he himself had always been an anti-Semite. A quotation from his maiden speech to parliament on foreign policy and the problem of Palestine in May 1921 gives the lie to this claim.

Document 8.8 Mussolini on Anti-Semitism

At this point I would like to make an aside, that is that no-one should read into my words any hint of anti-Semitism, which would be a new thing in this Chamber. I recognise that the sacrifice of blood on the part of Italian Jews during the war was great and generous.

Source: Opera Omnia, *XVI, 1957, p. 439*

In fact, Mussolini had rather fancied himself as the protector of Italy's Jewish communities after he had established them on a new legal footing in 1932. Subsequently, especially following the failure of his attempts to enlist the support of the Zionist organisation for Italian ambitions to take over the Palestine Mandate from the British, he attacked 'international Zionism'. But only a very small proportion of Italy's Jews were Zionists, and as late as 1934, Mussolini actually condemned Nazi anti-Semitism and allowed those fleeing the campaign – over 9,000 of them – a refuge in Italy.

Mussolini's other main argument to explain the development of Fascist anti-Semitism, that Italian racial consciousness had been heightened by the experience of the conquest of Ethiopia (and that it would have to be raised further if Italy was to hold on to her empire), is a little more plausible. But one can argue equally logically that Italy had already ruled an empire (Eritrea, Somalia and Libya) for fifty years before the invasion of Ethiopia without developing any discernible anti-Semitic tendencies, and this is borne out by the lack of an anti-Semitic element in the pre-First World War Nationalist movement.

The decision to introduce the Racial Laws appears to have been essentially motivated by the desire on Mussolini's part to 'keep up with the Joneses', or rather by an awareness that Italian Fascism was out of step with almost every other Fascist movement. It is no accident that in 1938, Austria (after the Anschluss), Hungary and Romania all introduced laws discriminating against the Jews. He also believed that a harsh policy towards the Jews and other 'inferior' races, together with a further militarisation of Italian society, would help create a totalitarian state on Germanic lines and would better prepare Italy for war. There is, however, no evidence that Mussolini was pressurised by Hitler to imitate his racist policies, contrary to what many Italians, including leading Fascists, suspected at the time.

Document 8.9 The Ten Points of Fascist Racialism

1. Human races exist
2. Big and little races exist
3. The concept of race is purely biological
4. The present population of Italy is of the Aryan race
5. The racial composition of Italy has remained unchanged for a millennium
6. A pure Italian race now exists
7. The racial question in Italy must be considered from an exclusively biological point of view, without any religious or philosophical implications
8. The Jews do not belong to the Italian race
9. The Hamitic and Semitic races are not Aryan
10. No miscegenation must be allowed to contaminate the Italian race

Source: La Difesa della Razza *[literally, 'The Defence of the Race', Fascist periodical), V, 10, 20 March 1942, p. 1*

The emphasis on the biological criterion for race is a clear reflection of German racial theory, even if Mussolini hotly denied being influenced in any way by those ideas. It also has to be said that points four, five and six are extremely dubious propositions in the light of the historical evidence about the effects of the Arab (Semitic race) invasions and occupations of Sicily in the eleventh and twelfth centuries.

Conclusion

If we accept that, ultimately, Italian Fascism was inspired by certain basic ideas, much of the 'ideology' produced from the late 1920s onwards seems to be a very improvised, artificial creation. Perhaps Mussolini believed that an elaborate ideology was essential to the prestige of the regime. Cassels's (1985, p. 56) claim that, 'It has always been suspected that Mussolini approached corporativism less out of cerebral conviction than out of the utilitarian calculation that Fascism lacked status without a political philosophy of its own', could apply equally well to the Doctrine of Fascism and introduction of anti-Semitism. Again, much of Fascist 'ideology' seems to have been an essentially propagandistic substitute for a real ideology of change. It is significant that the 1930s version of the myth of 'revolution' – that is, the glib anti-bourgeois sloganising of those years – took the farcical form of the so-called 'reform of custom': the replacement of the handshake by the Roman salute; the abolition of the formal 'you'; and ridiculous attempts to purge Italian of foreign words and phrases (for example, substituting *quisibeve*, literally 'here one drinks', for the word 'bar').

Much of Fascist ideology was for the consumption of the elite – Fascist intellectuals and the party leadership. Alternatively, it was manipulated to provide syntheses acceptable to the ideas and interests of the various individuals, groups and institutions with which Mussolini had made the alliances on which rested consensus for his rule. In this regard, De Grand's belief that Italian Fascism was essentially 'hyphenated', that it was a composite of different ideas representing different constituencies – such as 'clerico-Fascism' and agrarian Fascism – makes a great deal of sense. Thus, there was never really a single Fascist 'ideology' as such, but a cluster of Fascist 'ideologies' in tension, competition and even conflict with each other.

Fascism's synthetic 'ideologies' worked quite well in conciliating a number of very different schools of political and philosophical thought, as well as interest groups. What it failed to do was to provide the kind of 'compelling' ideas necessary to penetrate and mobilise all sections of the Italian population and thus effectively integrate them in a militarised, totalitarian state on a permanent basis. The broadly based constituency of Fascism's natural supporters – the middle and lower-middle classes – was not much influenced by them. The Fascist application of Corradinian nationalist ideas to the problem of assuaging Italy's 'national inferiority complex' was sufficient for them, as long as it fell short of waging a major war. These ideas (and to a lesser extent, racialism) eventually took root in some sections of Italian society and thus ensured the continued presence of neo-Fascism in post-war Italy.

9 The legacy of Italian Fascism

Introduction

Italian Fascism did not suddenly appear from nowhere. Its origins were deeply rooted in certain intellectual, social and political developments in the decades preceding the First World War, and there were many continuities between the Fascist regime and the Liberal state which it had displaced. It is also true that Fascism did not suddenly and finally disappear in 1945 without leaving any traces. On the contrary, it left behind a powerful legacy which ensured strong continuities between the Fascist regime and the democratic republic of the post-war period. Insofar as Fascism failed to solve the major economic, social and political problems facing Italy, there are even continuities between the pre-Fascist Liberal regime and the democratic republic. Indeed, according to the Marxist historian, Paolo Spriano, the legacy of Fascism conditioned, 'the entire life of the [Italian] nation' (Duggan and Wagstaff, 1995, p. 9). This is certainly overstating the case, but even allowing for other powerful factors – such as the Cold War and the consequent fear of Communism in Italy, the economic 'miracle' of the 1950s and 1960s and the massive social changes which it brought, and the American cultural 'invasion' from the 1950s onwards – much of Italy's development as a modern, democratic, capitalist state in the post-war period has been shaped by the legacy of Fascism. It has also become evident in the last few years that the Fascist legacy still has a potentially important role to play in shaping Italy's future.

Foreign Policy and National identity

As we have seen, Fascism's foreign adventures in the Second World War ended in disastrous failures with the result that in the international political sphere Italy effectively ceased to exist as an independent entity: just as Mussolini's Republic of Salo was essentially a Nazi puppet state, so the King's government in the South was a client of the Allies. Though the Allies formally recognised Italy as a 'co-belligerent' in the war against Germany after the armistice of September 1943, in practice the Italian government had little real power as opposed to the authority of A.M.G. (Allied Military Government of Italy). Italy was not to recover her international autonomy until the peace treaty was signed with the Allies in February 1947. As a result of that agreement, Italy lost most of her colonial empire, had to pay reparations to the countries against whom she had fought (including Russia), her armed forces were reduced in size and she lost territory on both her western and eastern borders.

Document 9.1 Italy After the Peace Treaty of 1947

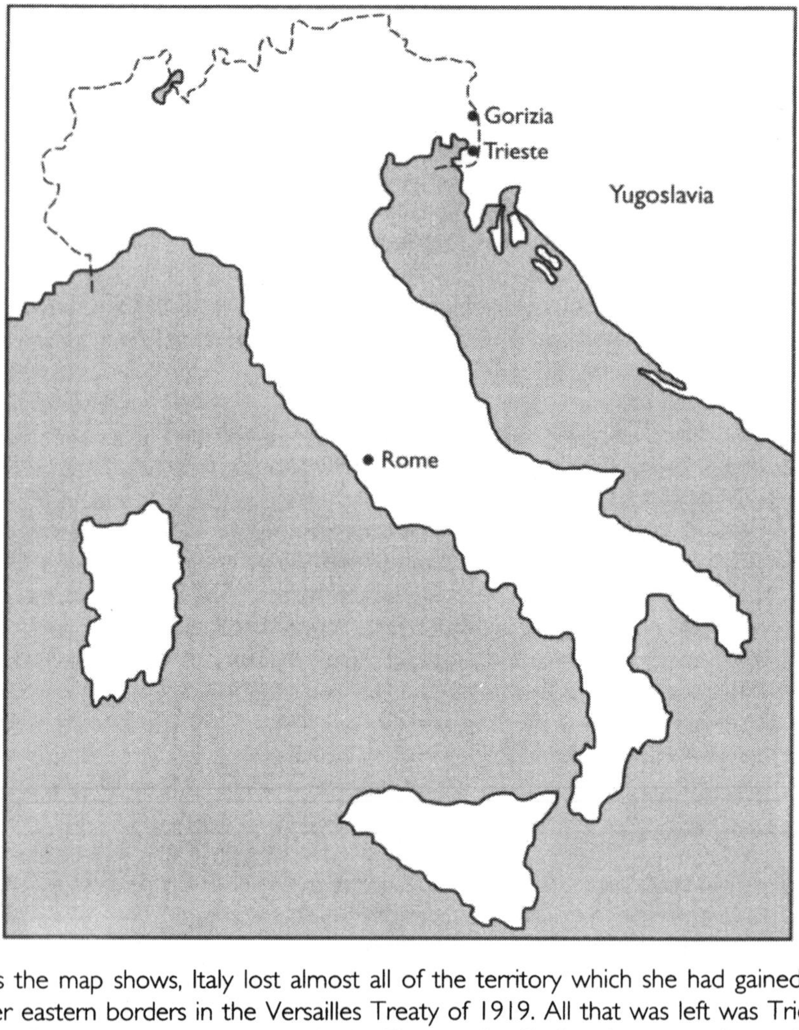

As the map shows, Italy lost almost all of the territory which she had gained on her eastern borders in the Versailles Treaty of 1919. All that was left was Trieste and Gorizia and a narrow coastal strip. Thousands of Italians became refugees from what was now Tito's Yugoslavia and Trieste remained a dangerous international flashpoint until the final settlement of the Italo-Yugoslav border in 1954. There was a special irony in the fact that, after fighting Bolshevism on the Eastern Front, thanks to Fascism's failures, Italy faced a Communist threat on her own border which constituted a part of the 'Iron Curtain' during the Cold War period.

Many Italian politicians and much of the population were outraged by the 1947 peace treaty: a sort of 'mutilated defeat' myth grew in right-wing circles as a result. But worse was to come. Italy in the post-war period faced an uphill struggle to reintegrate herself into the international community. Inevitably, Italy faced considerable suspicion on the part of its former enemies, especially the British, who were slow to forgive the foreign policy choices of Fascist Italy. It therefore became the guiding principle of the post-war prime minister, De Gasperi, and his foreign ministers to join every international organisation that emerged. Thus, despite strong neutralist tendencies in all sectors of the Italian political spectrum, Italy chose sides in the emerging Cold War situation by joining N.A.T.O. in 1949, and as moves were made towards European integration in the early and mid-1950s, Italy became an enthusiastic supporter: it is no accident that the founding conference of the European Community took place at Messina in 1956 and that the founding document is named the 'Treaty of Rome'. Democratic Italy carefully avoided the foreign-policy adventures of Fascism, choosing to defer to other powers, especially the most powerful of all, the U.S.A., until the early 1980s. Indeed, Italian reluctance to take the initiative in international affairs has led to the widely held opinion that Italy does not have a foreign policy in the real sense of the phrase.

The excesses of nationalism and racism under Fascism have also left Italians with a problem of national identity: after 1945 there could be no legitimate pride in Italy's war record or her empire. Strong patriotic pride was in any case frowned upon as virtually synonymous with Fascism, and many Italians have sought a 'safer' identity as Europeans: hence, repeated opinion polls have demonstrated the fact that the Italians are the most pro-European nation in Europe. Only since the 1980s, when Italy won the Football World Cup (1982) and the Italians claimed to have overtaken Britain in the world industrial league tables (1987), have Italians been able to feel more relaxed about their national identity. Even then, the emergence of the political movement known as the Northern Leagues, with their hostility to Rome and the South and their desire to 'reverse' the Risorgimento by threatening to secede from the Italian state, puts a serious question mark on Italian national unity and identity.

The Fascist Legacy and Post-war Politics in Italy

The memory of Fascism played an important part in the construction of the post-war Italian political system. First, the abolition of the monarchy by popular referendum in 1946 was partly the result of that institution's relationship with Fascism. Other characteristic features of the 1948 Constitution of the Italian Republic testify to the desire to avoid a repetition of Fascism: the creation of a weak executive (that is, presidential and prime ministerial power) and a powerful legislature – parliament; the return to the proportional representation voting system; and the introduction of other constitutional checks and balances, such as the constitutional court. And if the fear of the threat of Communism – the Italian Communist Party rapidly became the largest in the Western world – induced governments in the 1940s and 1950s to delay implementing the Constitution, it has to be said that this factor also ensured the survival of much repressive Fascist legislation, most notably in the area of police powers and public order regulations.

The Fascist Legacy as a Threat to Democracy

Other aspects of the legacy of Fascism constituted threats, sometimes potentially mortal, to the democratic system itself. In particular, the resurgence of squadrism, the use of violence for political ends, threatened to destabilise the new republic. Martin Clark has argued that the phenomenon of squadrism did not die with Fascism in 1945, that it remained a part of Italian political culture and practice, resurfacing at moments of acute economic and social crisis and political tension, its essential preconditions. In particular, he argues that a deep fear of Communism was a major stimulant to the resurgence of squadrism/right-wing political violence. Thus, he points to such a resurgence, albeit briefly, in the mid- to late 1940s, under the pressure of the Cold War and in the face of the emergence of a strong Communist Party (Clark, 1989, pp. 40–1).

But right-wing political violence most strongly manifested itself in the late 1960s and early 1970s. This was a period of student and youth agitation, new social movements, including women's and gay liberation, widespread social unrest and trade union militancy in Italy. This was accompanied by a massive increase in electoral support for the Communists – peaking at over a third of the vote in the 1976 elections. The neo-Fascist terrorist gangs of this period were a backlash against all this left-wing activity and also against the emergence of left-wing terrorist groups such as the Red Brigades. Whereas the left-wing terrorists tended to attack, maim and sometimes kill individual targets, such as ex-prime minister Aldo Moro in 1978, the terrorists of the right – who significantly used the names of the Fascist squads of the 1920s and 1930s (similarly, many left-wing terrorists looked back to the partisan bands of wartime resistance for inspiration), such as S.A.M. ('Mussolini Action Squad') – often planted bombs in public places which killed dozens of innocent bystanders and passers-by. All this was part of a so-called 'strategy of tension', a campaign designed to lead to a breakdown of law and order and a consequent collapse of public confidence in democratically elected government, precipitating a takeover by the army. Indeed, in the 1960s and 1970s there were several unsuccessful coup attempts.

Another important aspect of the legacy of Fascism was the survival, in increasingly powerful positions in the armed forces and security services, the judiciary and the civil service, of large numbers of Fascist sympathisers. The purge of Fascists in Italy in the mid-1940s, unlike the 'denazification' campaign in Germany, was not carried out by Allies but by the Italians themselves. The desire to preserve continuity and effectiveness of the state and return the country to 'normality' as quickly as possible meant that the purge failed to dislodge most Fascist sympathisers and so Italy after the Second World War was rather like Weimar Germany after the First: it had a new democratic constitution on paper, but many servants of the old authoritarian regime in key positions in the governmental machine whose sympathies were not democratic. These men were to play a key role in the 'strategy of tension' in the 1970s. Given the byzantine complexities of Italian politics in this period, and especially the rather murky involvement of the C.I.A., who did what and why will probably remain a mystery, but there is some salient evidence. First, Fascist sympathisers in the police and security services both aided and used terrorists of the right. According to an Italian senator, 'the judiciary identified at least forty instances of collusion between the security services and right-wing terrorists' (Willan, 1991, p. 128). Second, some policemen and judges were notoriously lenient towards Fascist terrorists, and even allowed some to escape punishment by fleeing to Greece, Spain or South America. Finally, a tiny minority of army generals and officials of the security forces were involved in coup plans and attempts, all of them unsuccessful.

On the positive side, the anti-Fascist resistance movement also had an enduring influence upon post-war Italy which helped to counteract the effects of the Fascist legacy. Even though its leaders were bitterly divided by ideological and class struggles, the resistance was inspired by certain ideals – a belief in democracy, equality and the rule of law. This is the foundation on which the post-war democratic republic was built. These were the principles which, in particular, influenced the framing of the republican Constitution of 1948. And even during the bitterest struggles of the Cold War in Italy in the 1940s and 1950s, and during the so-called 'years of lead' – the terrorism and attempted military coups in the late 1960s and 1970s – these principles and indeed the myth of the wartime resistance which incarnated them, helped Italian democracy to survive, uniting all the anti-Fascist parties, from the Communists to the Christian Democrats, and the overwhelming majority of the public against terrorism.

Church, State and Society after Fascism

The legacy of Fascism in the area of Church–state relations was to have an enormous influence on the political development of Italy after 1945. With Fascism's collapse and the subsequent abolition of the monarchy, the Catholic Church was easily the most powerful social and political institution in Italy, underpinned by a large stake in the economy. Moreover, it now had a close relationship with the U.S.A. So strong was the influence of the Church in the decade following the end of the war that Italy in this period has been described as 'The Papal State of the Twentieth Century' (Webster, 1960, p. 214). And the Communist Party leader, Palmiro Togliatti, was so afraid of the Church's influence that in 1947 he ordered his followers in parliament to vote for the acceptance of the Lateran Pacts in the new republican Constitution.

Document 9.2 Church and State in Democratic Italy

ARTICLE 7 OF THE CONSTITUTION OF 1948

The state and the Catholic Church are, each in their own ambit, independent and sovereign. Their relations are regulated by the Lateran Pacts. Such amendments to these Pacts as are accepted by both parties do not require any procedure of constitutional revision.

Source: J.F. Pollard in Eileen A. Millar, The Legacy of Fascism, *1989, p. 57*

Few modern, democratic states have countenanced such an explicit recognition of the independence of an ecclesiastical body in their midst. The consequences of this decision were momentous for Church–state relations in Italy. In the 1950s and 1960s Italian courts handed down a series of judgements which declared that since the Constitution had implicitly recognised the principle that Catholicism was 'the sole religion of the state' (as set out in the Lateran Treaty), then the protection of the interests of that religion had priority over the rights of religious minorities. The same principle inspired decisions affecting matrimonial law, church property and religious instruction in schools. As late as 1967, the Supreme Court made a judgement which imposed limits on freedom of religious discussion.

Under Fascism, the Church had managed to safeguard the autonomy and existence of its lay people's organisation, Catholic Action, when all other non-Fascist organisations were banned, by means of the Concordat of 1929.

Document 9.3 Article 43 of the Concordat, 1929

The Italian state recognises the organisations forming a part of the Italian Catholic Action, insofar as, in accordance with the instructions of the Holy See, they maintain their activity wholly apart from any political party and under the immediate hierarchy of the Church for the diffusion and practice of Catholic principles.

Source: J.F. Pollard, The Vatican and Italian Fascism 1929–32: A Study in Conflict, *1985, p. 214*

Thanks to the protection afforded by this clause, within Catholic Action it was possible to train a whole new generation of Catholic political leaders who, after 1943, played a major role in the new Catholic party, the Christian Democrats (henceforth D.C.). And with a membership of 2.5 million people, male and female, young and old, Catholic Action was able to mobilise massive electoral support for those leaders. In 1946 the D.C. won 35 per cent of the vote and became the largest party; two years later it obtained a parliamentary majority. The role of the D.C. as the officially sponsored Catholic party and political agent of the Church meant that it was guaranteed the continuing support of the bishops, clergy, Catholic organisations and press. This helped to ensure that it remained the largest party and therefore the dominant party of government for almost fifty years; more than twice as long as Fascism. Indeed, such was the domination of the Christian Democrats over the post-war political system that this period is often referred to as the 'Christian Democratic regime', echoing the 'Fascist regime' between 1922 and 1943.

The Economic Legacy of Fascism

The economic legacy of Fascism was enormous. Though much of it, the corporations, the industrial cartels and the tight regulation of foreign exchange and trade, was swept away immediately after the war, one aspect remained: the huge public sector. Thus, until recent privatisations, 40 per cent of manufacturing industry in Italy – everything from the production of iron and steel to the manufacture of Christmas cakes – was controlled by the state – and, more importantly, so was 80 per cent of all banking operations. This had very beneficial effects in the 1950s and 1960s when the Italian public sector played a key role in the economic 'miracle', creating new chemical, engineering and energy industries which private Italian capitalism was unable or unwilling to venture into, and initiating the network of *autostrade* on which cars produced in the private sector could drive.

On the other hand, more recently, the public sector has become an economic liability, artificially sustaining employment in 'lame duck' industries. Worse still, the huge public sector left by Fascism, and the large numbers of quangos which it created in the fields of health, welfare, social services and housing provision, played an important role in promoting the clientelism and corruption which became so widespread in the Christian Democratic regime in its last years. The governing parties, especially the Christian Democrats, took direct control of the public sector and used it to provide 'jobs for the boys'; in other words, for party members and voters.

Jobs in the other quangos were used in similar fashion, and control of most of the banks allowed politicians to grant credit and mortgages only to their supporters. Housing, health care, pensions and so on were also allocated on the same basis. And to add insult to injury, the funds of public companies, banks and the various quangos were plundered to provide financing for political parties and their hundreds of employees, large offices, fleets of cars and lavish publicity and entertaining. Politicians increasingly awarded public contracts to private business after receiving bribes: the so-called 'Bribesville' scandals of recent years were simply the tip of an iceberg of political corruption. All this, of course, cannot be *solely* blamed on the legacy of Fascism. There were other factors: a set of 'Mediterranean' values, especially in the South, that puts the interests of the individual and the family above the law and the common good; the lack of a clear political alternative to the Christian Democrats because the Communists were the only effective opposition. According to Lord Acton, 'All power corrupts but absolute power corrupts absolutely.' In the case of post-war Italy one might modify this axiom to say that *permanent* power corrupts absolutely.

Nevertheless, the legacy of Fascism did provide the *opportunities* for corruption on a scale which had hitherto not existed, and the Fascist use of the public sector in the 1930s and 1940s to win support provided a model to be imitated by post-war politicians. As McGregor Knox points out, 'The Fascist regime's foremost legacy to its successor was a tradition of bureaucratic elephantiasis, inept and corrupt intervention in the economy, and a static, mass-party patronage machine' (Knox, 1996, p. 132). Though the origins of these problems pre-dated the rise of Fascism (see Chapter 1) the policies of the regime undoubtedly helped to perpetuate and intensify them.

The Italian Social Movement

The most direct and visible aspect of the legacy of Fascism was a political force, the neo-Fascist Italian Social Movement (M.S.I.), which, as its name suggests, was nothing less than the heir of the Fascist Social Republic. The M.S.I. did not officially enter the Italian political stage until the general elections of 1953, but as early as the 1946 elections the Uomo Qualunque ('Every Man') movement, with scarcely disguised Fascist tendencies, won 1 million votes, chiefly in the South. Strictly speaking, a neo-Fascist movement should never have existed in post-war Italy, because the republican Constitution of 1948 specifically forbade it.

Document 9.4 The Constitutional Ban on Fascism: Constitution of the Republic of Italy, Transitory and Final Provisions

The reorganisation in any form of the dissolved Fascist Party is forbidden.

Notwithstanding Article 48 [on voting rights], the responsible leaders of the Fascist regime are excluded by law from voting and standing for office for a period of fifteen years from the date that this Constitution comes into force.

Source: Supplement to No. 4, Italy: Documents and Notes, *July–August 1965, p. 50*

The leaders of the neo-Fascist movement managed to get round this and the so-called 'Scelba Law' of 1952, which more explicitly banned it, by paying lip-service to parliamentary democracy. They were also helped by the complacent attitude of the ruling Christian Democrats who saw the neo-Fascists as a most useful counter to the Communists, kept the M.S.I. on the right side of legality and thus saved it from dissolution. So, despite these legal bans, despite the ignominious defeat of Fascist Italy in the Second World War and the consequent collapse of Fascism, and despite the anti-Fascist purges which were less than comprehensive or effective, by 1948 the M.S.I. had emerged with an ideology clearly derived from Mussolinian Fascism.

Document 9.5 Basic Ideas of Italian Neo-Fascism

CORPORATIVISM

Corporativism is a social, economic and political doctrine which seeks to create an organic society, one without classes, one which is both hierarchically and democratically organised, according to criteria of competence and responsibility, but always with respect for people's liberty . . .

The two essentials of modern corporativism are workers' participation and planning.

Corporativist participation in the economic system as a whole is achieved through representatives of categories of workers and employers.

Corporativist participation in the state is achieved through (party) political representation and through social bodies (the family, cultural and religious institutions, productive groups, firms and local authorities).

TRADE UNIONS

CISNAL [neo-Fascist trade union organisation] is based on 'national syndicalism', which is neither class based nor interclass, but seeks to transcend class and render the concept obsolete, within the framework of a corporative society that is organic and national.

THE STATE

[The state] is the necessary political and legal organisation of the national community, whose well-being it seeks to achieve: it is a creation of the spirit, which has a moral base.

On the material plane, its constituent elements are population, territory, sovereignty, the latter understood as being an autonomous capacity to rule . . . In the state advocated by the MSI–DN there is no place for totalitarianism, atomism or repression of any kind.

Source: The A to Z of the M.S.I.–National Right, *1980, pp. 15–16, 47 and 49–50*

Even allowing for some 'modernisation' of original Fascist ideas, and for an understandable desire to distance itself from some of the worst aspects of the Fascist regime (as in the last three lines), these ideas are not far removed from the Manifesto of the First *Fascio* (see Document 2.3) and the Verona Manifesto of the Fascist Social Republic. The strongest element of continuity between Fascism and post-war neo-Fascism was represented by the leadership of the movement which contained several survivors from the Fascist Social Republic, most notably Giorgio Almirante, formerly an under-secretary of state in the Salo government and General Secretary of the M.S.I. from 1969 onwards.

A number of factors made it possible for the M.S.I. to enter parliament. The Italian form of 'pure' proportional representation, unlike the form prevalent in post-war Germany, did not impose a percentage threshold before a minority party could enter the legislature. A large middle/lower-middle class of public employees who owed their jobs to Fascism survived in major cities such as Rome, Naples and Palermo. They repaid their debt by keeping alive support for Fascism in their families – many members of the Fascist youth organisations since the 1960s have come from this social background, and the ageing, nostalgic parents, especially the men, were enthusiastic voters for the M.S.I. Finally, the absence of an anti-Fascist wartime resistance in the South (most of the South was liberated by the Allies before the resistance movement began to flourish) combined with the continuing failure to resolve the serious economic problems of the major Southern towns. This left a sizeable element of hopelessly marginalised urban poor prey to the propaganda of the neo-Fascists as a non-Communist, anti-establishment party. This underlying characteristic of the social and geographical bases of post-war neo-Fascism, it should be noted, was profoundly different from the early 1920s when support for Fascism came almost exclusively from the middle classes of Central and Northern Italy.

With rarely less than 5 per cent of the vote and seats in parliament (7.5 per cent in the 1972 general election, thanks to an alliance with the monarchists), the Italian M.S.I. alone of post-war neo-Fascist movements in Europe maintained a place for itself in the political system, even if it never played more than a marginal role in national politics until the 1990s.

Italy in the Era of Post-Fascism

The succession of 'Bribesville' corruption scandals and trials from the spring of 1992 progressively discredited the majority of the Italian political class. On the eve of the general election of March 1994, for example, nearly half of the members of the Chamber of Deputies, the lower house of the Italian parliament, were under investigation on corruption charges. The result was that the parties which had governed in coalition for decades, the Socialists, the Social Democrats, Liberals, Republicans and, above all, the Christian Democratic Party, collapsed. New parties, like the Northern Leagues (a political force which had emerged in part as a protest against corruption) and Forza Italia, the party created from nothing by the media tycoon Silvio Berlusconi in 1993, sought to take their place, along with the surviving opposition parties, the Communists (now renamed the Party of the Democratic Left) and the M.S.I.

Of all these parties, the M.S.I. was the most successful in this endeavour with the result that in the March 1994 election, under the new name 'National Alliance', looking more and more like a party of the democratic, conservative right, it was able to win millions of votes in the South that had formerly gone to the Christian Democrats. It ultimately won nearly 14 per cent of the votes and six of its Deputies entered the government, one actually becoming deputy prime minister. One factor in the success of the National Alliance was the change of name, which reduced its Fascist association in the eyes of many voters. In fact, the M.S.I. had been becoming less and less 'Fascist' in ideological inspiration and policies since the death in 1988 of Giorgio Almirante. A second important factor was the cunning and charisma of the man who succeeded Almirante, Gianfranco Fini. A British journalist familiar with Italian politics, Peter Popham, described a speech which Fini gave in London:

> Fini pulled out all the stops to appear to be the Italian equivalent of a French Gaullist, a British Tory or an American Republican . . . but Fini is in essence a Fascist, and the first leader from the extreme right since the fall of Communism to have entered government in Europe.
>
> **(*Independent*, 25 March 1995)**

In March 1995, Fini sought to cut all links finally with the Fascist past. The M.S.I. was formally dissolved, with the result that the hard-core Fascists seceded to reform the M.S.I., with the name The Tricolour Flame, under the leadership of Pino Rauti. Along with Rauti went the even more extreme, violent fringe – 'the Nazi-skins'.

The events of the last few years raise many questions about the Fascist legacy:

1 Is Fascism/neo-Fascism finally dead in Italy, apart, that is, from the hard-core activists mentioned above?
2 Have the neo-Fascist leopards changed their spots?
3 Are we now really in a post-Fascist era, as Fini and his friends, and some Italian historians, contend?

Many people, both inside and outside Italy, would answer 'No' to all these questions. The French, for example, protested when Fini's colleagues entered the Italian government following the March 1994 election. And the behaviour of Fini and his political colleagues has been ambivalent in the extreme. On the one hand, he has condemned the 'Nazi-skins' for commemorating Mussolini's appointment as prime minister on 31 October, when he said of them, 'These young people have nothing in their brains, they should be sent to the mines'; on the other hand, he has also publicly declared that, 'Mussolini was the greatest statesman of the twentieth century' (*Independent*, 25 March 1995). And since his electoral success in 1994 there has been a recurrence of anti-Semitic and racialist graffiti. Just as worrying, the National Alliance Deputy who became chairman of the Italian parliament's foreign affairs committee immediately demanded the return of territories that now form parts of the republics of Slovenia and Croatia which were taken from Italy in 1945 and have been claimed by the neo-Fascists ever since. Perhaps the clearest evidence that Fascism is not completely dead in Italy is to be found in the 1994 manifesto of the National Alliance.

Document 9.6 Excerpts from the M.S.I./National Alliance Manifesto, 1994

The state is the image of the nation, epitomising its values by perpetuating them. It exalts the qualities of the people whose rights it safeguards; it tells them their duties; it promotes their development; it is the inspiring force behind national education and is the artificer of justice; it is the guarantor of social equilibrium . . . In this indissoluble identity the roots of the nation state extend deep into history, and it identifies the path to progress by pursuing the common good – the good of the nation – on the basis of which it ensures that all the needs of individuals and groups are met. With the disappearance of a sense of the state and the travesty of the state itself into a regime of parties, the sense of the nation has disappeared and with it the awareness of the value of the 'national community' . . .

Now a great chance for the introduction of a new model of political system has been created . . . The concomitant of a government made strong by direct popular investiture is a strong parliament with extensive powers of policy making and control.

It is because of its way of being, its history, its tradition, its presence in the country, that today the Youth Front [of the M.S.I.] must form the nucleus of a youth alliance [like the M.S.I.–D.N. in the National Alliance], a broad-based movement which enables different souls to identify with a political project in which such values as national identity, freedom, right to life, the family and solidarity provide the basis for the reconstruction of the nation.

Source: R. Griffin, Fascism, *1995, pp. 387–8*

As this extract shows, after fifty years, some of the essential ideas of Fascism, strong state power and palingenetic nationalism, have not entirely disappeared. They survive, albeit in a modernised, modified form, as the guiding ideas of the leadership of Italy's so-called 'new' right. It is extremely unlikely that a 'real' Fascist movement like that represented by the Nazi-skins and their older allies will come to power in Italy. Mussolini's rise to power was the result of a special set of circumstances created by the First World War which it is impossible to reproduce in today's world. But the entry into government in 1994 of a rightist party with Fascist antecedents, albeit in coalition with other parties, was bound cause serious concern about the future of Italian democracy, particularly in the light of the political instability that followed the 'Bribesville' scandals and the consequent collapse of the fifty-year-old Christian Democratic 'regime'. In this situation, a popular desire for political stability could easily be translated into a more sharply defined search for another 'strong man', as the present debates over constitutional reform in the direction of a presidential or semi-presidential system suggest.

The writings of the recently deceased Renzo De Felice, and other revisionists, have added some credence to Fini's claims that Italy is finally living in a post-Fascist era. They have sought to downgrade the idealism and political importance of the partisans and dismiss the significance of the Fascist Social Republic, placing the activities of the partisans on the same moral level as those of the Fascist and German security forces. They treat the events of 1943 to 1945 as a 'national tragedy', without laying too much blame at the door of Mussolini and Fascism: at most Mussolini is described as having made errors of judgement. And in line with the arguments about British responsibility for Italy entering the war in 1940, the Allies are also, very conveniently, made to take the blame for much of what went wrong from 1943 onwards: even Mussolini's death in April 1945 was said to be the work of the British Secret Service. The purpose of all this is to try to provide an acceptable past for Italians, one which they do not have to feel guilty about, one which, above all, does not divide them politically, or potentially 'disqualify' a major political force. The historical ignorance of Italian youth, which has been revealed in recent surveys, suggests that, in the long term, the revisionists might well succeed in their efforts.

Further reading

C.F. Delzell (ed.), *Mediterranean Fascism, 1919–1945* (1971) still provides the most comprehensive collection of documents on Italian Fascism in English. The omnibus collection of Mussolini's speeches and writings in E. Susmel and D. Susmel (eds), *Opera Omnia di Benito Mussolini* (1952–63) is also an invaluable resource.

Both W. Laquer (ed.), *Fascism: A Reader's Guide* (1976) and R. Eatwell, *Fascism – A History* (1996) help to set the Italian case in the broader context of the European experience of Fascism. R. Griffin, *The Nature of Fascism* (1991), also provides an interesting and controversial new definition of the general phenomenon. Comparative studies of Nazi Germany and Fascist Italy are to be found in R. Bessel (ed.), *Fascist Italy and Nazi Germany: Comparisons and Contrasts* (1996) and A. De Grand, *Fascist Italy and Nazi Germany: 'The Fascist Style of Rule'* (1996); Bessel is definitely the better of the two.

P. Morgan, *Italian Fascism, 1919–1945* (1995) and J. Whittam, *Fascist Italy* (1995) are both excellent, up-to-date surveys, but Morgan's analysis has more cutting edge. A very useful general reference work is P. Cannistraro, *Historical Dictionary of Fascist Italy* (1982). The best biography of Mussolini in English is D. Mack Smith, *Mussolini* (1981), though the author is inclined to dismiss the Duce with not a little Anglo-Saxon superiority. Quite the reverse is true of the eight-volume biography of Mussolini by R. De Felice (1965–90): but this is not for the faint-hearted, however good their Italian! De Felice was the doyen of Italian historians of Fascism, and a controversial one at that. For a critique of his interpretations of Fascism, see D. Mack Smith, 'Monument for the Duce' (1975).

On the history of Italy prior to the First World War see L. Riall, *The Italian Risorgimento: State, Society and National Unification* (1994), which contains a vital bibliographical survey and valuable insights. The history of Liberal Italy is still best explained by C. Seton-Watson, *Italy from Liberalism to Fascism* (1967). For the broad sweep of Italian history from unification to virtually the present day, M. Clark, *Modern Italy* (1996) is invaluable but controversial.

Seton-Watson (1967) *Italy from Liberalism to Fascism*, and A. Lyttelton, *Seizure of Power: Fascism in Italy, 1919–1929* (1987) contain extremely detailed analyses of the crisis of the Liberal state and the rise of Fascism between 1919 and 1922. Also very useful is the interpretation of those events by the political scientist P. Farneti in 'Social Conflict, Parliamentary Fragmentation, Institutional Shift and the Rise of Fascism' (1978).

S.V. Larsen *et al.* (eds), *Who Were the Fascists? Social Roots of European Fascism* (1980) and M. Revelli, 'Italy' (1987) are key texts in any study of the composition and development of the Fascist movement, as is F. Snowden, 'On the Social Origins of Agrarian Fascism in Italy' (1972). There is a wide range of studies of the rise of Fascism at a local level in both English and Italian – see T. Abse, 'A Survey of Local Studies of Italian Fascism' (1983) – and the classic is P. Corner, *Fascism in Ferrara* (1975).

H. Finer, *Mussolini's Italy* (1935) provides a penetrating contemporary critique of Fascism in power. E. Tannenbaum, *Fascism in Italy: Society and Culture 1922–1945* (1973) was the first major historical study of the workings of the regime. Since then, a whole literature has developed on various aspects of Fascist 'consensus' and social policies – see, for example, V. De Grazia, *The Culture of Consent: Mass Organisation of Leisure in Fascist Italy* (1982), and T. Koon, *Believe, Obey and Fight: Political Socialisation of Youth in Fascist Italy, 1922–1943* (1985). Fascism's relations with the Church are dealt with in J. Pollard, '"A Marriage of Convenience": The Vatican and the Fascist Regime in Italy' (1987); for an alternative view, see J. Gaillard, 'The Attraction of Fascism for the Church of Rome' (1990). For Fascist economic and social policy, V. Zamagni, *The Economic History of Italy, 1860–1990: Recovery after Decline* (1993) is indispensable; see also the entries for economic and social topics in P. Cannistraro, *Historical Dictionary of Fascist Italy* (1982).

Of all aspects of Fascism, its foreign policy has received most attention from Anglo-Saxon scholars. There is, as a result, a large and growing literature on the subject. The key works are A. Cassels, *Mussolini's Early Diplomacy* (1970), H.J. Burgwyn, *Italian Foreign Policy in the Inter-war Period, 1919–1940* (1997) and M. Knox, *Mussolini Unleashed 1939–1941: Politics and Strategy in Fascist Italy's Last War* (1986). In Italian, the best summary of Fascist foreign policy is M. Knox, 'Il fascismo e la politica estera italiana' (1991).

There is no complete study of Italy during the years of the Second World War, but W. Deakin, *The Brutal Friendship, Mussolini, Hitler and the Fall of Italian Fascism* (1966a) remains a vital source in English. R. De Felice's (1965–90) last two volumes – *Mussolini L'alleato: L'italia in guerra, 1940–1943* and *Mussolini L'alleato: Crisi e agonia del regime* – are the best works available in Italian.

Again, there is no fully comprehensive study of the ideology of Italian Fascism in English: A.J. Gregor, *The Young Mussolini and the Intellectual Origins of Fascism* (1979b) is interesting but inadequate. On the other hand, in Italian there is the excellent study by P.G. Zunino, *L'Ideologia dell'Italia Fascismo: Miti, credenze e valori nella stabilizzazione del regime* (1985). On Fascist racialism there is quite a lot in English, the best of which are M. Michaelis, *Mussolini and the Jews: German–Italian Relations and the Jewish Question in Italy, 1922–1945* (1978) and J. Steinberg, *All or Nothing; Hitler, Mussolini and the Holocaust, 1941–43* (1990)

A good account of the short-term Fascist legacy is provided by C. Duggan, 'Italy in the Cold War Years and the Legacy of Fascism' (1995). The essays by M. Clark, J. Pollard and C. Seton-Watson in E.A. Millar, *The Legacy of Fascism* (1989) are also useful on various aspects of that legacy. For the history of the post-war neo-Fascist movement, see R. Chiarini, 'The Movimento Sociale Italiano' (1991). Broad overviews of post-war Italian history are provided by M. Clark, *Modern Italy* (1996) and P. Ginsborg, *A History of Contemporary Italy* (1990).

Bibliography

This bibliography, while it is not a completely comprehensive list of all works available, is designed to provide a wide selection of source materials of different kinds to meet the needs of staff and students; including, in the latter case, specialist works for projects and dissertations.

Documentary collections and commentaries in English

The A to Z of the MSI–National Right. Rome. MSI–DN. 1980.

Ciano's Diary, 1939–1943, edited with an introduction by M. Muggeridge. London and Toronto: Heinemann. 1947.

The Constitution of the Italian Republic, in Supplement No. 4, *Italy: Documents and Notes*, July–August (1965).

Delzell, C.F. (ed.), *Mediterranean Fascism, 1919–1945.* New York: Walker. 1971.

Griffin, R. (ed.), *Fascism.* Oxford: Oxford University Press. 1995.

Halperin, S.W., *Mussolini and Italian Fascism.* Toronto, New York and London: Harper Torch Books. 1964.

Lyttelton, A. (ed.), *Italian Fascisms: From Pareto to Gentile.* London: Jonathan Cape. 1973.

Secondary sources in English

Absalom, R, 'The Armed Resistance in Italy 1943–45: The Politics of History', *Journal of the Association of Teachers of Italian*, 21 (1977), 7–18.

——, 'Fascist Foreign Policy and Italian Intervention in World War II', *Journal of the Association of Teachers of Italian*, 41 (1984), 15–33.

Abse, T., 'A Survey of Local Studies of Italian Fascism', in *Journal of the Association of Teachers of Italian*, 40 (1983), 19–34.

—— 'Italy', in J. Noakes (ed.), *The Civilian in War: The Home Front in Europe, Japan and the U.S.A. in World War II.* Exeter: Exeter University Press. 1992.

Acquarone, A., *L'Organizzazione dello Stato Totalitario.* Turin: Einaudi. 1965.

Allum, P.A., *State and Society in Western Europe*. Cambridge: Polity Press. 1995.

Arendt, H., *The Origins of Totalitarianism*. London: G. Allen & Unwin. 1967.

Baer, G.W., *The Coming of the Italo-Ethiopian War*. Cambridge, Mass.: Harvard University Press. 1967.

Barker, A.J., *The Civilising Mission: A History of the Italo-Ethiopian War*. London: Cassell. 1968.

Bessel, R. (ed.), *Fascist Italy and Nazi Germany: Comparisons and Contrasts*. Cambridge and New York: Cambridge University Press. 1996.

Bosworth, R., *Italy: The Least of the Great Powers*. Cambridge: Cambridge University Press. 1979.

——, *Italy and the Approach of the First World War*. London and Basingstoke: Macmillan. 1983.

Burgwyn, H.J., *The Legend of the Mutilated Victory: Italy, the Great War and the Paris Peace Conference 1915–1919*. Westport, Conn.: Greenwood Press. 1993.

——, *Italian Foreign Policy in the Inter-war Period, 1919–1940*. Westport, Conn.: Greenwood Press. 1997.

Cafagna, L. 'Italy 1830–1920,' in C. Cipdla (ed.), *The Fontana Economic History of Europe. The Emergence of Industrial Societies 1*. Glasgow: Collins/Fontana Books, 1973.

Cannistraro, P.V., 'The Radio in Fascist Italy', *Journal of European Studies*, 2 (1972), 127–155.

——, (ed.), *Historical Dictionary of Fascist Italy*. Westport and London: Greenwood Press. 1982.

Cardoza, A.L., *Agrarian Elites and Italian Fascism. The Province of Bologna, 1901–1926*. Princeton, NJ: Princeton University Press. 1982.

Carocci, G., *Italian Fascism*. Harmondsworth: Pelican. 1972.

Cassels, A., *Mussolini's Early Diplomacy*. Princeton: Princeton University Press. 1970.

——, *Fascist Italy*. Arlington Heights, Ill.: Harlan Davidson Inc. 1985, 2nd ed.

Cauldwell, L., 'Reproducers of the Nation: Women and the Family in Fascist Policy', in D. Forgacs (ed.), *Re-thinking Italian Fascism: Capitalism, Populism and Culture*. London: Lawrence & Wishart. 1986.

Chiarini, R., 'The Movimento Sociale Italiano: A Political Profile', in L. Cheles, R. Ferguson and M. Vaughan (eds), *Neo-Fascism in Europe*. Harlow: Longman. 1991.

Clark, M., 'Italian Squadrismo and Contemporary Vigilantism', in Eileen A. Millar (ed.), *The Legacy of Fascism*. Glasgow: Glasgow University Press. 1987.

——, *Modern Italy, 1870–1995*. London: Longmans. 1996.

Cohen, P., 'Fascism and Agriculture in Italy', *Economic History Review*, XXXII (1979), 70–87.

Collier, R., *The Years of Attrition, 1940–1941*. London: Allison & Busby. 1995.

Corner, P., *Fascism in Ferrara*. Oxford: Oxford University Press. 1975.

——, 'Fascist Agrarian Policy and the Italian Economy in the Inter-war Years', in J.A. Davis (ed.), *Gramsci and Italy's Passive Revolution*. London: Croom Helm. 1979.

——, 'Liberalism, Pre-Fascism, Fascism', in D. Forgacs (ed.), *Rethinking Italian Fascism: Capitalism, Populism and Culture*. London: Lawrence & Wishart. 1986.

Coverdale, J., *Italian Intervention in the Spanish Civil War*. Princeton: Princeton University Press. 1975.

Deakin, W., *The Brutal Friendship, Mussolini, Hitler and the Fall of Italian Fascism*. Harmondsworth: Penguin. 1966a.

——, *The Last Days of Mussolini*. Harmondsworth: Penguin. 1966b.

De Felice, R., *Mussolini il Fascista: L'organizzazione della stato fascista 1925–1926*, vol. IV. Turin: Einaudi. 1966.

——, *Interpretations of Fascism*. Cambridge, Mass., and London. 1977.

De Grand, A., 'Women under Italian Fascism', *The Historical Journal*, XIX (1976), 947–68.

——, *The Italian Nationalist Association and the Rise of Fascism in Italy*. Lincoln, Nebraska: University of Nebraska Press. 1978.

——, *Italian Fascism, its Origins and Development*. Lincoln, Nebraska: University of Nebraska Press. 1982.

——, *The Italian Left in the Twentieth Century: A History of the Socialist and Communist Parties*. Bloomington and Indianapolis: Indiana University Press. 1989.

——, 'Cracks in the Façade: The Failure of Fascist Totalitarianism in Italy, 1935–39', *European History Quarterly*, 21 (1991), 515–35.

——, *Fascist Italy and Nazi Germany: 'The Fascist Style of Rule'*. London: Routledge. 1996.

De Grazia, V., *The Culture of Consent: Mass Organisation of Leisure in Fascist Italy*. Cambridge: Cambridge University Press. 1982.

——, *How Fascism Ruled Women: Italy, 1922–1945*. Berkeley: University of California Press. 1992.

Delzell, C., *Mussolini's Enemies: The Italian Anti-Fascist Resistance*. Princeton: Princeton University Press. 1961.

Duggan, C., *Fascism and the Mafia*. New Haven, Conn., and London: Yale University Press. 1989.

——, 'Italy in the Cold War Years and the Legacy of Fascism', in C. Duggan & C. Wagstaff (eds), *Italy in the Cold War: Politics, Culture & Society, 1948–1958*. Oxford and Washington, D.C.: Berg. 1995.

Eatwell, R., *Fascism, A History*. London: Arrow Books. 1996.

Ellwood, D., *Italy 1943–1945*. Leicester: Leicester University Press. 1995.

Farneti, P., 'Social Conflict, Parliamentary Fragmentation, Institutional Shift and the Rise of Fascism', in J. Linz and A. Stepan (eds), *The Breakdown of Democratic Regimes*. London and Baltimore: Johns Hopkins University Press. 1978.

Ferraresi, F., 'The Radical Right in Post-war Italy', *Politics and Society*, XVI (1988), 76–97.

Finer, H., *Mussolini's Italy*. London: Frank Cass. 1935.

Forgacs, D., *Italian Culture in the Industrial Era, 1880–1980*. Manchester: Manchester University Press. 1990.

Gaillard, J., 'The Attraction of Fascism for the Church of Rome', in J. Milfull (ed.), *The Attraction of Fascism: Social Psychology and Aesthetics of the Triumph of the Right*. Oxford and Providence, R.I.: Berg. 1990.

Ginsborg, P., *A History of Contemporary Italy*. London: Penguin Books. 1990.

Gregor, A.J., *Fascism and Developmental Dictatorship*. Princeton: Princeton University Press. 1979a.

——, *The Young Mussolini and the Intellectual Origins of Fascism*. Berkeley: University of California Press. 1979b.

Grenville, J.A.S., *The Major International Treaties, 1914–1945. A History and Guide with Texts*. London and New York: Methuen. 1987.

Griffin, R., *The Nature of Fascism*. London and New York: Routledge. 1991.

——, 'The Post-Fascism of the *Alleanza Nazionale*: A case-study in Ideological Morphology', *Journal of Political Ideologies*, 1, 2 (1996), 123–45.

Hearder, H., *Italy in the Age of the Risorgimento, 1790–1870*. London: Longmans. 1983.

Kelikian, A.A., *Town and Country under Fascism: The Transformation of Brescia, 1915–1926*. Oxford: Oxford University Press. 1986.

Kennedy, P., *The Rise and Fall of the Great Powers: Economic Change and Military Conflict from 1500 to 2000*. London: Unwin Hyman. 1988.

Kent, P.C., *The Pope and the Duce: The International Impact of the Lateran Agreements*. London and Basingstoke: Macmillan. 1981.

King, B. and Okey, T., *Italy Today*. London: J. Nesbitt & Co. 1909, 2nd ed.

King, R., *The Industrial Geography of Italy*. London: Croom Helm. 1985.

Knox, M., *Mussolini Unleashed 1939–1941: Politics and Strategy in Fascist Italy's Last War*. Cambridge: Cambridge University Press. 1986.

——, 'Expansionist zeal, fighting power and staying power in Italian and German dictatorships', in R. Bessel (ed.) *Fascist Italy and Nazi Germany Comparisons and Contrasts*. Cambridge and New York: Cambridge University Press. 1996.

Koon, T.H., *Believe, Obey and Fight: Political Socialisation of Youth in Fascist Italy, 1922–1943*. Chapel Hill, NC, and London: University of North Carolina Press. 1985.

Lamb, R., *War in Italy, 1943–1945: A Brutal Story*. London: Penguin. 1993.

Laquer, W. (ed.), *Fascism – A Reader's Guide.* London: Penguin Books. 1976.

Larsen, S.V. *et al.* (eds), *Who Were the Fascists? Social Roots of European Fascism.* Bergen, Oslo and Tromso: Universitetsforlaget. 1980.

Lowe, C.J. and Marzari, F., *Italian Foreign Policy, 1870–1940.* London: Routledge and Kegan Paul. 1975.

Lyttelton, A., 'Fascism and Violence in Post-war Italy: Political Strategy and Social Conflict', in W.J. Momsen and G. Hirschfeld (eds), *Social Protest, Violence and Terror in 19th and 20th Century Europe.* London: Macmillan. 1982.

——, *Seizure of Power: Fascism in Italy, 1919–1929.* London: Weidenfeld & Nicolson. 1987, 2nd ed.

Mack Smith, D., *Mussolini as a Military Leader.* Reading: University of Reading. 1974.

——, 'Monument for the Duce', *Times Literary Supplement,* October (1975), 1278–80.

——, *Mussolini's Roman Empire.* London: Longman. 1976.

——, *Mussolini.* London: Weidenfeld & Nicolson. 1981.

——, *Italy and its Monarchy.* New Haven, Conn., and London: Yale University Press. 1989.

Michaelis, M., *Mussolini and the Jews: German–Italian Relations and the Jewish Question in Italy, 1922–1945.* Oxford: Clarendon Press. 1978

E.A. Millar (ed.), *The Legacy of Fascism.* Glasgow: Glasgow University Press. 1989.

Molony, J., *The Emergence of Political Catholicism in Italy: The Partito Popolare 1919–1926.* London: Croom Helm. 1977.

Morgan, P. 'The Italian Fascist New Order in Europe', in M.L. Smith and P.M.R. Stirk (eds), *Making the New Europe: European Unity and the Second World War.* London: Pinter. 1990.

——, *Italian Fascism, 1919–1945.* Basingstoke: Macmillan. 1995.

Nolte, E., *Faces of Fascism: Action Francaise, Italian Fascism, National Socialism.* New York and Toronto: New American Library. 1965.

Passerini, L., *Fascism in Popular Memory: The Cultural Experience of the Turin Working Class.* Cambridge: Cambridge University Press. 1987.

Pollard, J.F., *The Vatican and Italian Fascism, 1929–32: A Study in Conflict.* Cambridge: Cambridge University Press. 1985.

——, '"A Marriage of Convenience": The Vatican and the Fascist Regime in Italy', in J. Obelkovich, L. Roper and R. Samuel (eds), *Disciplines of Faith.* London: Routledge. 1987.

——, 'Post-war Italy: "The Papal State of the Twentieth Century"?', in E.A. Millar (ed.), *The Legacy of Fascism.* Glasgow: Glasgow University Press. 1989.

——, 'Italy', in T. Buchanan and M. Conway (eds), *Political Catholicism in Europe.* Oxford: Oxford University Press. 1996.

Revelli, M., 'Italy', in D. Muhlberger (ed.), *The Social Base of European Fascist Movements.* London: Croom Helm. 1987.
Riall, L., *The Italian Risorgimento: State, Society and National Unification.* London: Routledge. 1994.
Ricossa, R. 'Italy 1920–1970', in C.M. Cipolla (ed.), *The Fontana Economic History of Europe: Contemporary Economies – 1.* London and Glasgow: Fontana. 1976.
Robertson, E.M., *Mussolini as Empire Builder: Europe and Africa 1932–1936.* London: Macmillan. 1977.
Romano, R., 'Giolitti and the Crisis of the Liberal System', in E.A. Millar (ed.), *The Legacy of Fascism.* Glasgow: Glasgow University Press, 1989.
Sachs, H., *Music in Fascist Italy.* London: Weidenfeld & Nicolson. 1987.
Sadkovich, J.J., 'The Italian Navy in World War II: 1940–1943', in J.J. Sadkovich (ed.), *Re-evaluating Major Naval Combatants of World War II.* Westport, Conn.: Greenwood Press. 1990.
——, *The Italian Navy in World War Two.* Westport, Conn.: Greenwood Press. 1994.
Saladino, S., 'Parliamentary Politics in the Liberal Era, 1861–1914', in E.P. Noether and E. Tannenbaum (eds), *Modern Italy: A Topical History since 1861.* New York: New York University Press. 1974.
Salamone, A.W. (ed.), *Italy from the Risorgimento to Fascism: An Inquiry into the Origins of the Totalitarian State.* Newton Abbot: David & Charles. 1970.
Sarti, R., *Fascism and the Industrial Leadership in Italy, 1919–1940.* Berkeley: University of California Press. 1971.
——, 'Fascist Modernisation in Italy', in R. Sarti (ed.), *The Ax Within: Italian Fascism in Action.* New York: Franklyn Watts Inc., 1974a.
——, 'Politics and Ideology in Fascist Italy', in E. Tannenbaum and E.P. Noether (eds), *Modern Italy: A Topical History since 1861.* New York: New York University Press. 1974b.
Seton-Watson, C., *Italy from Liberalism to Fascism.* London, Methuen. 1967.
Snowden, F., 'On the Social Origins of Agrarian Fascism in Italy', *Archives Europeenes de Sociologie*, xiii (1972), 268–95.
——, *Violence and Great Estates in the South of Italy: Apulia, 1900–1922.* Cambridge: Cambridge University Press, 1986.
——, *The Fascist Revolution in Tuscany, 1919–1922.* Cambridge, New York and Melbourne: Cambridge University Press. 1989.
Sparke, P., *Italian Design, 1870 to the Present.* London: Thames & Hudson. 1988.
Steinberg, J., 'Fascism in the Italian South: The Case of Calabria', in D. Forgacs (ed.), *Rethinking Italian Fascism: Capitalism, Populism and Culture.* London: Lawrence & Wishart. 1987.
——, *All or Nothing; Hitler, Mussolini and the Holocaust, 1941–43.* London: Routledge. 1990.

Tannenbaum, E., *Fascism in Italy: Society and Culture, 1922–1945.* London: Allen Lane. 1973.

——, and Noether, E.P. (eds), *Modern Italy: A Topical History since 1861.* New York: New York University Press. 1974.

Thayer, J.A. *Italy and the Great War, Politics and Culture, 1870–1915.* Madison: University of Wisconsin Press. 1964.

Thompson, A.D., 'Between Two Waves: Mussolini's Interrupted Revolution' *Journal of the Association of Teachers of Italian*, 28 (1979), 9–22.

——, *State Control in Fascist Italy: Culture and Conformity, 1925–1943.* Manchester: Manchester University Press. 1991.

Toniolo, G., *An Economic History of Liberal Italy, 1850–1915.* London: Routledge. 1990.

Toscano, M., *The Origins of the Pact of Steel.* Baltimore: Johns Hopkins University Press. 1967.

Trye, R., *Mussolini's Soldiers.* Shrewsbury: Airlife. 1996.

Visser, R., 'The Fascist Doctrine and Cult of Romanita', *Journal of Contemporary History*, 27 (1992), 5–22.

Vivarelli, R., 'Interpretations of the Origins of Fascism', *Journal of Modern History*, January (1992), 29–34.

Von Plehwe, F.K., *The End of an Alliance: Rome's Defection from the Axis in 1943.* London: J.M. Dent & Son. 1971.

Webster, R., *The Cross and the Fasces. Christian Democracy and Fascism in Italy.* Stanford: Stanford University Press. 1960.

——, *Industrial Imperialism in Italy, 1908–1915.* Berkeley: University of California Press. 1975.

Whittam, J., 'The Italian General Staff and the Coming of the Second World War', in A. Preston (ed.), *General Staffs and Diplomacy and the Coming of the Second World War.* London: Cassell, 1978.

——, *Fascist Italy.* Manchester: Manchester University Press. 1995.

Willan, P., *Puppet Masters: The Political Use of Terrorism in Italy.* London: Constable. 1991.

Willson, P., *The Clockwork Factory: Women and Work in Fascist Italy.* Oxford: Clarendon Press. 1996a.

——, 'Flowers for the Doctor: Pro-natalism and Abortion in Fascist Milan', *Modern Italy*, 1, 2 (1996b), 44–63.

Woolf, S.J., *The Italian Risorgimento.* London: Longman. 1969.

——, *The Rebirth of Italy, 1943–50.* London: Longman. 1972.

Zamagni, V., *The Economic History of Italy, 1860–1990: Recovery after Decline.* Oxford: Oxford University Press. 1993.

Zucotti, S., *Italians and the Holocaust: Persecution, Rescue and Survival.* New York and London: Halban. 1987.

Document collections and commentaries in Italian

Bonfanti, G., *Il Fascismo*, 2 vols. Brescia: Editrice la Scuola. 1977.
Enciclopedia Italiana, vol. XIV. Rome: Istituto della Enciclopedia Italiana. 1932.
Susmel, E. and Susmel, D. (eds), *Opera Omnia di Benito Mussolini*, 36 vols. Florence: La Fenice. 1952–63.

Secondary sources in Italian

Abse, T., *Sovversivi e Fascisti a Livorno (1918–1922)*. Livorno: Quaderni della Labronica. 1990.
Bertoldi, S., *Salo: vita e morte della repubblica sociale italiana*. Milan: Rilldi, 1976.
Bocca, G., *La Repubblica di Mussolini*. Bari: Laterza. 1977.
Cannistraro, P.V., *La fabbrica del consenso*. Rome and Bari: Laterza. 1975.
Dall'Orto, G., 'Omosessualita e Razzismo Fascista', in *La Menzogna della Razza*. Bologna: Centro Fino Jesi. 1994.
De Felice, R., *Mussolini*, 8 vols. Turin: Einaudi. 1965–90.
——, *Rosso e Nero*. Milan: Baldin & Castoldi. 1995
Gentile, E., *Il Culto del Littorio: La Sacralizzazione della Politica nell'Italia Fascista*. Turin: Laterza. 1993.
Grandi, D., *25 Luglio. Quarant'anno dopo*, edited with an introduction by R. De Felice. Bologna: Il Mulino. 1983.
Guerri, G.B., *Galeazzo Ciano: Una vita 1901–1944*. Milan: Bompiani, 1979.
Jacini, S., *Storia del PPI*. Naples: Longaresi, 1971.
Knox, M., 'Il fascismo e la politica estera italiana', in R. Bosworth and S. Romano (eds), *La politica estera italiana, 1860–1985*. Bologna: Il Mulino. 1991.
Quartararo, R., *Roma tra Londra e Berlino; la politica estera fascista dal 1930 al 1940*. Rome: Bonacci. 1980.
Rochat, G., *Militari e politici nella preparazione della Campagna d'Etiopia: Studio e documenti, 1932–1936*. Milan: Franco Angeli. 1971.
Salvatorelli, L. and Mira, G. *Storia del fascismo*. Rome: Edizioni di Novissima. 1952.
Santarelli, E., *Storia del movimento e del regime fascista*. Rome: Editori Riuniti. 1967.
Savona, A.V. and Straniero, M.L., *Canti dell'Italia Fascista (1919–1945)*. Milan: Garzanti. 1979.
Scoppola, P., *25 Aprile. Liberazione*. Turin: Einaudi. 1995.
Togliatti, P., Lezioni sul fascismo. Rome: Editori Riuniti. 1970.
Valeri, N., *La lotta politica in Italia: All'Unita all 1925*. Florence: Le Monnier. 1973.
Zunino, P.G., *L'Ideologia dell'Italia Fascismo: Miti, credenze e valori nella stabilizzazione del regime*. Bologna: Il Mulino. 1985.

Fiction in translation

Bassani, G., *The Garden of the Finzi-Continis.* London: Quartet. 1978.
Brancati, V., *The Lost Years.* London: Harvill. 1994.
Levi, C., *Christ Stopped at Eboli.* London: Penguin. 1982.
A. Moravia, *The Conformist.* London: Secker & Warburg. 1952.
——, *Time of Indifference.* London: Penguin. 1970.
Silone, I., *Fontamara.* London: J.M. Dent & Sons. 1985.
——, *Bread and Wine.* London and Melbourne: J.M. Dent & Sons. 1986.

Audio-visual materials

'Mussolini's Rise to Power/Mussolini – the Dictator', Adrian Lyttelton and Denis Mack Smith, Sussex Tapes (1971).
'The Road to War: Italy', BBC documentary, London (1989).
'The Seventeenth Year', *Istituto Luce* propaganda film (1939), available for hire (comes with explanatory notes in English) from the Imperial War Museum, Duxford, Cambridgeshire.

Feature films about Fascism

Bertolucci, B., *Il conformista/The Conformist* (1970).
——, *Novecento/1900* (1976)
——, *Strategia del ragno/The Spider's Stratagem* (1970).
Blasetti, A., *Un giorno nella vita/A Day in the Life* (1946).
Cecchi Gori, M., *La marcia su Roma/The March on Rome* (1962).
De Sica, V., *La ciociara/Two Women* (1960).
——, *Il giardino dei Finzi Contini* (1970).
Fellini, F., *Amacord* (1973).
Genina, A., *Squadrone Bianco/White Squadron* (1936).
——, *L'Assedio dell'Alcaza/The Siege of the Alcazar* (1940).
——, *Bengasi* (1942).
Maselli, F., *Gli indifferenti/Time of Indifference* (1964).
——, *Sospetto* (1975).
Rosi, F., *Cristo si e fermato a Eboli/Christ Stopped at Eboli* (1979).
Rossellini, R., *Roma citta aperta/Rome Open City* (1945).
——, *Paisa* (1945).
Scola, E., *Una giornata particolare/A Special Day* (1977).

Index